Is God a Creationist?

Is
God a
Creationist?

The Religious Case
Against Creation-Science

EDITED BY

Roland Mushat Frye

Charles Scribner's Sons • **New York**

Library of Congress Cataloging in Publication Data
Main entry under title:

Is God a creationist?

   1. Creationism—Addresses, essays, lectures.
2. Creation—Addresses, essays, lectures. 3. Religion
and science—1946–   —Addresses, essays, lectures.
I. Frye, Roland Mushat.
BS651.I8 1983   213   83-11597
ISBN 0-684-17993-8
ISBN 0-684-18044-8 (pbk.)

1 3 5 7 9 11 13 15 17 19   F/C   20 18 16 14 12 10 8 6 4 2
1 3 5 7 9 11 13 15 17 19   F/P   20 18 16 14 12 10 8 6 4 2

PRINTED IN THE UNITED STATES OF AMERICA.

Contents

Preface and Acknowledgments

Disputes involving the biblical accounts of creation figure promi-
nently in and about American public education today. Many questions need to be raised in this regard. One of these concerns the biblical and theological legitimacy of the interpretations of divine
creation advocated by the so-called creationists and creation-scientists and proposed by them as educational models. The present volume addresses that question in its broad religious context.

My own professional study of such religious subjects began in the
late forties and early fifties when I was pursuing a doctorate at Princeton, where I combined the study of literary and cultural history at
the University with basic theological training at the Seminary. The
interdisciplinary approach which I began then has provided the focus of my teaching and scholarship in the intervening years, as I
have sought to combine literary and cultural history with theological
analysis and the history of Christian doctrine. As a result, the biblical doctrines of creation along with their interpretation in theology
and in vernacular literature have been in the forefront of my study
and concern. I hope that this anthology will serve to clarify and define the religious issues involved in the educational controversy, and
will do so in a way which is theologically informed, balanced in approach, and charitable in tone.

As editor, my responsibility has been to collect a group of essays
which would make clear the central understandings of divine creation within the mainstreams of biblical religion (including the Protestant, Roman Catholic, and Jewish traditions). On this issue the
ecumenical consensus is impressive indeed. Out of the available material I have selected eleven essays as most pertinent and useful for

the inquiring general reader. In addition to gathering and editing these, I have contributed an introductory "overview" which places the issues in the broad context of biblical interpretation, religious doctrine, and history. And I have provided an epilogue to suggest a course for the future which, while being true to past traditions, may provide a hopeful exodus from our present difficulties.

The assembling of these materials was sponsored by the Center of Theological Inquiry in Princeton. My research in 1982 was entirely devoted to this task, and I spent the fall semester of that year in residence as a member of the Center. Throughout, I have been particularly indebted for the understanding and encouragement given me by the Center's founder and continuing director, James I. McCord, who has recently completed a long and distinguished career as president of Princeton Theological Seminary. As one who has been privileged to work in many great research institutions in this country and abroad, I can say that I have nowhere found an atmosphere more conducive to serious study, reflection, and writing than that which the Center provides. To the Center, and to Dr. McCord, I extend my deep thanks.

My thanks are also due to the authors and copyright holders of the splendid essays collected here, contributions which will speak for themselves. In addition, churchmen, scholars, and friends here and abroad have been generous in giving consultation, advice, and support. The typescripts were prepared by Gloria Kramer at the Center, and by my secretary at the University of Pennsylvania, Eileen Cooper; for their untiring patience and accuracy I am indeed grateful. A final word of thanks is also due to my understanding publisher, Charles Scribner, Jr., and to my skillful editor, Jennifer Crewe. And of course to my wife, who while requiring no thanks can never be thanked enough.

R.M.F.

Is God a Creationist?

An Overview

Creation-Science Against the Religious Background

ROLAND MUSHAT FRYE

Foregrounds and Backgrounds

The controversy over teaching creationism in the public schools is creating a major crisis in American education, and indeed in the society as a whole. The essays gathered here analyze the creationist controversy calmly and judiciously, appraising it in the light of how major religious leaders, scholars, and mainstream denominations understand the doctrines of divine creation in the Bible and in religious tradition. The individual authors together represent a broad religious spectrum. They do not agree with each other on all points, but they do agree in three major ways: each is religiously committed to one of the major traditions of Protestantism, Roman Catholicism, or Judaism; each believes in divine creation as understood within those traditions; and each (whether implicitly or explicitly) regards creationism as a misreading of the basic religious evidence. Their arguments provide valuable insights for everyone who wishes to understand and appraise the contemporary controversy over "creation-science" and creationism.

From coast to coast today, advocates of creationism and of creation-science are demanding a place in our public school system and challenging the bases of both scientific and religious thought. The resulting controversies frequently generate more heat than light. Creationists attempt, often successfully, to inject into the American school curriculum the teaching of what is called a young-earth theory based upon a strictly literalistic reading of Genesis. These young-earth theories typically can allow no more than 144 hours to the whole process of creation, or, with a digital adjustment by which one day is taken to be a thousand years, they can extend that to 6,000 years. As for the total age of the universe, they allow only a few thousand years, up to a maximum of perhaps 10,000 or 20,000. Basically, that is the time scale, with its many implications, which creationism seeks to impose upon our scientific and religious understanding. It differs radically from the long time scale—running into several billion years—for which scientists find abundant evidence in nature. It also differs radically from the understanding of biblical records held by mainstream religion and theology.

Despite scientific, religious, and constitutional objections, bills which would require the teaching of so-called creation-science wherever evolution is taught are now pending in more than twenty state legislatures. Two such bills were passed by the states of Arkansas and Louisiana, and both have been struck down by the federal courts. It seems likely that any other bill requiring the teaching of creation-science would prove unconstitutional for the same reasons.

But the creationists do not concentrate only on passing laws, and indeed their major educational successes are scored in other ways. Even apart from legislative action, pressures on local schools in many different parts of the country have resulted in the teaching of creationist beliefs. Studies also show that a number of major high school textbooks now contain significantly less information than was once provided about evolution, and some have begun to feature creationist accounts, due to the skillful exertion of pressure on and through publishers. Creationist success in applying such pressures on American education, and more widely within American culture, has taken all observers by surprise. In purely political terms, the creationists obviously are very canny, whatever else may be said of them. More, however, must be said.

On the personal level, let us grant at the outset that most creationists are sincere and well-meaning. Indeed, most of us who strongly disagree with their program of scientific and religious education can still share their alarm over evidences of moral decadence in our society. Once that has been recognized, we can go on to other important issues. The creationists are claiming, after all, to represent both science and religion and wish to reshape the public school curriculum in both scientific and religious ways. It is therefore wise to appraise their credentials by the educational standards of both fields.

Because they are committed to having their own beliefs taught in science courses, the appraisal of the scientific community is clearly relevant, and that appraisal is overwhelmingly negative. The scientific repudiation of creationism as nonscientific is well known and widely publicized, and I know of no reason why that rejection should not be regarded as scientifically valid. We will therefore not consider that side of the question, nor will we consider the legal and constitutional issues, which have been appropriately tested in the courts, but will instead concentrate upon the religious issues involved.

The case for creationism arises more out of religious than out of scientific convictions, as most observers recognize, and at every point it is at least as much concerned with religion as with science. Here, too, the appraisal of the responsible community is negative, judging the creationists' biblical interpretations to be at best oversimplified and at worst incompetent. A recent and distinguished historian of creationism has observed that "leadership of the antievolution movement came not from the organized churches of America but from individuals like [William Jennings] Bryan and interdenominational organizations such as the World Christian Fundamentals Association, a predominantly premillenarianist body founded in 1919."[1] A respected journalist has summarized developments in this way:

> Nothing since the turn of the seventeenth century, when Galileo pointed out that the earth was not the center of the solar system, has so infuriated Christianity's fundamentalist fringe. . . . Why this should be so is a puzzle, because the ideas of evolution in no way contradict the fundamentals of general Christian belief in an all-powerful, personal deity, [or] in the redemptive sacrifice of Jesus. . . . It is only the Protestant fundamentalists who are incensed when evolution is mentioned.[2]

Creationists often belong to the major, historic denominations, and they even control some local congregations within these, but they do not represent the prevailing understanding of creation within those denominations, nor of their most eminent theological seminaries, nor of the ecumenical seminaries.

The creationists' deviation from the religious mainstream does not of course prove that they are wrong, but it is relevant to understanding the context of the current debate. Neither does the doctrinal eccentricity of the creationists suggest that they are less moral or less devout than the religious mainstream. But it is important to recognize that the movement represents a kind of "do-it yourself" approach to the knowledge of scientific and religious subjects. The underlying assumption seems to be that almost anyone is competent to judge education and to determine what should be taught. Without regard for scientific discovery, they are prepared to impose their own beliefs in science classrooms. Similarly for religious instruction, they are prepared to start anew in biblical interpretation, ignoring the ongoing consensus of biblical and theological scholarship and its understanding of God's creative actions. Seeking to impose their own anomalous interpretations upon education and religion, the major creation-scientists give the impression that they are strikingly uninformed about religious studies, whether current or historical. So far as I have been able to discover none of them has had the benefit of instruction by the great American theological seminaries and departments: surely the leading creation-scientists show no signs of theological education. That such people, however well-meaning, should be allowed to prescribe any part of the public school curriculum which concerns religion does not, to put it mildly, bode well for education. Educationally, the creationist leaders have shown themselves to be no better prepared in religious studies than they are in scientific fields.

Religious Opposition to Creationism

Let us now consider some recent critiques of creation-science made by major religious groups and leaders. In September 1982, the Episcopal Church in this country explained its objections as follows:

> The terms "Creationism" and "Creation-science" . . . do not refer simply to the affirmation that God created the Earth and Heavens and everything in them, but specify certain methods and timing of the creative acts, and impose limits on these acts which are neither scriptural nor accepted by many Christians. This dogma of "Creationism" and "Creation-science" as understood in the above contexts has been discredited by scientific and theological studies and rejected in the statements of many church leaders. "Creationism" and "Creation-science" is not limited to just the origin of life, but intends to monitor

public school courses, such as biology, life science, anthropology, sociology, and often also English, physics, chemistry, world history, philosophy, and social studies.[3]

The creationists described in that statement have been active in this country for more than a decade, but their efforts (as distinguished from those of the 1920s) did not become widely publicized until the recent Little Rock court case in which United States District Judge William R. Overton declared unconstitutional the Arkansas law requiring that creation-science be given equal time whenever and wherever evolution was taught in the Arkansas public schools.[4]

It is significant that the court action against that law was taken by a representative group of religious leaders, who retained the American Civil Liberties Union to plead the case for them. The case itself, *McLean v Arkansas Board of Education*, takes its name from the Reverend William McLean, the general presbyter or principal official of the Presbyterian Church in Arkansas. Officially joined with McLean as plaintiffs in this suit were the resident bishops of the Methodist, Episcopal, African Methodist, and Roman Catholic churches in the state, as well as the American Jewish Congress, the Union of American Hebrew Congregations, and the American Jewish Committee. The cooperation by these representatives of American Protestants, Jews, and Roman Catholics indicates one of the most important areas of modern ecumenical consensus: although many disagreements patently exist between these groups, they today affirm very similar understandings of what the biblical doctrines of creation do and do not imply.

That consensus indicates what is meant here by the mainstream of biblical religions, and the meaning of this consensus will become increasingly apparent as we proceed. Many members of the major denominations would dissent from the anti-creationism consensus, of course, and more members of the Southern Baptist and Missouri Synod Lutheran churches would even more surely dissent, but it is doubtful whether those two denominations (as well as some smaller sects) would ever wish to be described as part of the religious mainstream in this country. However, on the basis of the evidence of the Little Rock plaintiffs and of the church pronouncements to which we shall shortly turn, it is clear that both creation-science dogma and strategy are rejected by religious denominations and associations which represent the largest total proportion of Christians and Jews in this country. Thus, arguments for introducing creationism into the public school curriculum cannot fairly be based on an appeal for "equal time" or "equal representation," even if popular pressures were appropriate here, which they are not. What is most relevant for our concerns is the significance of an ecumenical consensus which rejects creationism on religious and biblical grounds.

In deciding on educational issues such as the content of school courses, professional standing and responsibility must be carefully weighed. In that regard, it is imperative to consider the professional competence of creationists to address the theological issues over which they claim a kind of authority. The judgment of contemporary theologians has been summarized by Professor Langdon Gilkey of the Divinity School of the University of Chicago, who observed in his testimony on the Arkansas law that none of the supporters of creationism represented "the established and professional religious and theological communities," that none of "the spokesmen for the type of religion represented by the creationists were recognized, established religious leaders," and furthermore that "they could not, I warrant, have found a single biblical scholar or theologian" of major standing who would support them.[5] The same must of course be said about the "scientists" who argue for creation-science, but our concern here is with the religious evaluation.

In addition to the successful ecumenical challenge of creationism in the Arkansas case, doctrinal statements have been made on the highest ecclesiastical levels during recent years within the Roman Catholic, the Episcopal, and the Presbyterian churches. Each of these denominations of course affirms God's creation of the universe, but on the basis of that affirmation they deny the eccentric interpretations of creation which creation-science seeks to impose. The most comprehensive and detailed of these statements was adopted on June 28, 1982 by the General Assembly of the United Presbyterian Church, U.S.A. Entitled "Evolution and Creationism," and running to nine pages, this Resolution with Supporting Information identifies and opposes creationist efforts on three major fronts: it describes any legislative requirement that creation-science be taught as a violation of the Constitution, it condemns pressures on schools and school boards as infringing on the "academic freedom of both teachers and students," and it opposes pressures to modify academic textbooks as threats to "professional authority and freedom."[6] The Presbyterian statement also maintains that creationism represents a faulty understanding of science, of religion, and of the relations between them.[7] In rejecting the religious bases of creationism, the General Assembly explicitly cited the theological consensus of Protestant, Roman Catholic, and Jewish understanding. Suggesting that the dispute over creation-science "is not really over biology or faith, but is essentially about biblical interpretation, particularly over two viewpoints regarding the characteristics of biblical literature and the nature of biblical authority," the Resolution proceeded to affirm

> that the imposition of a literalist viewpoint about the interpretation of Biblical literature—where every word is taken with uniform literalness and becomes an absolute authority on all matters, whether moral, religious, political, historical, or scientific—is in conflict with the perspective on Biblical interpretation characteristically maintained by Biblical scholars and theological schools in the mainstream of Protestantism, Roman Catholicism, and Judaism. Such scholars and, we believe, most Presbyterians find that the scientific theory of evolution does not conflict with their interpretation of the origins of life found in the Biblical literature.[8]

The Episcopal statement is briefer, but also very much to the point. I have already cited its explanation defining creationism, which clarifies the grounds on which the major biblical religions object to creation-science. In the resolution itself, the 67th General Convention of the Episcopal Church acted, in September 1982, to "affirm its belief in the glorious ability of God to create in any manner," rejected "the rigid dogmatism of the 'Creationist' movement," and supported "scientists, educators, and theologians in the search for truth in this Creation that God has given and entrusted to us."[9]

The Roman Catholic statement, made by the pope himself, does not specifically mention the uniquely American controversy over creationism, but it does unequivocally deny the fundamental assumptions of creation-science. Addressing the Pontifical Academy of Sciences before its meetings on Cosmology and Cosmogony in October 1981, Pope John Paul II reaffirmed the statement of Pope Pius XII that the universe was created "milliards of years ago" (which in the American idiom means billions of years ago) "by the creating mind . . . calling into existence, in a gesture of generous love, matter teeming with energy." On the basic issue of the age of the cosmos, the papal views are thus directly contrary to those of the creationists. But there is an even more fundamental difference, involving how the Bible is to be understood, and to what purposes it is to be studied. On those issues, the present pope declared that

> The Bible itself speaks to us of the origin of the universe and its make-up, not in order to provide us with a scientific treatise, but in order to state the correct relationship of man with God and the universe. . . .

> Any other teaching about the origin and make-up of the universe is
> alien to the intentions of the Bible, which does not wish to teach how
> heaven was made, but how to go to heaven.[10]

On any intelligible reading of the pope's statement, the attempt to
base science on Genesis "is alien to the intentions of the Bible,"
which speaks of the origin of the universe "not in order to provide
us with a scientific treatise, but in order to state the correct relationship of man with God and the universe."

It is important here not to miss the pope's allusion to the greatest
earlier misreading of the Bible in terms much like those employed
by twentieth-century creationism, when an imperialist Vatican
sought to silence the heliocentric arguments of Galileo. Galileo had
defended himself against such pressures by saying that "the intention of the Holy Ghost is to teach us how one goes to heaven, not
how heaven goes."[11] By his unmistakable paraphrase of that famous
statement, the pope provides a graceful, yet forceful warning against
repeating that tragic seventeenth-century effort to dominate science
by a literalistic interpretation of Genesis.

The Creationist Movement

Those are potent disavowals, from important religious groups, but
even where such disavowals have not been made explicit it is clear
that the principal historic denominations neither endorse nor support the creationist movement. Later in this chapter I shall place creationism in the broader perspective of Christian history, but it is
well to recognize at the outset that it is a distinctive product of
twentieth-century America. We can begin the story about sixty years
ago, using William Jennings Bryan as a representative example of
creationist concerns.

Bryan was a very distinguished man, much admired in his own
time, although today he is best remembered for his discredited role
in the 1925 court case (the so-called "Monkey Trial") in Dayton,
Tennessee, which sought to exclude the teaching of evolution from
the public schools by making an example of high school biology
teacher John Thomas Scopes. Although the local judge decided against
Scopes and evolution, the larger public effect was to discredit the arguments Bryan presented, arguments derived from the leaders of the
fundamentalist movement which had been organized some fifteen

years before. That movement was in itself a protest against the Christian and especially Protestant mainstream, as we shall later see, but what concerns us here is the early manifestation of its efforts to oppose the teaching of evolution in the public schools. Historically, Bryan provides a good starting point for approaching the creationist campaign which has once again become conspicuous in our own time.

In the first place, Bryan serves to illustrate why and how generally admirable people can be drawn into efforts which most members of the religious and scientific communities regard as wrongheaded and even dangerous. However much Bryan was inclined to take oversimplified approaches to complex issues both political and religious, his personal life and his services to the nation were impressive indeed. A liberal Democrat, he was three times nominated for the presidency by his party, later served as secretary of state under Woodrow Wilson, and throughout his public life spoke out for the economically underprivileged. Internationally, he contributed significantly to world peace and to opposing militarism and imperialism of all kinds. Although none of our contemporary creationists have Bryan's public stature, and although most apparently favor political conservatism rather than his political liberalism, the underlying similarities between them are greater than the differences.

After World War I, Bryan became increasingly convinced that the acceptance of evolution would require the rejection of that fundamentalist reading of the Bible which undergirded his beliefs, his personal ethics, and his vision of a moral society. This is an extremely important point, and difficult to overemphasize. Whereas nonfundamentalist Christians and Jews who are just as devout and strong in their faiths as are the creationists do not find their life-systems threatened by evolution, people like Bryan did, and today they still do. However much other religious Americans (and nonreligious Americans also, but for a different set of reasons) disagree with their beliefs, creationists like Bryan deserve understanding, even as the debates continue.

In addition to representing a fundamentally religious view which in an even more restricting form still permeates the creationist leadership, Bryan also illustrates some of the ethical concerns of that movement. Bryan felt that modern society was more and more modeling itself upon the laws of the jungle rather than upon the humanitarian example and teaching of Jesus Christ. Here he was equally troubled by the decline in personal conduct and the widespread social acceptance of new models, which were at once less elevated and less elevating. All of this he ascribed to the influence of Darwinism. The fact that such a cause-and-effect relationship was at best an oversimplification or misunderstanding and at worst a distortion of historical developments did not concern him, nor was he impressed by the fact that many evolutionists shared his own alarm about moral decay. Temperamentally averse to complexity, he declared quite simply that "All the ills from which America suffers can be traced to the teaching of evolution."[12]

Bryan's inclination to propose very simple solutions for very complex problems is clearly illustrated here. Directly after the sentence just quoted, he went on to say: "It would be better to destroy every other book ever written, and save just the first three verses of Genesis." Even so literalistic a reader of the Bible as Bryan would presumably have objected to a literal interpretation of that statement, which is literally absurd. But even granting all due allowance for an old campaigner's flights of rhetoric, when that statement is read in Christian terms it comes very close to dangerous heresy, elevating a few verses at the beginning of the Bible over all the rest of scripture, and indeed of all other known writings.

Another insight into creationism is provided by Bryan's counsel to antievolutionists: "Commit your case to the people." In the half-century which has elapsed since Bryan's time, creationists have achieved their most notable successes before state legislatures and school boards, and from pressures exerted upon local schools. Bryan neither foresaw nor planned these later tactics, but they continue to implement his advice: "Forget, if need be, the high-brows both in the political and college world, and carry this cause to the people. They are the final and efficiently corrective power."[13]

Bryan thus represents a typical pattern of the individual twentieth-century American creationist: a sincerely devout person without significant training in theology but with strong religious and ethical commitments, he sought to settle intellectual and educational policy by skillfully exerted popular pressures. From Bryan's time into our own, such creationist pressures have been generated by concerned individuals banded together into groups (often shifting and plagued by division).[14]

Many individuals less well-known than Bryan have followed courses similar to his. Thus in 1961 a California housewife and mother named Nell Segraves learned that the U. S. Supreme Court had decided the suit of Madalyn Murray so as to protect atheist students from required prayer in the public schools. Murray's success in defending her child from mandatory exposure to religion "suggested to Segraves that creationist parents like herself 'were entitled to protect our children from the influence of beliefs that would be offensive to our religious beliefs.' "[15] Along with another like-minded California housewife named Jean Sumrall, Mrs. Segraves urged the State Board of Education to include the literalist understanding of biblical creation alongside evolution in the public school textbooks, and the Board was persuaded to do so. It was a bad decision on educational grounds, and at least questionable on constitutional grounds, but however much we disagree with the creationists, the human concerns of such people should be neither ridiculed nor ignored.[16]

The typical group pattern seems to be for biblical literalists of this kind to form or join ad hoc associations to challenge the established wisdom both educationally and religiously. Although the creationist movement as such is now a little more than fifty years old, it has not only been unable to attract significant support from the principal religious denominations, but has even been unable to establish stable, permanent connections within its own ranks. One major historian observes that "a serious and long-standing problem among antievolutionists [has been] their failure to agree on a theory of creation."[17] As a result, they have displayed a succession of internal dissensions and the consequent dissolution of groups into other groups. Out of these shifting patterns, the most influential association to emerge in recent decades is centered about Henry M. Morris, a civil engineer, and Duane T. Gish, a biochemist, at the Institute for Creation Research in San Diego, California. In the dozen years or so since its foundation, that Institute has issued publications of its own and has attracted widespread attention in the media, as well as inspiring and leading local pressure groups throughout the country.

Creation-science as we know it today is identified with this Institute, but its ideological pedigree has been traced back to a divine inspiration which, according to Ellen G. White, the nineteenth-century prophetess of Seventh-day Adventism, revealed to her that the fossil records cited by evolutionists were merely deposits left by Noah's flood. Also fundamental here was her Adventist insistence that the "days" of creation were exactly twenty-four hours long, no more and no less. The teachings of White influenced a young member of the Adventists named George McCready Price (1870–1963) and convinced him to become a strict creationist rather than an evolutionist. Price's formal education consisted of two years' study at an Adventist college, and the completion of teacher-training at a normal school in Canada, but he was a bright man and he read widely in search of ways to discredit evolution.[18] As a self-trained geologist, he issued his first book in 1906, *Illogical Geology: The Weakest Point in the Evolution Theory*, a clever argument for recent creation, but not one which leading scientists and theologians could take seriously. In 1923 his *The New Geology* appeared, equally clever but no more convincing, and on the basis of these writings he became known as "the principal scientific authority of the Fundamentalists," even though the better educated fundamentalists could not accept his arguments.[19] After the debacle of the Scopes Trial in 1925, such creationist efforts were somewhat muted, but only for a time.

In 1961, Henry Morris, who today heads the Institute in San Diego, collaborated with a minister of the Grace Brethren church named John G. Whitcomb, Jr., on a book entitled *The Genesis Flood*. One reviewer described this work as "a reissue of G. M. Price's views, brought up-to-date," but so effective was its "revival" of those views that it can now be seen as launching the controversy once again.[20] The authors began by affirming "the verbal inerrancy of Scripture," taking it literalistically as a guide to understanding the origin and structure of the universe, and despite their claims to scientific authority they maintained that "the real issue is not the correctness of the interpretation of various details of the geological data, but simply what God has revealed in His Word concerning these matters."[21] They contended that the universe was created as recently as a few thousand years ago (most strict creationists hold to a limit between 6,000 and 10,000 years), that the second law of thermodynamics resulted from the fall of man, and that most of our presently visible geological strata and fossils were laid down during Noah's flood. On this basis, they believe, evidence for many millions of years of evolutionary development can be dismissed both scientifically and religiously. Leading scientists and religionists rejected these arguments as scientifically or biblically naive, but many literalists accepted them, and the modern confrontation was generated.

What is new is the claim that Morris, Gish, and others have developed a scientifically viable alternative to the subject of universal origins. This approach was developed after "the Supreme Court made it clear in 1968 that laws forbidding the teaching of evolution were flatly unconstitutional." With no more possibility of excluding evolution from the public schools by legal means, the creationists turned to demanding "equal time" for what they began, rather ambiguously, to call "creation-science."[22] This new tactic has allowed "creation-scientists" to claim authority in two different fields of study, but Federal Judge William R. Overton found in the Arkansas case that they do not engage in the constructive professional activities of either science or theology, that they do not read papers at professional meetings or publish in the recognized professional journals of either, and that they have earned professional respect neither from scientists nor religionists. Lacking such respect, their claims to reshaping education can only appear dubious. But the grounds for rejecting those claims are historic as well as contemporary.

Biblical Accounts and the History of Christian Understanding

Having surveyed the development of creationism and creation-science in the twentieth century, we need now to go back in time to examine the biblical accounts themselves and to understand the traditions of biblical interpretation within the Christian church. If we look carefully at the references to creation in the Bible, it will become as apparent to us as it has been to leaders in religious studies and in the major denominations that the Bible cannot be forced into a single uniform "science" such as the creationists propose. A number of the Old Testament treatments of creation were not, strictly speaking, original, but represent significant monotheistic and Judaic alterations of widespread ancient cosmologies. Even the first two chapters of Genesis contain different accounts, as was recognized by Augustine and others long before these differences came to be ascribed to separate documentary traditions now known as the Priestly (P) and the Yahwist (J).

Here let us perform a kind of mental experiment, by temporarily assuming a literalistic approach to the Genesis stories. If we do so, we will see that a consistent "creationist" account cannot be extracted even from the first chapter of Genesis, and still less so from the first two chapters. Consider, for example, the question of a time scale of six twenty-four hour days: such days must be based upon the diurnal appearances of the sun, but the Genesis story says that the sun was not created until the fourth *yōm* in the narrative series of six. Obviously, then, the first three *yōmīm* must be calibrated by a different measure from that applied in the last three. Furthermore, whereas the first chapter treats the whole work of creation as occupying six separate *yōmīm*, the second chapter refers to the single *yōm* in which the Lord God created the earth and the heavens (Gen. 2.4). Clearly, the Hebrew word *yōm* cannot here be calibrated into a specific chronological measure as creation-science presupposes: it must be understood, not as an inflexible twenty-four hour unit, but as a time of flexible and uncertain duration, within the overall symbolic context of biblical parable. That is only one example from Genesis, and others could also be cited to the same effect.

If we move beyond Genesis, the problems raised for a literalist interpretation become even more intractable. Thus the thirty-eighth chapter of Job suggests that the creation occurred on a single morning during which "the morning stars sang together," while Proverbs 8.22-31 implies an indeterminate time during which a personified Wisdom was associated with the divine action. Other references to creation, which the so-called creationists literally ignore, occur when we are told that God "drew a circle on the face of the deep and made firm the skies above" (Prov. 8.27-28), or that he "has set a tent for the sun" (Ps. 19.4), or that he "stretched out the heavens like a curtain and laid the beams of his chambers on the waters," and made the clouds his chariot (Ps. 104.2-4).

The same Psalmist then went on to say that the Lord "laid the foundations of the earth, that it should not be moved forever" (Ps. 104.5). That statement about an immovable earth was once used by literalist forebears of the present-day creationists to "prove" that the earth could not move about the sun, as Copernicus and Galileo had discovered that in fact it did. Creation-science advocates today do not so interpret that passage, but they would do so if they were really consistent in the literalism which they wish to impose on American education. Indeed, if their own anti-Darwinian interpretations of scripture as a literalistically infallible criterion of science are valid, then those anti-Copernican interpretations must be equally valid. In this example we can see once more, as leading biblical scholars have long recognized, that an extreme literalism is counterproductive and that it is also impossibly self-contradictory, as my other examples have also indicated.

But such literalistic efforts really miss the point of the Bible on this issue. The various biblical references to creation are magnificent descriptions, sublime in their symbolic vision, inspiring in their religious faith, but there is simply no way that we can derive from them a single, literal "creation-science." Nor should we. Their frame of reference is different.

In the patristic period, the fathers of the Christian Church were fully aware of these and other problems, and generally refused to be trapped in any such dogmatic and educational cul-de-sac as the modern creationists have devised. St. Augustine, probably the most influential church father and one who is equally respected in Roman Catholicism and in Protestantism, found it impossible to impose a time frame on the biblical treatments of creation, and regarded them as pervasively figurative.[23] Augustine examined major alternative views of the age of man, and finding in his time no conclusive scientific or historical evidence to the contrary (evidence such as we have today), he accepted as most convincing and consistent the view that humanity (but not the entire universe) had been created about 5,000 or 6,000 years before.[24] Yet the primary concern was not the number of years since the beginning, but the fact of a beginning, however recent or remote. Unequivocally opposing cyclical, self-generating, and eternal conceptions of the cosmos, he allowed broad latitude for the actual time involved. To questions raised by his adversaries as to why humanity was created at one particular time and not at an earlier time (questions linked to pagan conceptions of an eternal, noncontingent universe), he replied in a way which illustrates his flexibility about the time scale: "if there had elapsed since the creation of man, I do not say five or six, but even sixty or six hundred thousand years, or sixty times as many, or six hundred or six hundred thousand times as many, or this sum multiplied until it could no longer be expressed in numbers, the same question could still be put. . . ." On any of these counts, he held, "controversy about the commencement of this world's history would have had precisely the same difficulties as it now has."[25] In the Bible, he said, "God did not intend to teach men about the inner structure of nature."[26] As in Augustine's time, so also today that recognition is absolutely basic to any responsible interpretation of scripture.

Such interpretations were part of a broad conception of biblical communication, usually called accommodation or associated with it. Accommodation is an interpretive device or principle which allows an interpreter to preserve valid meaning found in a text without a sterile literalism, and it informed Christian exegesis through the first sixteen or seventeen centuries. A few representative examples will indicate the value of the continuity of that tradition. Approximately 300 years after Augustine, the Byzantine theologian Maximus Confessor treated biblical symbolism as "an accommodation . . . to human ways of thinking. Scripture spoke in a way that was not literally accurate in order to enable its readers to grasp what transcended literal accuracy."[27] Still later the scholastic philosopher Thomas Aquinas wrote that "the use of metaphors . . . befits sacred doctrine. . . . Poetry uses metaphors to depict, since men naturally find pictures pleasing. But sacred doctrine uses them because they are useful and necessary."[28] Still later the Reformed theologian Amandus Polanus wrote that the true or genuine "is not opposed to the figurative but to the false."[29] Such principles, which twentieth-century creationism ignores, denies, or violates, were standard in the patristic, scholastic, and reformation eras.

On this basis, it was possible to avoid many (although unfortunately not all) unnecessary and time-consuming conflicts between religion and science. Francis Bacon was thus firmly within the Christian and the Reformed tradition when he referred to the two books of God: Nature, the particular subject of science, and Scripture, the particular subject of theology. He was equally orthodox when he protested against the absurdity of attempting "to found a system of natural philosophy on the first chapters of Genesis, on the Book of Job, and other parts of the sacred writings . . . because from this unwholesome mixture of things human and divine there arises not only a fantastic philosophy [or science], but also an heretical religion," which he illustrated by those narrow dogmatists who assumed that the earth is flat because of their interpretation of Genesis.[30] Augustine had been just as stern in his rebuke of ignorant believers who "talk utter nonsense" *(dēlīrāre)* about scientific issues which they do not understand, to the great injury of all who listen, and to the discrediting of the faith.[31] John Calvin in the sixteenth century was similarly insistent that science not be condemned just "because some frantic persons are wont boldly to reject whatever is unknown to them."[32]

For Calvin, the principle of accommodation always intervened between God, the words of scripture, and human understanding.[33] As an example of the folly of taking science from Genesis, Calvin chose the reference in Genesis 1.16 to the sun and moon as the two great lights of heaven. Although Genesis treats these as the major luminaries, he wrote, "astronomers prove, by conclusive reasons," that others are in fact greater, and he went on to say, "Here lies the difference: Moses wrote in a popular style things which, without instruction, all ordinary persons, endued with common sense, are able to understand; but astronomers investigate with great labor whatever the sagacity of the human mind can comprehend." The purpose of the biblical account of creation was not to instruct people in astronomy or in any other science, but rather in their human nature and destiny, and in their relation to God. Calvin taught that the author of Genesis "as became a theologian . . . had respect to us rather than to the stars."[34] He nonetheless took repeated pains, in his commentaries and in *The Institutes*, to praise and commend the study of science. The question of whether individual scientists are themselves believers or unbelievers is quite irrelevant to what Christians should properly learn from them, as Calvin declared: "If the Lord has willed that we be helped in physics, dialectic, mathematics, and other like disciplines, by the work and ministry of the ungodly, let us use this assistance." Otherwise, "if we neglect God's gift freely offered in these arts [i.e., in our terms, sciences], we ought to suffer just punishment for our sloths." Calvin summarized these views when he asserted that we can "neither reject the truth itself, nor despise it wherever it shall appear, unless we wish to dishonor the Spirit of God."[35]

Such considerations surely facilitated, even if they did not by themselves cause, the rise of modern science. But by the time of Darwin, they had been very largely overshadowed by other theological emphases. The general flexibility which I have illustrated from Augustine through Calvin, and the implementing principle of accommodation, were not entirely lost, but they were progressively upstaged by the concordism and physico-theology which sought ways to coalesce scientific and biblical accounts into a kind of unitary system. In the history of thought, concordism is defined as "the effort to read the Bible as though its apparently literal expressions were teaching the facts of science." Physico-theology is an eighteenth-century term to the same general effect, and it even more graphically suggests a mechanical reading of Scripture for scientific as well as religious messages, which appealed to the mechanistic post-Newtonian world.[36] On the scientific side, eighteenth- and nineteenth-century culture found great satisfaction in a mechanical view of nature and the world, assuming a one-for-one and virtually univocal correspondence between scientific formulae and the data to which they referred; such a worldview would naturally also take satisfaction in claiming a similarly mechanical correspondence between the words of a biblical text and the data to which those words were said to refer. Although exegesis of this kind did not reach the extremes we see today, it was well along the way. Popular nineteenth-century readings of the Bible often and perhaps even typically showed a literalism, less tempered by metaphoric and symbolic understanding, a literal reading which went far beyond the characteristic exegesis of earlier periods.[37] Thus even so intelligent a person as Charles Darwin could say of his years at Cambridge, when he was expecting to enter the Anglican ministry, that "I did not then in the least doubt the strict and literal truth of every word in the Bible"—a statement which could not have been made in anything like the same sense by Augustine and Calvin, as we have seen.[38]

In that context of an accepted physico-theology, the publication of Darwin's *Origin of Species* in 1859 may be likened to a volcanic eruption or great earthquake which shook everything in its range and changed the contours of the land. Scientists and religionists alike struggled within their own ranks, and between them, to come to terms with this new conception. In retrospect we can now see that, by the time of Darwin's death or thereabouts, both the scientific and religious leadership had begun to lay out the general lines along which his ideas would become accepted and would develop. New paradigms were established in both fields, and within these paradigms both the principal scientific and religious understandings have continued into our own time.

The religious leaders who opposed Darwinism were not the only voices of Christianity, and the future fortunately lay with others.[39] Two examples will have to suffice in this survey. Harvard's Asa Gray, probably the most influential Darwinist in nineteenth-century America, delivered an elegant lecture series at the Yale Divinity School in 1880 in which he affirmed his acceptance both of classical Christianity and of evolutionary theory. In the course of developing that larger conception, Gray observed that "There are perplexities enough to bewilder our souls wherever we look for the causes and reasons of things; but I am unable to perceive that the idea of the evolution of one species from another, and of all from an initial form of life, adds any new perplexity to theism."[40] Others were speaking to the same effect. James McCosh, the Scottish theologian and philosopher who crossed the Atlantic to become president of Princeton in 1868, had from the beginning been a stalwart and outspoken advocate of evolution, and in 1888 he published an influential book in which he declared like Gray that "no difficulty arises on the theory of [evolutionary] development which does not meet us on the theory of the immediate creation of every new individual and species," and similarly affirmed that Christians should "look on evolution simply as the method by which God works."[41]

When Christians like Gray and McCosh rejected the mechanical reading of Scripture which accompanied physico-theology, and accepted the different paradigm in which historic biblical religions would primarily develop, they did so in good measure because of the rise of Darwinian evolution, but also because of the recognition or recovery of the older nonliteralistic traditions in exegesis, and finally because of then current developments in biblical study itself. Even before the nineteenth century, new methods of historical research were introduced into the analysis of the Bible, its origin, growth, and content. Such research continued through the Darwinian period and into our own time, providing a fuller understanding of the Bible in its historical contexts and in its own terms. As a result, it became increasingly apparent, on the basis of solid historical and archaeological evidence, that the Bible as we know it was itself formed through an evolutionary process. The book of Genesis did not spring in its present form directly from Moses' pen, as had once been supposed. Indeed, the entire corpus of the Pentateuch was apparently brought together from four independent documents. That process of redaction took place at identifiable stages between the tenth and the fifth centuries before the Christian era, although each of these formative documents obviously contained far more ancient materials and traditions. Again there were different responses to these discoveries. The literalists objected to the evolution of the biblical Books just as vehemently as they objected to the evolution of species. People who represented the new paradigm, however, accepted them, not as damaging the Bible, but as enriching and enlivening it. Again we may take Asa Gray as a representative example.

In addition to his intimate professional involvement with current scientific research, Gray, as a well-informed Christian layman, was aware of these developments in biblical scholarship. In his brilliant Yale Divinity School lectures, not only did he repudiate the kind of literalism developed during the preceding two centuries, but he adopted in its place a combination of very ancient and very modern approaches to the Bible. First invoking the long-standing tradition of accommodation, he wrote: "We may take it to be the accepted idea that the Mosaic books were not handed down to us for our instruction in scientific knowledge, and that it is our duty to ground our scientific beliefs upon observation and inference, unmixed with considerations of a different order."[42] Gray also emphasized new development in the historical understanding of the Bible:

> I trust that the veneration due to the Old Testament is not impaired by the ascertaining that the Mosaic is not an original but a compiled cosmology. Its glory is, that while its materials were the earlier prop-

erty of the race, they were in this record purged of polytheism and Nature-worship, and impregnated with ideas which we suppose the world will never outgrow. For its fundamental note is, the declaration of one God, maker of heaven and earth, and of all things, visible and invisible,—a declaration which, if physical science is unable to establish, it is equally unable to overthrow.[43]

Gray was certainly not the first or even the most important Christian scholar to bring together the ancient doctrine of accommodation with the modern knowledge of the evolution of the biblical accounts, but he did so in a way which is, for our purposes, conveniently illustrative.

The Current Controversy

Broadly speaking, the kind of understanding illustrated by Asa Gray is common among American theologians and church leaders today, and is virtually unchallenged in British and Continental churchmanship. Against the background of such a consensus, European Christians find the creationist movement difficult to understand, even find it difficult to believe that such a movement could arise in the twentieth century. It has arisen here largely because of distinctively American experiences, especially perhaps because of an over-simple revivalism, the frontier's separation from educational and cultural centers, and various kinds of populist anti-intellectualism and antiprofessionalism. Those factors and others contributed to nurturing and sustaining a literalism which had become virtually extinct in other countries. Fundamentalism is thus a distinctively American movement, and it is significant that even the words "fundamentalist" and "fundamentalism" are twentieth-century neologisms, coined in this country.[44]

Fundamentalism was launched in reaction against the broader Christian mainstream which I have described, and from its inception it represented a narrowing of the accepted theologies. When that has been said, it is also important to note that it counted among its early leaders a number of intelligent and learned theologians who could not be classified as anti-intellectual. Nor was it unanimous in its opposition to evolutionary theory. The essays which launched the movement were published in Chicago between 1910 and 1915, and were called *The Fundamentals*, from which the name of the movement derived. Among these essays by various contributors on different subjects, there were three principal fundamentalist analyses of science and religion, two of which acknowledged that the earth could be much older than literalistic interpretations of Genesis allowed and even held that evolution was not necessarily incompatible with Christianity.[45] In the Scopes "Monkey" Trial in 1925, that redoubtable fundamentalist William Jennings Bryan showed a flexibility of belief about the age of the universe which would today exclude him from being an accredited member of the creationist elite, unless he were willing to recant.[46] But in the decades since Bryan's time, there has been a progressive narrowing of an already constricted base.

After the debacle of the Scopes trial, even more extreme choices were faced and often made. For example, so-called dispensationalist groups increased in strength and stressed even more emphatically, among other things, an approach to the Bible as a prophetic puzzle which can be solved by appeal to the literal inerrancy of all that it contains. Much of fundamentalism thus appears to have moved from literal to more literal positions. In the process, some adherents fell away to accept more broadly based religious beliefs, while others, comfortable with the maximum of literalism, developed or embraced creation-science.[47] Once religious belief and religious life are entirely based upon this extremely literalistic interpretation of the first chapters of Genesis, then any form of evolution is seen as irreconcilable. The choice is therefore presented as mutually exclusive: one or the other, either scientific evolution or biblical religion.

Although fundamentalists like Bryan, and the even more rigid creationists of our time, have failed to convert the major denominations or capture the Christian leadership, they have succeeded in preserving and activating a certain popular (or perhaps we should say populist) cast of mind. And although the aggressive proponents of creation-science operate from a base which is almost as narrow proportional to the historic and worldwide Christian mainstream as it is narrow in theological and intellectual content, this latest and most extreme form of biblical literalism has managed over the last dozen or so years to challenge the major judgments of science, religion, and education in America.

Is the creation-science controversy, then, no more than a tempest in a teapot? Those who think so would, I respectfully suggest, change their minds if they would study the issue with some care—either by talking to people across the country who are under these pressures or by reading, for example, the reports on the creationist campaign which appeared in *Science '81* and *Science '82*, the monthly magazine of the American Association for the Advancement of Science. In an editorial for that journal, senior editor Boyce Rensberger admitted that "the debate seems so unnecessary because there are few issues that were not thrashed out a hundred years ago." Yet, as he said, a "minority kept to its literal reading of Genesis," so that today, "though few in number, the creationists are loud and effective. They must be reckoned with."[48] Indeed they must.

They cannot and should not be defeated simply by pointing out that they are a minority. Minorities can, and sometimes do, present valuable alternatives to majority views, or even improve upon and supplant them, but they do not always or automatically do so. What counts is the quality of the case represented by a particular minority, and in this case that quality is poor. The creationists, after all, claim to represent both science and religion, but their interpretations are rejected by the most respected leaders of both fields. Whatever other differences, suspicions, and disagreements may exist between individual scientists and religionists, a concurrence on this particular issue is present and should be more widely recognized. A broader public awareness of that concurrence will not change the minds of the creationist leaders, but it might and I suspect would help to deflate the pressures they can exert upon public education. State legislatures, school boards, and local schools and teachers, along with ordinary followers of creationism and the intelligent public at large, should be aware, in short, that creation-science cannot be regarded as representing either responsible science or responsible religion. In those terms, the case for injecting it into our educational curriculum can, as a practical matter, be more effectively appraised on every level.

My purpose thus far has been to outline the religious history and the religious issues which underlie the contemporary controversy, as an introduction to this anthology. Most of the principal Christian and Jewish groups in this country concur in their understanding of the biblical doctrine of creation, despite the major differences separating them on other theological issues. The essays which follow have been selected to illustrate that consensus about what the biblical accounts of creation do and do not mean, and to show why most biblical scholars and denominational leaders disagree with the creationist arguments.

Following this general overview, provided as an introduction, Part One presents three essays which explore the often unstated assumptions underlying the controversy on both sides, clarifying these in personal and social terms and also in logical terms. Part Two consists of articles by three authorities who specifically rebut the creationist claims for religious competence and for inclusion in the school curriculum. Part Three includes two papers by eminent scientists and Christian laymen who exemplify what many others have also found, that it is possible to affirm in all honesty both the Christian faith and the established scientific accounts of the origins of the universe. The fourth section presents, through three papers, the biblical and theological affirmations of divine creation which are made in the Roman Catholic, Jewish, and Protestant traditions. This final group of essays does not so specifically address the evolution-creationism issue as do the others, but it is necessary for laying out the religious bases for avoiding such conflicts as now plague us, or for defusing their explosive and destructive potential.

Throughout this volume, all the essays are relevant to each other, and together they present a comprehensive picture of central religious responses to, and rejections of, the oversimplified and misapplied literalism of modern creationism and creation-science. Finally, the epilogue suggests constructive ways in which we may move on from here, recognizing similarities and differences but living with them constructively and creatively in a spirit of reason, reverence, and good will.

Notes

1. Ronald L. Numbers, "Creationism in 20th-Century America," *Science* (Nov. 5, 1982), 216:539.
2. John Skow, "Creationism as Social Movement," *Science '81* (December 1981), p. 54.
3. Explanation of the "Creationism" Resolution adopted by the 67th General Convention of the Episcopal Church, September 5–15, 1982, meeting in New Orleans, La.; resolution proposed by Deputy Robert Schwartz, representing the Diocese of West Missouri (Reference No.: D-090 Substitute; Referred to: HD; Committee #11).
4. See the Judgment and Opinion dated January 5, 1982, of the Hon. William R. Overton, United States District Judge in the Eastern District of Arkansas in the case (LR C 81 322) *Rev. Bill McLean, et al., plaintiffs* v *The Arkansas Board of Education, et al., defendants.*
5. Langdon Gilkey, "Creationism: the Roots of the Conflict," *Christianity and Crisis* (April 16, 1982), 42:112–13, also published in somewhat re-

vised form in *Science, Technology, and Human Values* (Summer, 1982), 7:67–71.

6. "Resolution and Supporting Information on Evolution and Creationism," adopted June 28, 1982, by the 194th General Assembly of the Presbyterian Church, U.S.A. Sections opposing legislative action occur on pp. 1 and 2, pressures on school boards in Affirmations 3 and 6, and textbook interference in Affirmation 3 and Supporting Information, p. 4.

7. *Ibid.*, Supporting Information, pp. 3–4.

8. *Ibid.*, Paragraph 4 and Affirmation 2.

9. Episcopal resolution on creationism (see note 3).

10. John Paul II, "Science and Scripture: The Path of Scientific Discovery," *Origins* (1981), 11:277–80, with quotation on p. 279. See also the pope's first address to the Pontifical Academy and his address to German scholars and students at Cologne, "Faith, Science and the Search for Truth," *Origins* (1979–80), 9:389–92, and "Science and the Church: A Dialogue," *Origins* (1980), 10:395–98. As examples of Roman Catholic analyses of evolution over the course of the past quarter century, see: Nicolas Corte, *The Origins of Man*, trans. by Eric E. Smith (New York: Hawthorne, 1958) (volume 19 in Henri Daniel-Rops, ed., *The Twentieth Century Encyclopedia of Catholicism*); Walter J. Ong, S. J., ed., *Darwin's Vision and Christian Perspectives* (New York: Macmillan, 1960); Johannes Metz, ed., *The Evolving World and Theology* (New York: Paulist Press, 1967) (volume 26 of *Concilium*); Jean de Fraine, *The Bible and the Origin of Man* (Staten Island, N.Y.: Alba, 1967); while Zachary Hayes, O.F.M., *What are They Saying about Creation?* (Ramsey, N.J.: Paulist Press, 1980), provides a brief summary of recent Roman Catholic thought. As these works contain a number of reflections upon the *Humani Generis* of 1950, see Pius XII, *The Encyclical "Humani Generis" with a Commentary*, ed. by A. C. Cotter, S.J. (Weston, Mass.: Weston College Press, 1952).

11. Galileo, "Letter to the Grand Duchess Christina," in Stillman Drake, ed. and trans., *Discoveries and Opinions of Galileo* (Garden City, N.Y.: Doubleday Anchor, 1957), p. 186. Perhaps it is appropriate to cite here another remark attributed to Galileo, "but it does move," applying it in this instance not to the earth but to the Vatican. For a clear and balanced analysis, see Owen Gingerich, "The Galileo Affair," *Scientific American* (1982), 247:132–43.

12. Richard Hofstadter, *Anti-Intellectualism in American Life* (New York: Knopf, 1966), p. 125.

13. *Christian Fundamentalist* (1929), 2:13, as cited by Numbers, "Creationism in 20th-Century America," p. 539.

14. Numbers, "Creationism in 20th-Century America," and Skow, "Creationism as Social Movement."

15. Numbers, "Creationism in 20th-Century America," p. 543. Here again,

the opinions of Bryan are relevant. In his populist view, it seemed preposterous that a few thousand scientists should be allowed "to establish an oligarchy over forty million American Christians" and to dictate how their children would be educated. See P. E. Coletta, *William Jennings Bryan* (Lincoln: University of Nebraska Press, 1969), pp. 3 and 230.

16. In addition to the humanly sympathetic while doctrinally opposite views expressed in this anthology, see also the two essays on "The Creationism Controversy" by Francis J. Flaherty and Anne Brennan in *Commonweal* (Oct. 22, 1982), 109:555–61.

17. Numbers, "Creationism in 20th-Century America," p. 540.

18. Numbers, "Creationism in 20th-Century America," pp. 539 f.

19. Numbers, "Creationism in 20th-Century America," pp. 539–40.

20. Review by R. M. Allen, *Journal of the American Scientific Affiliation* (June 1965), 17:62.

21. Henry Morris and John G. Whitcomb, Jr., *The Genesis Flood* (Philadelphia: Presbyterian and Reformed Publishing Co., 1961), p. 55, and a joint statement published in *Journal of the American Scientific Affiliation* (June 1964), 16:60.

22. See the admirably dispassionate articles on "Creationism as a Social Movement" by John Skow and "Creationism as Science" by Allen Hammond and Lynn Margulis in the special insert section of *Science '81* (December 1981), pp. 53–60, with quotation from p. 59.

23. For a succinct account, see the analysis by John O'Meara: *The Creation of Man in St. Augustine's "De Genesi ad Litteram,"* in the St. Augustine Lecture Series of the Augustinian Institute (Villanova, Pa.: Villanova University Press, 1980). Other Augustinian reflections may be found in *De Genesi contra Manichaeos* and in the last two books of the *Confessions*. In a seminal treatment of Christian exegesis, James Samuel Preus summarizes Augustine's methodology for overcoming "the unedifying literal"—see *From Shadow to Promise: Old Testament Interpretation from Augustine to the Young Luther* (Cambridge, Mass.: Harvard University Press, 1969), especially pp. 14–15.

24. Augustine, *The City of God* (trans. by Marcus Dods et al.), in *Basic Writings of Saint Augustine*, 2 vols. (New York: Random House, 1948), 2:188–90.

25. *Ibid.*, XII.xii, pp. 190–91.

26. Augustine, *De Genesi ad Litteram*, in *Patrologia Latina*, 34/270.

27. Quoted in Jaroslav J. Pelikan, *The Christian Tradition* (Chicago: University of Chicago Press, 1974), 2:14, citing *Patrologia Graeca*, 90/621, 812.

28. Aquinas, *Summa Theologica*, I, Q.1 Art. 9, in A. M. Fairweather, ed. and trans., *Nature and Grace* (Philadelphia: The Westminster Library of Christian Classics, 1954), pp. 46–47.

29. Quoted in Heinrich Heppe, *Reformed Dogmatics set out and illustrated from the sources*, trans. by G. T. Thomson (London: Allen and Unwin,

1950), p. 638. For the Reformation's inclusion of the metaphoric within the "plain" sense of Scripture, see also pp. 37–39.

30. Francis Bacon, *Novum Organum*, lxiv, lxxxix, in Edwin A. Burtt, ed., *The English Philosophers from Bacon to Mill* (New York: Modern Library, 1939), pp. 45 and 63.

31. John O'Meara, *Augustine's "De Genesi ad Litteram,"* pp. 22–23.

32. John Calvin, *Commentaries on Genesis*, ed. by John King (Grand Rapids, Mich.: Baker, 1981), p. 86.

33. See Edward A. Dowey, Jr., *The Knowledge of God in Calvin's Theology* (New York: Columbia University Press, 1952), pp. 3–17 and *passim*; Ford Lewis Battles, "God was Accommodating Himself to Human Capacity," *Interpretation* (1977), 31:19–38; Roland M. Frye, *God, Man, and Satan* (Princeton: Princeton University Press, 1960), pp. 3–17 and *passim*; C. A. Patrides, "*Paradise Lost* and the Theory of Accommodation," *University of Texas Studies in Language and Literature* (1963) 5:58–63.

34. John Calvin, *Commentaries on Genesis*, pp. 85–87. Another treatment of the two great lights, as found in Psalm 136.7, occurs in Calvin's *Commentary on the Psalms*, ed. by James Anderson (Grand Rapids, Mich.: Baker, 1981), 5:184–85.

35. John Calvin, *Institutes of the Christian Religion*, ed. by John T. McNeill (Philadelphia: Westminster, 1960), vol. 1, 2.2.16 and 2.2.14–15.

36. For the definition of concordism, see Robert Gleason, S.J., in Walter J. Ong, S.J., ed., *Darwin's Vision and Christian Perspectives*, p. 105. The term physico-theology is taken from the title of the Boylean Lectures delivered in 1711–1712 by William Derham, and this particular approach reached its apogee in 1802 in William Paley's *Natural Theology*, but the conception was doomed by the development of evolution. I am using the term in a somewhat broader way than the original sense because the hyphenated joining of "physico" with "theology" suggests the kind of mechanical reading of scripture which I am about to describe. It can, of course, be seen as an intellectual evolution from the mechanistic views of Descartes, Hobbes, and others, about whom Ralph Cudworth wrote that "they made a kind of dead and wooden world, as it were a carved statue, that hath nothing neither vital nor magical at all in it," in Thomas Birch, ed., *The True Intellectual System of the Universe* (London, 1845) 1:221.

37. From the patristic period through the Age of Reformation, there was a strong (although admittedly varying) emphasis on the *sensus literalis*, but we should not read back into the Latin of that technical phrase our modern sense of literalism, because that would gravely distort the meaning. Where appropriate, the *sensus literalis* was intended to include the metaphoric, and the phrase was understood to apply to the broadly literary meaning of a text. For useful treatments of this subject, see for example the following essays and books: Brevard S. Childs, "The

Sensus Literalis of Scripture: An Ancient and Modern Problem," in H. Donner, R. Hanhart, and R. Smed, eds., *Beiträge zur Alttestamentlichen Theologie. Festschrift für Walther Zimmerli zum 70. Geburtstag* (Göttingen, Vandenhoeck and Ruprecht, 1977), pp. 80–93; and (also by Childs) "The Old Testament as Scripture of the Church," *Concordia Theological Monthly* (1972), 43:709–22; Anthony Nemetz, "Literalness and the *Sensus Litteralis*," *Speculum* (1959), 34:76–89; and James Preus, *From Shadow to Promise: Old Testament Interpretation'from Augustine to the Young Luther* (Cambridge, Mass.: Belknap Press, 1969). Treatments may also be found in P. R. Ackroyd, et al., eds., *The Cambridge History of the Bible*, 3 vols. (Cambridge: The University Press, 1963–70), and Beryl Smalley, *The Study of the Bible in the Middle Ages* (Notre Dame, Ind.: Notre Dame University Press, 1964, reprint).

38. Nora Barlow, ed., *The Autobiography of Charles Darwin* (New York: W. W. Norton, 1969), p. 57. That apparently unthinking literalism, uninformed by theological depth or understanding, never broadened into an intelligible and defensible faith as the years passed, and Darwin consequently moved toward agnosticism.

39. It has been noted that "the attempt by Wilberforce 'to destroy the Darwinian theory by theological weapons damaged the current theology more than the theory,' despite the well-known fact that the bishop had, for the most part, simply served up scientific arguments learned from [the anti-Darwinian anatomist Richard] Owen, seasoned with his own acidulous wit." The then popular physico-theology allowed for such crossings over between theology and science. For a fascinating and informative account of the doctrinal developments and debates in science and theology, see James R. Moore, *The Post-Darwinian Controversies: A Study of the Protestant Struggle to come to Terms with Darwinism in Great Britain and America, 1870–1900* (Cambridge: Cambridge University Press, 1979). The larger quotation is from Moore, p. 61, with the inner quotation derived from Francis Warre Cornish, *The English Church in the Nineteenth Century*, 2:224, appearing as vol. 8 of E. R. W. Stephens and William Hunt, eds., *A History of the English Church* (London: Macmillan, 1910).

40. Asa Gray, *Natural Science and Religion: Two Lectures Delivered to the Theological School of Yale College* (New York: Charles Scribner's Sons, 1880), p. 64. He also notes that "the high Calvinist and the Darwinian have a goodly number of points in common" (p. 102). Gray was not the only scientist-Christian to accept evolution, as George M. Marsden states: "In fact, with the exception of Harvard's Louis Agassiz, virtually every American Protestant zoologist and botanist accepted some form of evolution by the early 1870s"—quoted from his "Understanding Fundamentalist Views of Science," ms. pp. 9–10, forthcoming from Oxford University Press in an anthology edited by Ashley Montague.

41. James McCosh, *The Religious Aspect of Evolution*, 2d ed. (New York:

Charles Scribner's Sons, 1890), pp. 58 and 68.

42. Gray, *Natural Science and Religion*, p. 8.

43. Gray, *Natural Science and Religion*, p. 9.

44. For a balanced and authoritative history of this development, see George M. Marsden, *Fundamentalism and American Culture, the Shaping of Twentieth-Century Evangelicalism, 1870–1925* (New York and Oxford: Oxford University Press, 1980).

45. James Orr, "Science and the Christian Faith," and George F. Wright, "The Passing of Evolution," in *The Fundamentals: A Testimony to the Truth*, 4:91–104 and 7:5–20, respectively. I owe this citation to George M. Marsden's "Understanding Fundamentalist Views of Science," unpublished ms., pp. 10–11 and n.22.

46. Numbers, "Creationism in 20th-Century America," p. 540, with cross reference to Numbers' essay in *Spectrum* (January 1979), 9:24. See also Marsden, "Understanding Fundamentalist Views of Science," unpublished ms., n.42.

47. Marsden, "Understanding Fundamentalist Views of Science," unpublished ms., pp. 11–13 and 15–16.

48. Boyce Rensberger, "Darwin vs. Dogma," *Science '81* (December 1981), p. 5.

part one

Understanding the Misunderstandings

Chapter 1

Hidden Agenda Behind the Evolutionist/Creationist Debate

EDWIN A. OLSON

Professor of Geology and Physics at Whitworth College in Spokane, Washington, Edwin A. Olson is primarily interested in geochemistry, and has done research on the accuracy of radiocarbon dating. His essay, first published in the evangelical magazine Christianity Today, *gives a balanced introduction to the basic issues (both spoken and unspoken) in the debate over creation-science, defining terms, explaining what constitutes genuine science, and approaching all sides in the controversy with what might best be called an existential sympathy and understanding. In a charitable and rational way, he analyzes the basic complaints which motivate the creationists, yet he opposes both their methods and their conclusions. Olson's essay thus provides insight into the current debate which avoids stereotypes and invites a discriminating comprehension.*

Once again the evolution/creation controversy makes front-page news. Here are all the ingredients a newsman could ask for. We see

This chapter is reprinted, by permission, from *Christianity Today* (April 23, 1982), 26:26–30.

the champions riding out to do rousing, albeit verbal, battle. Behind each of the two groups is a home front, a good-sized segment of America's general public. One side the mass media find easy to caricature or portray as the buffoon. The other side, speaking from a rostrum of academic prestige, is learning to flavor its pontifications with enough salt to satisfy the media taste.

How delightful a battle, so human yet so bloodless! Who would be churlish enough to ask for definition of terms or clarification of the issue? But do it we must. We begin by asking whether evolution and creation are necessarily antithetical alternatives. And the answer depends on how the two words are defined.

Defining Evolution

Evolution is a term that can conjure up a host of images and conceptual extrapolations—nature red in tooth and claw, social Darwinism, robber barons and laissez-faire capitalism, reductionist materialism, aggressive atheism, ethical relativism, human perfectibility, a self-existent universe. To the scientist acting as a scientist, however, such ideas are simply not germane. Evolutionary theorizing is merely a way of explaining in natural terms the history and mechanism of change within the universe as a whole, in certain parts of it such as stars and the earth, and in life on our planet (i.e., cosmology, stellar evolution, historical geology, and organic evolution).

Usually the scientist is simply investigating whether there exist long-term, large-scale, natural processes analogous, for example, to the development of a baby from a fertilized egg. More often than not, he has no theological or philosophical ax to grind, and is likely to be a bit irritated when a nonscientist carries his ideas beyond what he feels to be their legitimate bounds. Obviously that irritation is not a preventive against unwarranted extrapolation, for each idea listed above has turned to scientific evolution for support. The point is that a scientific concept must be considered independently of its perversions.

Defining Creation

The word creation, too, evokes different responses. Many scientists shun it altogether because it connotes situations and events impossible to understand through empirical data. Theistic scientists, to be sure, do not shy away from the word, for they see the material realm as contingent upon a creator. To them, the stuff of the world, its behavior patterns and changes over time, are all cradled in the hand of a transcendent God. Among today's theistic scientists, however, is a group called creationists, who require the word "creation" to mean much more. For them, believing in creation means adhering to a specific chronology of events which they believe the Bible unequivocally describes. Compressed into perhaps 10,000 years or less, it is a chronology sufficiently idiosyncratic as to call for a new name—"creationism."

Daniel Wonderly describes another group of creationists who have been around "since the latter part of the 19th century" (some say the 18th century). Including himself among them, he describes them as "a large body of Catholic and Protestant creationists who accept the geologic evidence for long periods of time, including the entire sedimentary record." Many within this group, according to Wonderly, "believe that matter and the basic forms of life were originally created by divine fiat, with extensive speciation following the creation." Wonderly's group is not at the center of the current controversy, so that here the terms creationist(s) refer exclusively to those who insist upon a very young earth and the rejection *in toto* of the geological timetable.

It is the habit of these creationists to apply the label "evolutionist" to almost anyone who differs from them in the slightest degree. They fail to recognize that there are many who hold to divine creation while rejecting the label "creationist." Such people consider themselves faithful to the Christian Scriptures but see no reason to exclude God from slow processes which result in novelty. They are creationists in the traditional sense, but now find themselves standing in the gray area between "creationists" and "evolutionists." By omitting them and their contributions, current discussions are so starkly black and white that a balanced examination of the issues is impossible.

Evolutionary Theorizing

In most cases, evolutionary theorizing begins with pre-existing stuff which evolves; that is, changes. Given that stuff, its energy and its basic laws, scientists face the task of drawing historical and mechanistic conclusions from presently accessible empirical data. They do not ask "Who?" and "Why?" Rather it is "How?" and

"When?" that concerns them as scientists. The theists among them will certainly use the term "creation" to describe the origin of the basic stuff of the universe; but what about subsequent developments? How does one label changes that turn primordial matter into new entities? Do theists label them "creation" so as to affirm their theism? Do they also require that the processes be supernatural, fearing that natural (and gradual) processes are somehow beyond the purview of God?

As a Christian, I necessarily recognize both my own creatureliness and that of the entire material realm. Furthermore, I have no problem at all with divine creation by fiat if the evidence requires it. In another time my position would have clearly marked me as a creationist, but today that appears not to be the case. Now it seems that one can claim to be a creationist only by rejecting the possibility that God's activity includes time-consuming natural processes.

There is a tendency for today's self-styled creationists to subsume all such processes under the term "evolution" and then apply the term pejoratively at the first hint that someone does not accept their scenario. I do not know whether they respond from an *a priori* bias against process, or are fully convinced that Scripture negates it. For whatever reason, what they regard as evolution is anathema to them, and its association with divine activity is considered incongruous.

Often those who do battle with "creationists"—call them evolutionists—are equally rigid in separating process from God. Prominent among them is Stephen Jay Gould, the Harvard paleontologist (see his "Evolution as Fact and Theory," *Discovery*, May 1981). With the alternatives limited by such a dichotomy, it is no wonder that the current battle between the extremes of evolutionists and "creationists" generates more heat than light.

The Lesson of Big-Bang Cosmology

Although evolutionary theorizing generally begins with pre-existent material, a few scientists try to fit even the origin of matter into a naturalistic framework. Most notable are advocates of the steady-state cosmology that envisions the continuous *ex nihilo* creation of matter atom by atom over endless time. At present this cosmologic view is being eclipsed by big-bang cosmology, a concept that includes a seeming "beginning" of the universe. Supposedly there was a moment about 15 billion years ago when all of the matter in the universe exploded from a point and moved out to form the expanding universe of today. The status, even the existence, of that universe-in-a-point are problematic, to say the least.

How one eminent scientist responded to this apparent beginning and how others have responded to him are instructive here, for the whole affair bears upon what I consider to be an implicit conviction of creationists—namely, that if in the present universe we can find evidences of former catastrophes, abruptness, discontinuity, or currently inexplicable processes or events, then we will have irrefutable proof that the universe was made by almighty God. A logical extension is that many will be drawn irresistibly to a theistic conviction, perhaps even to Christian faith.

Unfortunately, the case of astrophysicist Robert Jastrow does not follow the above script. At the 1978 meeting of the American Association for the Advancement of Science, Jastrow gave an address entitled "God and the Astronomers" (now available in a small book of the same name [New York: Norton, 1978]). Jastrow made the dramatic statement that "now we see that astronomical evidence leads to a biblical view of the origin of the world." Nowhere did he say straight out, "I believe that God exists." But he came so close that a number of noted scientists have taken up the cudgels against him.

Jastrow's God, it turns out, is basically the God-of-the-gaps. Where empirical knowledge fails, invoke God. He says:

> Scientists cannot bear the thought of a natural phenomenon which cannot be explained, even with unlimited time and money. . . . Every effect must have its causes, there is no first cause. . . . This religious faith of the scientist is violated by the discovery that the world had a beginning under conditions in which the known laws of physics are not valid, and as a product of forces or circumstances we cannot discover . . . the scientist's pursuit of the past ends in the moment of creation! . . .
>
> For the scientist who has lived by his faith in the power of reason, the story ends like a bad dream. He has scaled the mountains of ignorance; he is about to conquer the highest peak; as he pulls himself over the final rock, he is greeted by a band of theologians who have been sitting there for centuries.

Jastrow began his talk by stating his own agnosticism, and he maintained that position when quizzed following the formal talk. A Christian physicist in the audience, Paul Arveson, asked him, "In light of all this evidence and in light of your own honesty in taking it at face value, why are you still an agnostic?" Jastrow replied, "I keep coming close to the edge of faith, but I never quite make it over. . . . In my later years I may reconsider this. You know how old men often turn to such thoughts."

One wonders why Jastrow went to the trouble of sticking his professional neck out so far while continuing to be an unbeliever through it all. It would seem that theistic conviction does not automatically follow when a person becomes aware that scientific knowledge has its limitations.

If the astronomic evidence and Jastrow's inferences from it were unsuccessful in making even Jastrow a believer, it is not surprising that others were unconverted. Fred Hoyle, British astrophysicist and proponent of a universe infinite in space and time, was interviewed after Jastrow's lecture and said that he thought "the main controversy is whether the so-called origin of the universe really has to be taken literally or whether this is a physical transition from a preceding state." He added, "I personally have little doubt that there has to be a preceding stage, perhaps even an evolutionary process." Even a Christian astronomer, Owen Gingerich of Harvard, was cool to Jastrow's conclusion. His response, quoted in *Time* magazine (February 5, 1979), was that *"Genesis* is not a book of science. It is accidental if some things agree in detail. I believe the heavens declare the glory of God only to people who've made a religious commitment."

Scientist-writer Isaac Asimov was notably unrestrained in responding to Jastrow. He wrote:

> If I can continue to read the English language, Jastrow is implying that since the Bible has all the answers . . . it has been a waste of time, money and effort for astronomers to have been peering through their little spyglasses all this time. Perhaps Jastrow, abandoning his "faith in the power of reason" (assuming he ever had it) will now abandon his science and pore over the Bible until he finds out what a quasar is. . . . Why should he waste his time in observatories? ("Science and the Mountain Peak," *The Skeptical Inquirer*, winter 1980–81, p. 43).

Such an intemperate response shows that Asimov holds deep convictions that Jastrow has disturbed. Asimov is an avowed atheist and Jastrow has pointed to what he considers to be evidence for God. He has touched a sensitive spot beneath the skin of Asimov's formal scientific knowledge.

Do Creationists Have a Hidden Agenda?

It seems to me that similar sensitive spots exist in the "creationist/evolutionist" debates, but are being covered over in an effort to portray the discussion as purely scientific. The fact is, the "creationists" have a hidden agenda. And, because they are sincere Christian people, I believe it contains supremely important issues, issues that transcend the minutia of science and strike at the heart of what it is to be human. The question of God's existence is certainly one, as illustrated by the Jastrow affair. But also crucial are God's relationship to the universe as well as the purpose and destiny of human life.

In the debate now going on, however, such issues are not overtly discussed. We are led to think, by the "creationists" at least, that what is being debated is totally a scientific matter, a question to be argued in the same way as any of the many scientific issues in history. Ostensibly the Bible is kept out of the discussion, although the biblical wellspring of the "creationists" is clear to all who are familiar with its history. It is only because of the American commitment to separation of church and state that mention of the Bible is muted. As a result, the wrong battle is being fought and a potent weapon silenced.

Suppose the "creationists" were to win their case, or at least to insinuate their position into the public schools. Would a proclamation of the Christian gospel thereby be assured? Does human uniqueness flow only from a creationist cosmology? Is "proof" of a 10,000-year-old earth a key to revealing Christ's redemptive act on the cross? To me, the answers are obviously No. Thus, I consider the creationist approach to be poor strategy for a truly Christian impact on the world. I do not believe it will accomplish what its promoters desire (and what I desire)—namely, widespread and effective dissemination of the good news of God, including a respect for the divine authorship of the material realm.

The Aberration of "Creationism"

Scientists in general, and many Christians among them, regard the "creationist" movement as aberrational and cultic, an irritant rather than a force for creating understanding. While many of its leaders have earned doctoral degrees from prestigious universities, most are in the fields of engineering, mathematics, physics, and chemistry—areas lacking in the historical dimension crucial to the issues being debated. Admittedly, some are biologists, but geologists and astronomers are almost unrepresented.

More important than academic background, however, is the way in which "creationists" participate in the scientific enterprise. Having set in concrete their view of events in the mist of distant history, they come to lecture from a rostrum of certitude. They separate themselves even from scientists who are committed Christians. The Creation Research Society, for example, was founded by people who withdrew from the American Scientific Affiliation, not because ASA members were unable to recite the Apostles' Creed with full affirmation but because the ASA was supposedly "soft" on evolution.

The only contacts that "creationists" have with the scientific community at large are through campus debates where their ablest speakers generally acquit themselves very well. However, rather than face-to-face debate before generally uninformed audiences, creationists should be making their case through established scientific channels. After all, science is not static. Its history records a myriad of cases where people with new ideas supported by new data have overturned the status quo. And they have done it directly by confronting their peers. The journals and the scientific meetings are there for those who would participate.

What we see, in fact, is "creationists" talking to creationists. They speak about research that they have done. What that research seems to involve, however, is a search of the orthodox scientific literature to cull out statements that reinforce creationist prejudices. How odd that the honesty of establishment scientists in expressing their failures as well as their successes should not be matched by a similar honesty by "creationists," whose scientific convictions seem surprisingly free of ambivalence and uncertainty. Consider, for example, this ingenuous statement of an establishment anthropologist, David Pilbeam of Harvard University, in his review of Richard Leakey's book, *Origins:*

> Perhaps generations of students of human evolution, including myself, have been flailing about in the dark; that our data base is too sparse, too slippery, for it to be able to mold our theories. Rather the theories are more statements about us and ideology than about the past. Paleoanthropology reveals more about how humans view themselves than it does about how humans came about (*American Scientist*, May/June 1978, pp. 378–379).

Such a statement no doubt evokes different responses. Creationists probably say, "I told you so," and add another arrow to their quiver. Some professional anthropologists with phylogenies well worked out in their own minds may be upset and rush to reply.

My own response is two-fold: first, to admire the author's candor as well as the give-and-take of the intellectual environment from which it springs and then to add the author's remarks to my mental storehouse of information about human nature. There it joins with data, both secular and biblical, to provide the grist for my own thinking about the mechanism (not the Mechanic) behind human origin. Currently I see sufficient ambiguity to make me cautious about endorsing a particular mechanism of human origin. About human nature, however, I have no hesitation. I believe that the Bible unequivocally affirms that we humans, in spite of our all-pervasive sin, are the apple of God's eye, significant enough to be redeemed by the death of his only Son.

Reasons for Creationists' Success

If "creationists" have been unable to dent scientific orthodoxy, what accounts for their success in capturing headlines and influencing state legislators? I believe there are two factors that any successful salesman can quickly recognize. First, there is zeal issuing in hard work, and, second, a new product for which there is clearly a wide market.

For many years, a host of Christian people with a simple faith and little knowledge of science has been suspicious of scientists as a group. In their reading of the Genesis account, God brought the current universe into being as it is now in six 24-hour days. All this scientific theorizing about evolutionary processes is simply introducing complications where there is obvious simplicity. Besides, scientists seem always to be attacking the Christian faith and acting as if they could accomplish anything through science.

For a long time such Christians saw the alternatives as science or faith—choose one. And they chose their faith. Then came the new generation of "creationists" with the message that Christians can now have their cake and eat it too. The Bible has been right all along; science is now seen to affirm the simple story to which the faithful have been holding for so long. Thus, the new twist of "creationism" is to argue that the facts of science point to "creation" rather than to "evolution." This is reflected in the title of the current creationist bible, *Scientific Creationism* (ed. Henry Morris, Creation-Life Publishers). Its message is that about 10,000 years ago God created by fiat a universe much like that of today. The earth's multitude of plant and animal species shares a simultaneous birth rather than any common ancestry, and the fossil-filled rock record is primarily a consequence of the flood of Noah.

In publications galore, this message has been disseminated through religious bookstores all over America. It has been picked up by a diverse readership—pastors, speakers, youth workers, and Sunday school teachers. Most of them are not scientifically trained. So the message they send forth is often garbled or incomplete or just plain wrong. Though their message is often lacking in accuracy or balance, it is heard by many Christian people, and it creates the widespread conviction that the scientific establishment is engaged in a conspiracy to keep the truth hidden so that atheistic secular humanism can have its way.

Seemingly in support of such a conclusion is the scarcity of books written by Christian authors who oppose recent earth "creationism." Many scientifically qualified people fall into this category, people with an orthodox faith in Jesus Christ and a deep commitment to divine creation. For a diversity of reasons they have not felt constrained to expose in writing the faulty foundation of "creationism." For some it is the unpleasantness of writing polemics against fellow Christians; for others it is a conviction that nothing will change the minds of those who want to believe the "creationist" paradigm. Still others recognize the many tentative areas of historical science and refuse to be drawn into a debate where rigidity seems to dominate.

An Analysis of the "Creationist" Phenomenon

How is it that one group of Christians has magnified the importance of a particular view of animate and inanimate history so that it rivals the redemptive message of the Christian gospel? What can explain, for example, the masthead of the *Bible-Science Newsletter*, which lists "A Young Earth" side by side with "Christ as God and Man—Our Savior"? It seems to me that the answer is a mixture of three ingredients: biblical interpretation, human personality, and the current American context.

Creationists, in my judgment, are hyper-literalists in their interpretation of the first chapter of Genesis. They require the days to be consecutive 24-hour intervals, and that makes humanity a mere five days younger than the oldest stars and rocks. Furthermore, the genealogies in later chapters are seen to confine humanity to the past 10,000 years or less; so that must also be the age of the entire universe. The incredible amount of scientific evidence for the earth's great age is swept aside with seeming ease. Henry Morris, for instance, writes: "The biblical cosmologist finally must recognize that the geological ages can have had no true objective existence at all, if the Bible is true" (*Biblical Cosmology and Modern Science*, 1970, Baker, p. 23).

Yet W. B. Riley, premier American evolution fighter of an earlier generation, had no trouble accepting the geologic ages. Furthermore, a later host of conservative Bible scholars considers an ancient earth fully compatible with Scripture. These are people with evangelical credentials and a commitment to biblical inerrancy—men such as J. Oliver Buswell, Jr., E. J. Young, and Gleason Archer. How unwise to ignore their contributions.

But behind the conviction that the Genesis 1 account of creation is to be taken in uniformly literal sense are also some very able people, the second ingredient in creationism, its leaders who write and debate and speak. As mentioned previously, they have scientific or engineering credentials. Above all, their zeal is based on a belief that they are serving God in a world that is godless. In withdrawing even from Christian scientists of different persuasion, they are like Elijah in their inability to recognize a cadre still loyal to God. Furthermore, a society increasingly aboveboard in its opposition to Christian faith almost confirms the wisdom of their withdrawal. Here is where the third strand enters: American culture in the later twentieth century.

One need not be a very perceptive observer of current American society to discern the erosion of Christian behavioral standards. The opposition to Christian mores has moved from insidious to blatant, forcing a defensive posture on those who would style their lives according to biblical principles. Furthermore, atheism clad in religious and intellectual garb is heralded more openly and more frequently. Thus pressured, Christians seek help in standing firm. Some reach out for symbols and causes that seem to echo the noble words of Martin Luther, "Here I stand: I can do no other!"

"Creationism," I believe, is one such cause. I understand it, but I cannot support it. To me it is a caricature of the true Christian view of men and things. In its isolation and inflexibility "creationism," in my judgment, is doing more harm than good.

Science—An Ally Not an Enemy

It is my belief that the scientific enterprise, as it exists today, is plodding along the path that leads to accurate knowledge of the material realm. This is not to sanction all that goes on in the name of science; rather it is to affirm that at its core the scientific enterprise is sound. Who can deny the significant progress already made toward understanding the material world? In addition, science seems to operate in ways that eventually weed out error and define profitable avenues of attack. This seems as true for unraveling earth history as for elucidating the nature of the atom.

Of course, no Christian would grant ultimacy to scientific truth, for the heavens and the earth are destined to pass away. But this is no reason for Christians to abandon science or participate only as kibitzers. As fellow passengers on planet Earth, Christian scientists should be in the thick of things, contributing and receiving, correcting and being corrected. Participation is not implying that the scientific enterprise will one day usher in an age of the ultimate, or even of total material truth. Rather, Christians within the scientific establishment are needed both to point out the impossibility of such goals and to witness to the divine message which redeems the material world.

When a Carl Sagan or a Jacob Bronowski is carried beyond the scientific data to personal speculation, who but a Christian scientist is more qualified to resist being hoodwinked and to articulate an accurate response? The challenge is to respond precisely and clearly when God's Word is clear, with restraint and admitted uncertainty when dogmatism is biblically unjustified. Our model is He who was full of grace and truth.

It is my conviction that Christians need to strive continually to integrate scientific truth with biblical truth, never demeaning one or the other, never setting one against the other. After all, the God who made the world also authored the Word. Only when we honor them both can he be glorified fully.

Chapter 2

The Beginning

RICHARD W. BERRY

Richard W. Berry, Professor of Geology at San Diego State University in California, has been notably active in geological research and publication. As a layman prominent in the affairs of the Presbyterian Church, he has helped to organize and lead week-long conferences on Genesis and Geology (held at Ghost Ranch, New Mexico) in a program which combines geological principles and fieldwork with biblical study. In the chapter which follows, Berry shows why the arguments of an imperialist scientism and an imperialist literalism can succeed only in talking past each other. Whereas he finds creationism too narrow and too imperialist in its methods and conclusions, so too are certain equally pretentious forms of scientism. Berry argues persuasively for a broader and more judicious approach than can be found in extreme and exclusivist positions on either side. He says that he began this article, which first appeared in the quarterly journal Theology Today, *"as a means of pulling my own thoughts together, and I now hope it will have a positive and healing effect on the controversy."*

Creationism or evolution? Can you be a Christian and believe in evolution? Is creationism a part of science or part of a fundamental religion? Is evolution a part of science or is it the work of humanists

This chapter is reprinted, by permission, from *Theology Today* (October, 1982), 39(3):249–59.

and the devil? These questions and many others like them are stirring our times and may be the sign of a deep schism developing in our society. Issues which first came into prominence during the Scopes Monkey Trial of 1925 are still being debated in legislative bodies and before various courts of our nation. Laws and courts have been able to do no more than give both sides time to rest and prepare to rejoin the battle.

One thing is abundantly clear—people are interested and concerned about what happened in the beginning. The interest in evolution and creationism should therefore come as no surprise, but what does surprise and even dismay people is the intensity of emotion and the degree of irrationality which come to the surface when these two ideas are debated. The conflict which is centered on evolution and creationism is convincing evidence that stories about creation are very important to the people who are telling them.

The objective of this article is to analyze the evolutionist and creationist positions and explain why the debate is so intense and the controversy so inflamed with passion. We will first examine what is meant by "stories of ultimate meaning" and what happens when they are told.

I

We all have areas in our lives where factual data are absent or inadequate to allow us full understanding of what is true, real, and meaningful. When faced with such a circumstance, humans usually tell a story about what they believe to be true, real, and meaningful. The more vital an area of a person's life which is involved, the more important the story becomes until it develops into a story of ultimate meaning, a story which expresses the ultimate truth about life and death. The more people who share the same story, the more powerful it becomes.

The absence or inadequacy of factual data leading to stories of ultimate meaning occurs in two different ways. In the first instance, the necessary or desired data are available but technological limitations prevent their acquisition. The flat earth story is an example. It was invented, had meaning, and was accepted as truth by those who needed to have a concept of the earth's shape but were unable to measure it accurately. The second reason for data being absent is that there simply are none in existence. Typical of this condition are stories which concern the presence, absence, and nature of God. No amount of technological advance will allow humanity to either prove or disprove stories about God. We are faced, therefore, with two varieties of stories of ultimate meaning. One variety is testable but for some reason has not yet been verified (or falsified). The second variety of story is inherently untestable and cannot be verified or falsified.

Most people found it relatively easy to accept the demise of the flat earth story when data showed it to be false. Flat earth people certainly felt frightened and threatened as their story was destroyed, but most of them moved ahead with a new and better story about an earth with the shape of a ball. For some flat earth people, the transition was devastating because their story about the shape of the earth was all tangled up with their story about God. Let us examine why it may have been relatively easy for some to change from a flat earth story to a spherical earth story while for others it was not. To do this we must observe the differences in the ways the shape-of-the-earth stories and God stories interacted.

Those who found it easier to shift to the spherical earth story might have said, "The earth is flat and God is in heaven." The statement really tells two independent stories. Destruction of the flat earth story does not threaten the God story. In contrast, those who found it difficult to accept a spherical earth story in the face of overwhelming evidence might have said, "The earth was created flat by God who is in heaven." This last statement resembles the first statement because it also consists of two totally different stories. Where it differs from the first statement is in the ultimate tangling of the two stories with each other. They are so closely interdependent that the destruction of the flat earth story, at the very least, called into serious question God's existence and place of residence. When faced with a threat to their concept of God, it is understandable why some flat earth people refused to reject the flat earth story. It is also understandable why it was easier for some to deny rational evidence, personal testimony, and overwhelming masses of data concerning a spherical earth than it was to deny God. Any time culture or a significant segment of society tells a story that is inherently not verifiable (a God story) and makes it dependent upon another story which is testable (verifiable), we risk intense and divisive conflict.

When stories are told about our life, death, and origins or about the forces which control our lives, their meaning takes on ultimate importance. Stories of ultimate meaning share much in common with stories which John Westerhoff refers to as myths. He says, "Myths explain that this is the way life really is in spite of any evidence to the contrary. Myths are not false stories." He goes on to say,

"They explain the meaning and purpose of life. They are true stories, in the most important sense of those words, for they explain our world. Everyone lives by some collection of myths. No one lives with meaning or purpose without them." Westerhoff gives further insight into the nature of myths and he says, "Sacred stories speak to our deepest, unconscious longings and questions, our problems and predicaments, our inner and outer struggles in human life. They exist in the form of truth that only intuition and imagination can provide, truth just as significant and real as that which comes through logical analysis and scientific probing."[1]

Stories of ultimate meaning which inherently are not verifiable (God stories) are clearly the same as Westerhoff's myths. But what about stories of ultimate meaning which *are* testable but which for some reason or another have not been verified? Are these also myths? The answer depends upon how the stories are viewed by the people who own or tell them. Clearly they are myths in the sense of Westerhoff's definition, if the people who own the stories which are falsifiable will only accept evidence in support of the stories and ignore all evidence to the contrary. These testable (refutable or verifiable) stories become inherently untestable in the minds of those people who own or tell the stories if they decide that the stories are true despite all contradictions. Falsifiable stories are elevated to the same uncontradictable status as the inherently untestable God stories when the two types of stories are ultimately tied together. It becomes easier to deny the refuting evidence than to deny God.

Two additional points need to be made about stories of ultimate meaning (inherently untestable and testable alike). The first is that these stories usually cannot be changed. They can be destroyed and a new one accepted in the place of an old one, or they can be added to, if the original story is maintained unchanged in the process. The reason it is so threatening to have even a small part of a story of ultimate meaning called into question is that it calls the whole story into question. The second point about stories of ultimate meaning is that the more people who believe the story, the more powerful the story becomes in the eyes of those who own the story. This is part of the motive for a group, denomination, or sect to evangelize people to believe in their particular story. The more who believe the story, the more resources there are available to defend the story and the greater the validation of the truth and importance of the story.

Society can get itself into deep trouble when a large segment tells a story of ultimate meaning which is believed immutable but which is also potentially refutable. Why does society do such a disservice to itself? At least two reasons come to mind. The first reason is simple and straightforward. Many of the testable stories were believed to be inherently untestable when they were first told. The flat earth story was told by people who could not conceive of the earth beyond the horizon. Not only that but they couldn't conceive of traveling far enough to see what did indeed exist beyond the horizon. As far as they were concerned, the earth looked flat from their perspective and beyond that the story was untestable. The second reason why society will ascribe untestable qualities to a story which is indeed testable is slightly more complicated and indirect. We can start first with the God stories. Despite the fact that such stories of ultimate meaning are inherently untestable, we humans are tempted (even driven) to try to test the untestable. Many, perhaps all humans have some degree of yearning to prove or disprove the existence of God on a more concrete basis than faith. It is insidiously easy to tie a testable story of ultimate meaning to the God story for when the testable story is verified it also gives a sense of verification of the God story. All is well unless the testable story is refuted; then the God story is called into question at the same time. At this point the story-teller must either ignore the refutation or risk losing God.

For either of the two reasons, society has placed many booby traps in its stories of ultimate meaning. One of the causes of society's uneasiness in these modern times is that science and technology are revealing mythic booby traps at a rate which we find difficult to accommodate. As science and technology challenge stories of great or ultimate meaning, they also engender a growing sense of anti-science/anti-technology.

II

Creationists are telling a story about our beginnings which is rooted solely in the first two chapters of the book of Genesis. When we look at the Genesis account, we see that there is both a God story ("In the beginning God created . . .") and a story about the order and timing of creation. The first story is inherently untestable, whereas the second story is quite testable. Creationists find the theory of evolution to be very threatening, as legislative tactics and court actions attest.

Exactly why evolution is so threatening is not obvious. Evolutionists intend no threat to the God story. Christian evolutionists share the God story about who was responsible for creation. Atheist evolutionists find the God story irrelevant to their study of the *process* of development of life on earth. A study of the process of creation (evolution) is as little affected by Christian or atheistic beliefs as a study of combustion would be affected by who lit the fire. The God story concerns the who of creation whereas evolution concerns the when and how of creation, so there is no direct threat to the God story.

At one time, creationists demanded that evolution be taught as a theory. Scientists were quick to agree. Most scientists who are actively involved in research pertaining to evolution view it as a theory or concept which has much merit and is generally valid. They also agree that the understanding of the details of evolution needs refining and much more research is necessary before the theory is substantiated in all its parts. The theory of evolution is testable, and the testing is going on continuously. The creationists had made a demand, and the evolutionists had acquiesced. For a while it appeared that the threat to the creationist's story had been removed. Since there was no direct threat to the God story, this should have resolved the controversy and the creationists and evolutionists were free to go their separate ways. The creationists soon revealed, however, that the threat to them had not been removed. If a controversy had indeed been resolved, it was the wrong controversy. The battle quickly resumed.

The question remains, what is it that the creationists find so threatening in evolution? Evolution does not directly threaten the supremacy of God as Creator because it concerns itself with the "how" of creation, not the "who" or "why." Evolution does not threaten creationism by claiming to be an immutable law of science or the universe because it isn't. We must conclude by process of elimination that evolution is threatening to creationists even in the form of a *theoretical alternative* to the two accounts of creation which are given in Genesis. Creationists respond to the threat by calling evolution "non-Christian" and "humanist" inspired. This doesn't tell us why evolution is threatening but it does help delineate the threat and gives us a direction to follow in our inquiry. Despite the fact that creationists assert that one cannot be an evolutionist and a Christian, there are many Christians who are not at all troubled by the theory of evolution. Let us pursue the difference in response of Christians to evolution in an attempt to understand more fully the threat as perceived by creationist Christians.

Most, if not all, Christians share the story of God's responsibility for creation, so we must look elsewhere for the reason for the different responses to evolution. This leaves the Genesis accounts of the order and timing of creation to which some Christians respond as evolutionists and some as creationists. Why don't all Christians turn to creationism in the face of the theory of evolution? It is because despite the sharing of the story of God as the "who" and "why" of creation, not all Christians tell exactly the same story about the "how" of creation. We all share the same words but the story is not quite the same.

To some, the steps and timing of creation in Genesis represent what the ancient Hebrews and their predecessors were able to understand about creation. To others, these same words and passages are a poetic statement, and the structure of the language in which the verses were spoken, and then written, did more to control the nature and order of events which were included than did any insight into fact. When creationists use these same words in Genesis they tell yet another story which is that the Genesis account is the way that God actually chose to create the universe. All of these examples are consistent with the idea of God as Creator. All of them are interpretations of Genesis to be found in Christendom today. Only one of the examples is told by people who find evolution to be threatening. The creationist not only finds evolution threatening to the biblical steps of the creation story, but it is also threatening to the ultimate role of God as Creator even to the point of threatening the existence of God.

Creationists have set themselves apart from other Christians by intimately interweaving their story of the "who" of creation with the "how" of creation. For them, it is the flat earth problem all over again. Creationists have taken a theory of creation which is testable and tied it to an inherently untestable story about God. In the process, they have declared a testable theory to be also inherently untestable. As was pointed out earlier, this works fine, if the testable story is verified. Controversy has arisen because evolution has not verified the creationist's story. At best, research has shown the Genesis account of the "how" of creation to be incomplete. Because the creationists have tied their story of the "how" of creation to their story of the "who" of creation, any doubt cast upon the "how" also casts doubt on the "who." Creationists follow a predictable pattern as they find it easier to deny physical evidence than to deny God. Physical evidence, no matter how overwhelming, can be dismissed as the work of the devil. Christians who find evolution acceptable, or at least not threatening, are those who have managed to keep their stories of the "how" of creation separate from the "who" and "why" of creation.

In simplest terms, creationists reject the theory of evolution not because evolution is bad, in and of itself, but because for them it threatens, indirectly yet potently, the very existence of God. Scientific arguments in support of evolution will have little if any effect because creationists are not really arguing about the validity of the theory of evolution but the existence of God.

III

Surely the idea of creationism holds no threat to evolutionists. Where would the threat come from? Those who work to improve and refine the theory of evolution are scientists for the most part. Evolution is a scientific theory. Creationism is not science, so how could it threaten science? Creationism is in part theology, philosophy, history, and even, perhaps, sociology, but it isn't science. Furthermore, calling it "Creation Science" or "Scientific Creationism" does not make it science. The heart of science, the scientific method, is to test hypotheses and theories with the objective of verifying or falsifying them. Since the Genesis story is held by creationists to be untestable, then creationism which is based solely on Genesis cannot be science. I am not trying to diminish the importance of creationism by stating that it is not science—only trying to establish proper labels and to do away with inappropriate terminology. If creationism is not a scientific theory in competition with evolution, then why are evolutionists and scientists in general so threatened by it?

Robert Dott has noted that "much of the rhetoric from the conventional scientific community about creationism has been so dogmatic—even hysterical—as to be counter-productive."[2] Such rhetoric is no more rational than creationist rejection of substantiated data. Both types of behavior represent a response to threats to stories or beliefs of ultimate importance in the lives of the people concerned. We have already established the nature of the threat to the creationist. We must now seek out the source of the threat to evolutionists. I do not refer to threats to academic or political freedom as a result of laws passed recently and currently being reviewed in the courts of several states. These kinds of threats, important as they are, usually elicit rational responses through politics, the courts, or various media of communication.

We must search for a threat to scientists which would be viewed by them to be as profound and potentially injurious as we found the threat to the creationists' God. What does creationism call into question which is parallel to evolution calling the creationists' God into question? What is the story of ultimate meaning which is shared by the scientific community (theist and atheist alike)? How does creationism threaten this story? It cannot be a story about God's existence, for if it were, there would be no evolutionists who were also Christians. We need to discover what it is in science that is accepted widely, principally because it has worked well in the past and continues to work well. What is it in science which seems intuitively obviously true but which defies proof or is inherently untestable in a rigorous way?

The only thing that comes to mind is the *scientific method of inquiry*. The scientific method is so important that no more painful or damning criticism can be leveled at scientists than that they depart from the scientific method. This is the means by which science approaches truth and documents the approach. It is used to test ideas and proposals of the scientific community.

But we must ask, "Who or what is testing the test?" I do not doubt the validity of the scientific method nor do I mean to raise doubts about it. It has served well and not been shown significantly to be errant in decades, even centuries of use. I do suggest, however, that it qualifies as a story of ultimate meaning to scientists. When the scientific method is called into question, it also calls into question the concepts derived by means of the scientific method.

The threat of creationism to the scientific method is subtle but potent. Science is faced with an idea which is called science but is not science. Beyond this, creationism is held up to society as being "true science" which is outside normal science and as such is equal to or better than any theory which could come out of the scientific community (specifically, evolution). Furthermore, any attempts on the part of the scientific community to use the scientific method to verify evolution or refute creationism are ignored or belittled by creationists. When the general public votes (directly or through their elected representatives) to establish creationism to be either on equal terms with or superior to evolution in science education, it also calls into question the validity or potency of the scientific method by means of which the theory of evolution was derived. Hence, the threat of creationism to evolutionism is minor in the face of the much more serious and fundamental threat to the scientific method and even to scientific objectivity.

In simplest terms, the evolutionist rejects and fights the idea of creationism not because it is bad, in and of itself, but because it is presented as being science and thus threatens the validity of the scientific method and scientific objectivity. Theological arguments or factual nit-picking by creationists with regard to evolution will have little if any effect because the evolutionist is not arguing about the validity of creationism but on behalf of the scientific method and scientific objectivity.

IV

The complexity of the controversy and the reasons for it being so heated begin to become clear. Ostensibly there are two groups of people arguing the relative merits of the concepts of evolution and creationism. The two sides are having little effect on each other except to make each other angry. Arguments are put forward, proofs are presented but no resolution is in sight except for what is imposed through political or judicial action. It is no wonder that the controversy continues because what was just described is what is *apparently* going on, not what is *actually* going on. What the creationists are really saying is that God is real and responsible for creation, so scientific proof in support of evolution seems irrelevant to them. What evolutionists are really saying is that the scientific method is valid and is the most effective means of maintaining objectivity in the search for truth, so philosophical or theological arguments in support of creationism seem irrelevant. Is it any wonder that neither side is successful in influencing the other? They only appear to be debating the evolution/creationism controversy; each side is actually debating and defending something quite different.

It is ironic that neither side recognizes or is willfully attacking what the other side is defending. Scientists, those who are also Christians, agree with the story of God as Creator. Scientists who are atheists are interested in what is happening in the universe but couldn't care less if someone wants to make God responsible for it all. Most creationists neither understand nor care about the scientific method. Accordingly, we have two groups who appear to be defending one thing while they are actually defending something else. Proofs and arguments not directed at the appropriate targets become meaningless while provoking anger at the same time. It is easy to understand why both sides of the controversy have turned to propaganda and power politics to attain resolution. Sadly, any resolution to the controversy which is reached by these means is likely to be uneasy and temporary. The Scopes Monkey Trial will be brought back to trial again and again under various guises until both sides recognize what is really being argued and so come to a mutually satisfactory agreement. The resolution must be one that avoids threatening either side's story of ultimate meaning.

V

It is important that effective steps be taken to bring about reconciliation between creationists and evolutionists, at least to the degree that they believe that they can co-exist, peacefully. Much more is at stake than evolution and creationism. Men and women who assumed leadership roles on both sides of the conflict when it first began, did so for the very highest moral and ethical motives. Many who remain involved today maintain the same motives. Unfortunately, controversy draws religious and scientific opportunists like honey draws flies. Such people exacerbate the confusion while professing to be helpful. But their objectives are often simply self-aggrandizement, financial profit, and power. The judicial and political maneuverings that are now occurring in several states are being rendered unnecessarily complex by the mixed motives of protagonists and antagonists. To quote Lucy in a Peanuts cartoon by Schulz, "It's becoming increasingly difficult to tell the 'Phonies' from the 'Realies'."

There is an urgent need for reconciliation between the two sides before irreparable harm is done both to science and religion in our nation. I make no claim to having the complete solution to the problem, but there are steps that can be taken to reduce the threats to the stories of ultimate meaning on both sides.

(1) One step is to stop calling creationism a scientific concept. Most creationists admit that it isn't science. If creationists are concerned with presenting the Genesis view of creation to the young people of our country it should be labeled properly. The case for having the creationist view of beginnings presented in a believable and supportable way would be strengthened by labeling it theology, which it is, rather than science, which it is not. The shift in labeling does not reduce the importance of the concept of creationism nor does it belittle the importance of God. It allows argument about the relative merits of theological and scientific stories of creation without so severe a threat to the underlying stories of ultimate meaning.

(2) Another step is to stop inundating creationists with data in support of evolution, except when truly necessary (as in a court case). These data are irrelevant to the actual case of the creationists and will only cause them to nit-pick the scientific literature to find anything that might cast doubt on the integrity of the scientific method or of scientists themselves. Such counterattacks are usually shown to be without substance, but the general public sees the scientific community belittled on grounds which cannot be evaluated immediately, thereby furthering the tendency toward anti-science and anti-technology.

(3) A third step is for creationists to view evolution as a supplement to the Genesis account of creation rather than as a replacement of it. Although stories of ultimate meaning cannot be amended, they can be appended. The Bible reveals that God communicated with humanity in accordance with humanity's ability to comprehend. God's revelation became more profound and complicated as our ability to reason and understand became more sophisticated, from Abraham to Moses to Jesus. It is my hope that creationists view the Genesis accounts of creation as being the word of God spoken in terms that people could understand, thousands of years ago. It is my further hope that creationists believe that God gave us brains to appreciate and study what has been created. From this position, I urge creationists to consider accepting evolution as doing no more than supplying the details for the biblical account; details which would have been mostly incomprehensible to Old Testament Hebrews.

I have been asked why God did not include evolution in Genesis if evolution was indeed God's procedure of creation? When answering this, I ask the questioner to visualize a hill under starry skies, somewhere in the vicinity of Jerusalem. A young shepherd is sitting on the hill watching the sheep and wondering how it all came into being. At this point a strong, comforting voice calls the shepherd by name, "Hameed." The shepherd answers, "Yes, Lord," with more than a little fear and trembling. The voice continues, "Listen while I tell you how I created the universe." Hameed thanks God and settles down to listen, and God says. . . !

So I ask the questioner to *assume* that God did indeed use something akin to our concept of evolution to create the universe as we know it. Based on this assumption would God have gone on to talk about electrons and protons, genes and DNA, plate tectonics, and continental drift, or would God have given Hameed an explanation something like the Genesis accounts? This approach usually helps the questioner understand that given the time and person with whom God was communicating, the account of creation had to be simple, much simpler than the actual process God chose. For this reason, the absence of the theory of evolution from Genesis cannot be used to prove that evolution is not part of God's means of creation. With this in mind, it may be possible for creationists to add evolution to their story of ultimate meaning rather than believing that it contradicts or threatens it.

The last suggested step is a suggestion to creationists and evolutionists alike. Avoid saying that one cannot believe in both God and evolution. There are many of us who believe in both.

There is little hope of reconciling the evolutionist and creationist positions until both sides start talking about the real issues. We must all stop pretending that the controversy pertains to no more than evolution and creationism. Profoundly important stories of ultimate meaning are involved, the God story of the creationist and the scientific objectivity story of the evolutionist. Until it is recognized by both sides what it is that the battle is really about, resolution is unlikely.

Notes

1. John H. Westerhoff, III, *Bringing Up Children in the Christian Faith* (Minneapolis, Minn.: Winston Press, 1980), pp. 37, 39.
2. Robert H. Dott, Jr., "The Challenge of Scientific Creationism," *Journal of Sedimentary Petrology* (1980), 51(3):701–4.

Chapter 3

Creationism: The Roots of the Conflict

LANGDON GILKEY

Langdon Gilkey is Shailer Mathews Professor of Theology at the Divinity School of the University of Chicago. He has written two important books on the relations of science and religion (Three Essays on Science and the Sacred *and* Religion and the Scientific Future, *both published in 1981) and a seminal study of the biblical teachings on creation,* Maker of Heaven and Earth: A Study of the Christian Doctrine of Creation *(1959). He has probably been more intimately involved in the creation-science debate than any other leading Protestant theologian, and he served brilliantly as an expert witness in the court case involving the Arkansas "creationism law." Few legal issues in recent years have attracted such wide public interest as this one. The Arkansas law (Act 590 of 1981) required that equal time be given to creation-science where evolution was taught in the schools. On January 5, 1982, U.S. District Judge William Ray Overton found the law unconstitutional under the First Amendment's ban against any establishment of religion, thus upholding the challenge to that law by a group of plaintiffs, most of whom represented religious groups. The following essay contains some of Gilkey's reflections on various important issues represented in that case, reflections which include but also go much deeper than the legal questions involved.*

Adapted, by permission, from an article that appeared in Science, Technology & Human Values (Summer, 1982), 7:67–71. Copyright © 1982 by the Massachusetts Institute of Technology and the President and Fellows of Harvard College. A version of this article also appeared in Christianity and Crisis (April 26, 1982), 42:108–15, and the version printed here conflates the two.

The Arkansas "creation-science" case raised issues of such importance for religion, for science, and for society as to require the careful consideration of all thoughtful persons. The case was argued by the lawyers of the American Civil Liberties Union on behalf of leaders of the major Christian Churches in Arkansas, three national Jewish groups, and other concerned citizens. Like many other Christians, I was grateful by Judge Overton's decision declaring the Arkansas law unconstitutional. It should be understood, however, that the struggle is not over in the courts; new and differently nuanced versions of the Arkansas law, enacted or awaiting passage in other state legislatures, remain to be tested.

Apart from the constitutional issues, moreover, the creationist controversy raises other questions having to do with the relation of scientific truth to religious truth and with the degree to which scientists on the one hand and "religionists" on the other comprehend these questions. The problems rise out of the very nature of an advanced scientific and technological culture that also remains a religious culture. We are all aware of the fundamentalism that operates within parts of the religious culture; as will be seen, there is another kind of fundamentalism manifested by scientists—including some on both sides of the issue argued in Little Rock.

The law tested in that case, Arkansas' Act 590, represented an effort to avoid the First Amendment test. In requiring that "evolution science" and "creation science" should receive balanced treatment in science classes (roughly, "equal time"), it specified that no references to "religious doctrines" or "religious materials" were to be made; it tried to define each of these "scientific models" very broadly, and it said that whenever either one was taught, then the other should also be taught.

On the face of it, this law seems innocent, even virtuous enough. It pleads for objectivity and fairness, the rough justice of equal time. It promises to avoid religion; it seeks to break open a probably quite real liberal, humanistic . . . establishment of ideas in the scientific and academic communities. Yet it is an exceedingly dangerous law whose enactment in any wide extent would represent a disaster to our society. Why? Clearly the legal issue, as the lawyers for the American Civil Liberties Union saw, was that this law contravened the First Amendment. But there are also other, deeper issues involved. Although each of us will give a different emphasis to these elements, I suggest that the following represent the *main* reasons that defeat of this and similar laws is of such overriding importance.

An Official Religion

(1) First, the law endangers the free practice of religion in our society by the establishment in the public schools of one particular tradition (Christianity) and, indeed, one particular interpretation of the Christian religion. It does this by presenting as "science" a particular, even sectarian, interpretation of the Christian symbol of the creation and so of the Book of Genesis—thus ruling out not only other religious and philosophical traditions than the Christian but also other Christian views of creation, my own included. It tacitly equates religion, and Christianity, with a literalistic fundamentalism. This equation would be a disaster for the religious communities of America. That was the central reason most of the plaintiffs [against the law] were church leaders and individual churchgoers—and why we witnesses from religious studies were present.

(2) Act 590 and its equivalents in Louisiana and elsewhere parade as science a model or theory which in fact is not science, and insert this theory into the scientific classroom. The result of such legislation almost certainly would be *either* deep confusion about what science is and what theories most branches of contemporary science hold, *or* the refusal by responsible educators to teach either model and thus the disappearance of genuine science instruction in our secondary schools. This would in turn represent a disaster for American science as a whole comparable to the fiasco of Soviet biology during the Lysenko era. Our society is now technological to the core; its institutional foundations would be severely shaken if the level of its scientific instruction were seriously damaged.

(3) Act 590 and its siblings represent a dangerous challenge to academic freedom. Here the State is not only legislating on the subjects to be taught in a curriculum; it is going further and requiring a given profession—the science teachers—to teach certain definite theories or models. In doing this the State replaces, or seeks to replace, the consensus of the community of working scientists as the authority capable of determining the methods and content of science. The scientifically legitimate "models" to be discussed and studied are made the business of legislatures. No longer is the question what is science and what may be taught in its name to be answered by the community of scientists in its relation to the individual teacher of science (a relation that can take a number of varied forms); it is answered authoritatively by the State's insistence on these two theories and no others. Expanded into other, even more sensitive areas such as history, civics, political and economic theory and philosophy, this precedent could well subvert the authority of each professional community to determine its own criteria, canons or methods and its subject matter—and result in a disaster to public education. According to our lawyers, this

important, not to say crucial, element of the case was too elusive legally or constitutionally to be made central to the argument. As a result, it was more implied than stressed in the presentation of the case.

Confusions Over Kinds of Knowledge

The basic error reflected in the Arkansas law is to regard these two models—one religious (creationism) and the other scientific (evolution)—as equivalent, logically comparable and therefore mutually exclusive theories or interpretations. Creationist documents present both as parallel explanations of "origins." Paradoxically, both are argued to be "scientific" or "equally scientific," yet both are called equally "religious"—one model representing a believing, Christian and biblical religion and the other espousing an "atheistic" or "humanistic" religion. The person who believes in evolution cannot also believe in God or the Bible, this attitude argues; correspondingly, a person who believes in God, and finds some sort of truth in Genesis, must deny evolution. Only as equivalent hypotheses can both models be regarded as scientific explanations, can one model be regarded as the representative of valid religion, and can the State be viewed as having an apparently legitimate responsibility to accommodate both. This error of regarding evolution and Genesis as comparable and therefore mutually exclusive "explanations" is not confined to the fundamentalist community; it represents the confusion out of which this controversy as a whole has arisen. The following two points descriptive of the creationists' arguments contain innumerable further confusions about not only religion but also science, especially its formal structure, methods, and canons.

First, the creationists claim that creationism is not religion but science—a "scientific model" based on "scientific evidence" or "scientific facts" and thus "at least as scientific as evolution." It is not religion because it neither appeals to scriptural or doctrinal authority nor talks about God "religiously" (e.g., as a personal, loving savior and so on). Neither creation nor evolution, they argue, can be "scientifically proved" because origins, however interpreted, lie beyond direct observation and so beyond experimental testing. Thus, the relative status of each model depends on the "scientific evidence" to which each can appeal, and the capacity of each model to "explain intelligibly" these data.

Second, creationists' writings, and the Arkansas law itself, assume that what the creationists call a "naturalistic explanation"—and, by extension, any theory of science based on such an explanation—is inherently atheistic. If a theory leaves out God—as the scientific theory of evolution certainly does—then it is clearly false and so cannot be *really* "science."* Evolution, therefore, to them means not merely a tentative theory full of empirical or scientific "holes"; it represents a deliberate and powerful expression of naturalism or atheism. And in some of the creationists' religious writings, the same authors portray evolution as an instrument of aggression by cosmic forces of evil, by the Devil himself.

What sorts of confusions are represented here? First, there is confusion about what science is. The creationists—many of whom are trained scientists—speak of "scientific facts" and "scientific evidence"; they see science as located in its facts, rather than in its theoretical structure. There is little recognition of the "canons" of scientific method, the logical conditions that make a theory a part of *science,* and creation-science contravenes each of these major "canons." The creation-science "model" is, therefore, not an example of science at all: it involves a supra-natural cause, transcendent to the system of finite causes; it explains in terms of purposes and intentions; and it cites a transcendent, unique, and unrepeatable—even in principle, uncontrollable—action. It represents, therefore, logically and linguistically, a re-edition of a familiar form—that is, "natural theology," which argues that certain data point "rationally" to a philosophical/religious conclusion, namely, to the agency of a divine being.

.. Second, the creationists fail to distinguish the question of *ultimate* origins (Where did it *all* come from?) from the quite different question of *proximate* origins (How did A arise out of B, if it did?). They ignore the (scholastic) distinction between the *primary* causality of a First Cause, with which philosophy or theology might deal, and *secondary* causality, which is causality confined to finite factors. Assuming that it is science's role to deal with the truth and, therefore, with *all* of the truth, they conclude that a scientific explanation of origins must be an *exhaustive* explanation and must be inclusive of all possible related factors or causes. If evolution theory deals with proximate origins, it must also deal with the question of ultimate origins. If, in this process, evolution theory has left out God, then it

---

*In a scientific culture, science is regarded not only as *true* but also as *defining* *truth.* As a consequence, some religious people in such a culture can believe that an atheistic science must *ipso facto* be not science but *false science* (i.e., they do *not* say that science is false but that *this* is false science).—LG

must be asserting that there is no God, or that the divine is in no way the Creator of the process of secondary causes. At the Arkansas trial, the creationists therefore interpreted the scientific witnesses' demurrals that "science does not raise the question about God at all" as meaning that science rules out the presence of God in any way.

The creationists ignore—or possibly are unaware of—the restrictive canons of the scientific method (e.g., that no super-natural causes may be included in a theory) and the distinction of ultimate from proximate origins. As a consequence, they fail (as do many) to understand that, although science provides testable and relatively certain conclusions, its conclusions or answers are limited and not exhaustive. As in the parallel cases of historical inquiry, law, or psychology, the "atheism" of natural science is *a priori* and methodological. No acceptable historical or legal hypothesis can include the *divine* as a central cause of an historical event or of a crime. If, as another example, objective psychological inquiry cannot locate experimentally (behavioristically) any sign of my inward freedom, this does not mean either that such freedom is not, in fact, there or that psychological inquiry denies human intentionality—unless, of course, one specifies in advance that the results of *only* such inquiry are to be considered "real." In the same way, scientific explanations of proximate origins are confined to using *finite* causes as principles of explanation and thus leave quite open the question of God. The charge that evolution is "atheistic" is, as a consequence, a simple tautology, an analytic judgment equivalent to the assertion "this is a scientific theory."

Confusions about the nature and rules of the scientific method, about the distinction between scientific and other forms of knowing, and so about the limitations of scientific inquiry—and the subsequent distinction of ultimate from proximate questions of origins—have bred the theoretical confusions that made this case possible. These same confusions are not confined to fundamentalist groups. In a culture in which science represents the paradigmatic, if not the exclusive, mode of knowing, knowledge is apt to be regarded as all on one level. As a consequence, scientific and religious explanations are bound to conflict and may be regarded at one moment as "science" and at another as "religion." At the same time that naturalistic humanism parades itself as "what we scientists now know," therefore, fundamentalist creationism challenges evolution science with the claim to represent an *alternative* "science." Which one is more confused about both science and religion is hard to say.

The Theological Testimony

The logic of the plaintiff's case in *McLean v. Arkansas* was directed at the confusions embodied in the law itself and in this "scientific" defense of the law. The plaintiffs wished, first of all, to establish that the creationist model represents a particular form of religion, one exclusive of not only all non-Christian religions but also most recognized forms of Christian faith. The theological testimony at the trial dealt with these arguments *theoretically*.

In a monotheistic culture, the testimony went, all that is religious has to do with God and all that has to do with God is religious. For monotheistic religions, God is the principle of ultimate reality and therefore is the source of all other reality, the principle of authority in revelation, the source of every religious way of life, and the founding agent of the religious community. Religion refers essentially and exclusively to God. This religious reference includes *all* of God's actions, his or her creative activity in establishing the world, and divine redeeming action in reuniting with us. For this reason, all supra-natural beings who create are as much "gods" as are all such beings who save. To speak of a creator of all things, therefore, is to speak religiously, even if a philosophical argument may also be produced to give secular warrants for this notion. Not all religions have gods and surely not all worship God, but all that has to do with God is certainly religious.

When, in order to circumvent this argument, the authors of the Arkansas law sought to separate the Creator implied by creation-science from the notion of "religion," it was ironic that they came close thereby to the "first and worst" Christian heresy—the denial of monotheism (i.e., the belief in two gods, one of them the morally dubious creator and the other the good, loving Savior God). It was no accident . . . that the first article of the earliest Christian creed witnessed to "one God, the Father Almighty, and Maker of Heaven and earth." Further, if religious statements are referent to God and not to finite causes—and this defines most Western religious assertions—then, of all the statements about God that could be made, the proposition that God creates "out of nothing" is the *most* religious. By definition, no other agent was present because this act established all other agents. The Arkansas law, therefore, is religious not because it refers explicitly to a doctrine or appeals to scripture, but because the notion of the agency of a supra-natural being is essential to each of the constitutive elements of the creationist model—and that is, *ipso facto*, religious speech. Finally, the creationist model proposes a *particular* religious view of creation, different from that of other religious traditions and different from other Christian interpretations. It is not a scientific model at all but a theological one and thus (as Judge Overton held in his opinion) contravenes the First Amendment.

Testimony by scientists at the Arkansas trial supported this line of argument. Creation-science is not, they said, science at all. In making its own case as legitimate science, creationism has misunderstood the methods of science, many of its fundamental laws, and many of its present theoretical conclusions. In denying that evolution is valid science, in asserting that it is disguised religion, and in rejecting the testability of evolution theory's major conclusions, the creation scientists reveal that they do not understand how the relevant sciences proceed, how theories are composed and tested, and what scientific status various hypotheses can claim. The distinction between alternative *scientific* accounts and a *religious* account of origins was fundamental to the plaintiffs' strategy. Time and again, scientists testified "but *that* is not science"—a statement dependent for its force on the mostly unexplicated distinction between scientific and religious speech and understanding, a distinction operative in types of questions asked, in procedures and authorities invoked, in the forms of speech used, and in the shape of the resulting system of symbols.

At the Interface of Inquiry and Belief

The Arkansas case does *not* represent simple warfare between the enlightened forces of science on the one hand and the darkening forces of religion on the other—as fundamentalists, the secular intelligentsia, and the media have frequently implied. The makeup of the list of plaintiffs and their witnesses in the Arkansas case shows this. Almost all the mainline churches were represented on the "science" side and only *one* scientific organization, and on our own team half the witnesses represented religion. Arguing in defense of creationism, a whole battery of "scientists" provided the theoretical backing and gave the central testimony. Several scores of these "creation scientists" hold advanced degrees in science from major universities; they could not, I warrant, have found a single biblical scholar or theologian with the same level of professional degree to support them. If one then says, "But these are not recognized, established scientists, working members of the scientific community," one can answer, neither were the spokesmen for the type of religion represented by the creationists "recognized, established" religious leaders.

Historians of science now recognize that the image of a warfare between science and religion was not even true in the 19th century. Such a picture of a conflict between two separate forces, old-time religion and new world science, is, in our advanced technological culture, sheer mythology. Technology and science in some form or other characterize now all levels of society, and correspondingly, so do "faith" and the religious in some sense or other. Moreover, the religion represented in the creationist case is itself a function, a product, an aspect of that technological and scientific society, not a carry-over from the old. Fundamentalist and cultic forms of religion have grown in our lifetime *because of* the dilemmas of a technological society, not *despite* the character of that society. Both technology and religion are permanent and essential aspects of the culture as a whole; both are potentially very creative and both potentially infinitely destructive.

If this litigation is not merely the last episode in a continuing contest but is, in fact, a much more complex problem of misinterpretation, on many levels, of two essential and pervasive aspects of cultural life, then how are we to understand it? First, much of the blame for misinterpretation rests with the churches and the schools of theology. One of theology's major tasks in the last two centuries has been to understand reflectively how religious faith (and, by extension, Christian religious faith—even in Genesis) can be reinterpreted in the light of modern science. Yet, a satisfactory (i.e., intelligible) understanding of the relationship between religion and science has not permeated American church life (or, I might add, all of American society). Many people still assume that to believe in God or the Bible one must reject the notion of evolution. For example, following my testimony in Arkansas, a *Time* Magazine reporter asked me "If you are a Christian theologian and believe in revelation, how can you accept Darwin?" I replied, "On many counts I don't. I understand there are today a number of scientific reasons for questioning elements of Darwin's theory." The reporter seemed even more baffled by my reply.

The responsibility of the religious community is clear enough. What is not so obvious is the scientific community's responsibility for this same problem. Many scientists share with the fundamentalists the confused notion that so-called religious knowledge and scientific knowledge exist on the same level and that, as science advances, scientific knowledge simply replaces and dissolves religious myth. Religion is viewed primarily as "belief," an early and very shaky stage of human *cognition* and understanding and an enterprise that reaches its culmination in modern science. Religion is thus regarded as "pre-science," "early science," or "primitive science," and can be expected to vanish, as do all denizens of the night, when the daylight of science appears and spreads—a view theologians often characterize as the "Walt Disney theory" of cultural history. While scientists who believe this interpretation reject *all* of religion as pre-science, the creationists cling to certain aspects of science associated with their religious faith and reject only scientific hypotheses that compete with the doctrines of that faith. One encounters this view of science as dissolving religious truth in the writings of Julian Huxley, Gaylord Simpson, Jacob Bronowski, and Carl Sagan; a recent volume of readings in evolution theory edited by C. Leon Harris, for example, classifies Genesis under the heading of "pre-scientific myth" and cites the great St. Augustine under the bizarre title "The Infanticide of Science: Augustine and the Dark Ages." This is about as informed and sensitive as listing Einstein and Fermi under the heading "The Development of Destructive Weaponry."

Not only do the scientific naturalists and the fundamentalists agree in theory that religious truth and scientific theory are direct competitors and so mutually exclusive, but each perspective tends to breed and encourage the other. Much of scientific naturalism has gestated out of parental fundamentalism or orthodoxy. Correspondingly, the new fundamentalist reaction against evolution has arisen in part because of the frequently careless and uninformed way evolution science is being taught. Each time a child comes home and reports, "I learned in school today that Genesis is wrong," the seed is planted for creationist reaction. As fundamentalism originally arose in the late 19th and early 20th centuries as a reaction against liberal and modernist Protestantism, so creation-science has arisen in our day in reaction to scientific naturalism, which is a global (and, therefore, "religious") *weltanschauung* based on science but extending beyond science to encompass and frame all of human experience.

In a scientific culture it is rightly taken for granted that the modern educated person should understand at least enough science to be aware of its methods and limits, of its most general conclusions, and, above all, of the "world" of reality, truth, and value which science implies. Because of the myth of the absoluteness and self-sufficiency of scientific knowing and because of a confidence in the imminent disappearance of religion, the reverse has not been the case. Scientists have not been expected to be aware of the wider implications of their methods and, by and large, have not been encouraged to reflect on the relations of scientific truth to *other* ways of knowing such as historical inquiry, art, morals, philosophy, or religion.

The myth that religion will vanish in a secular and scientific culture is itself vanishing under the pressure of repeated historical falsification. Part of the counterfactual data is the reappearance of fundamentalism, the appearance (in unexpected variety and strength) of non-Western religious cults, and the appearance in political and economic ideologies of historical myths that unify, empower, and direct modern technological societies much as traditional religions unified and directed archaic societies—for example, the myth of democratic, liberal, and scientific Progress or the myth of Marxist Communism. None of these new forces represents traditional religion carried over from the past, as do Western Christianity and Judaism. These new religious forms appear and reappear *out of* and *because of* a scientific, technological culture in response, first, to the demand for a credible system of symbols giving structure, meaning, and direction to nature, history, society, and the self, and, second, to the particular sharp anxieties—and even terrors—of a technological age, especially one in apparent, although not admitted, decline.

The creative as opposed to the destructive effects of scientific knowledge and technology *depend* on other aspects of culture: on its political and legal structures and processes, on its moral integrity and courage, and on the forms of its religious faith. Our century has also shown the persistence, the permanence, the ever-renewed power, as well as the deep ambiguity, of religion. But religion in one form or another does and will continue to exist—like science—in both demonic *and* creative form. The relations between these two essential and permanent elements of culture represent a recurrent, fundamental issue that should be a part of the training and self-understanding of both the scientific and the religious communities. In such times as these, the religious dimension tends to expand, and, unfortunately, to grow in fanaticism, intolerance, and violence; science and technology tend accordingly to concentrate more and more on developing greater and greater means of destructive and repressive power. The combination represents a most dependable recipe for self-destruction. Let both the scientific and the religious communities, then, re-think their roles in this light; let each especially reflect upon its relations to the other community in our total social life. Only then can we prevent the proliferation of laws such as Act 590 which unite science and religion in ways destructive of the genius of each.

Science and religion will unite in some form or another in any case: in theocratic or fundamentalist form, in political, ideological form—or in the more desirable form of a relation respectful of the autonomy and yet the creative power of each. Such a desideratum, however, requires critical reflection both ways, joint dialogue and deliberation; above all, mutual respect, interest and forbearance. It is not too late for these two important communities to embark on such mutually vital communication—let us begin.

part two

Rebutting Creationism

Chapter 4

Creationism: Creative Misuse of the Bible

BRUCE VAWTER

Author of two books on Genesis, the first in 1957 and the second in 1977, Father Bruce Vawter, C. M., is one of the most widely respected Roman Catholic biblical scholars in America today, and is held in equally high esteem by non-Roman scholars and theologians. He has taught at the Pontifical Biblical Institute in Rome and at numerous theological seminaries, both Catholic and Protestant, in the United States. His writings have been concerned with the New Testament, the Old Testament, and theology, and he is now Professor of Theology at De Paul University in Chicago. Incisive without being heavy, his essay provides a classic and exemplary critique of the arguments for creation-science, with just enough salt to give flavor. He read this paper at the Conference on Creationism in American Culture and Theology, held at the Lutheran School of Theology in Chicago on October 9, 1982.

I plan to frame my objections to what has recently come to be termed "creationism" or "creation science" under the headings of three separate propositions. The first is that creationism seriously misconstrues the meaning and purpose of the Bible, both in part and in whole. In connection with this proposition I shall have some remarks to make with regard to the concept of biblical authority as it is understood by the proponents of creationism. My second proposition will be that creationism introduces a false dichotomy between religion and science by assuming that belief in a Creator God is incompatible with an acceptance of the scientific hypothesis that existing life-forms came into being through an evolutionary process. That some evolutionists share this same assumption proves nothing, of course, beyond the commonplace that fallacious conclusions can be drawn by just about anybody, whether that body be scientific or pious. Finally, as my third proposition, I shall argue that so-called creationism or creation science is a concept both theologically and philosophically unsound, derived from bad premises.

I shall take up these propositions in order and then, I hope, offer a few suggestions that may mitigate to some extent the impression that my outlook on this situation or controversy is entirely a negative one. For I do see some benefit to the development of the human comedy that has emerged in the creationist/evolutionist confrontation. I would like to say, "the creationist/evolutionist dialogue," but, of course, there has been precious little dialogue. Perhaps no real dialogue was ever conceivable, given the vastly different mind-sets that are involved. In any case, the benefits that I can discern as emerging from the confrontation I shall have to identify according to my own optimism, which may not be shared by others.

Literalism

Literal and Literalistic

We frequently hear it said that notions like creationism come from a "literal" reading of the creation stories in the book of Genesis. I think we need to achieve a better definition of terms in this connection. I would call the creationist interpretation of Genesis 1-3 not "literal" but rather "literalistic." I admit that the terminology is ambiguous and that etymologically "literal" does indeed mean what the very letter of a text or a statement signifies. However, I think we generally understand as the literal sense of a writer or speaker the meaning that he wished to convey by the words he used—not what the words themselves might mean independently of his use of them. The literal meaning of a metaphor is not what its component words signify by dictionary definition but what their combination means in a context that challenges the imagination. A metaphor metaphorizes, that is, it transfers the surface sense of its words to apply to another area of existence, an analogue. When I say that "it was raining cats and dogs," surely no one would suspect that I was affirming that the streets had been littered with the corpses of pekes, dalmatians, and tabbies after a recent downpour. Literalistically I had said that. Literally, I had not. It is the same with idiom. Idiom is, by definition, idiosyncratic. As anyone who has ever done any translating knows, idiom is not translated from one language to another, or from one thought-world to another, by transposing one word to another; it is the idea encompassed by the words that has to be transposed. "Grandfather is All" was the name of a book published some years ago in celebration of the heritage in this country of what is called "Pennsylvania Dutch." The phrase is meaningless in standard English, there is no doubt. To extract meaning from it, it is necessary to recognize that it is a literalistic rendition of a German idiom which means "Grandfather is dead."

Now it is true, the so-called literalist interpreter of the Bible has, in these days, learned to recognize such linguistic facts of life. He speaks the common language. He knows that there are such things as poetic license, hyperbole, metaphor, and he does not automatically exclude them from the Bible, even though he is reluctant to find them there. Because he is reluctant to find them there, he does not of course find them there as often as they are present; and this fact is due to the doctrinal bias that I shall discuss in a moment. But he does, in general, accept the principle.

What the literalist does not recognize is that the Bible itself—not its words only, not only its figures of speech or its varied literary forms, conventional or exotic—the Bible itself is a document so far removed from our own by language, culture, idiom, that it needs translation and transposition before it can ever be properly understood. The Bible itself is a literary form of which the biblical literalist is by religious dedication willfully ignorant. I will discuss this phenomenon in the context of the notion of biblical infallibility or, as I prefer to call it, the superstition of bibliolatry.

At this point, some may think that I have strayed from the issue that is before us, by insinuating that "creationism" or "creation science" is the result of a simplistic reading of Genesis rather than, as it claims to be, an account for cosmic and human origins based wholly and entirely on empirical evidence without reference to religious belief.

Only the naive will think that I have strayed from the point. Indeed, I have put my finger on the essential point which is, I regret to say, the hypocrisy of the so-called creationist movement as it has emerged in America. Whether studied or committed fecklessly in obedience to a simple-minded piety, it is hypocrisy in either case. An essentially religious—and quite sectarian religious—outlook on the origins of life has, for purely pragmatic reasons dictated by American constitutional law which separates church and state, intruded into American legislatures and courts under the guise of a secular science. Consider, if you will, the terms of Act 590 of 1981, the legislation passed by the 73rd General Assembly of the State of Arkansas "to require balanced treatment of creation-science and evolution-science in public schools." This act (in Section 4 [a]) defined "creation science" as:

> the scientific evidences and related inferences that indicate: (1) Sudden creation of the universe, energy, and life from nothing; (2) The insufficiency of mutation and natural selection in bringing about all living kinds from a single organism; (3) Changes only within fixed limits of originally created kinds of plants and animals; (4) Separate ancestry for man and apes; (5) Explanation of the earth's geology by catastrophism, including the occurrence of a worldwide flood; and (6) A relatively recent inception of the earth and living kinds.

Can anyone read or hear this and not agree that what is being called creation-science is simply an attempt to validate a vision of cosmic and human origins that has been extracted from a literalistic reading of the early chapters of the book of Genesis? District Judge William R. Overton, who found in favor of those who challenged the constitutionality of Act 590 and permanently enjoined its implementation, in a model of judicial opinion certainly recognized that the proponents of the act had been engaged in a "religious crusade" and that the act itself had "as its unmentioned reference the first 11 chapters of the Book of Genesis." It was amusing, to say the least, that when the creationists had won their apparent victory with the enactment of Act 590 mandating "equal time" for "creation-science" and "evolution-science," they discovered there were neither teachers nor textbooks for any such enterprise. Creationism—that unneeded neologism and a barbarism as well—had obtained no advocates outside the circles of fundamentalistic biblical piety. The creationists who had insinuated a sectarian religious viewpoint into a state's legislation under the pretense that they were serving the secular commonweal now found themselves hoist with their own petard.

In truth, there are many myths of creation among the many peoples of the earth, ancient and modern. Barbara C. Sproul (*Primal Myths: Creating the World*) has recently collected an enormous number of them, from every conceivable part of the world. But there is no doubt where the "creationists" myth comes from. It comes straight from the book of Genesis, literalistically interpreted. Judge Overton saw this plainly, and he ruled accordingly.

Biblical Inerrancy

As James Barr perceptively concluded in his 1977 study, *Fundamentalism*—and it is the fundamentalist biblical mentality that we raise when we scratch the rash of creationism—the fundamentalist is no literal reader of the Bible. Rather, he will use every logical or factual means at his disposal to avoid what the Bible literally says in order to harmonize what he thinks to be its meaning with what he thinks to be logical, factual, or historical reality. This he does in obedience to his belief in what he calls biblical inerrancy or infallibility.

Every biblically based religion, Jewish or Christian, recognizes the authority of the Bible and, within varying degrees, its normative character. "Biblical inerrancy," however, though the term has been used officially or casually by practically every biblically based religion, is a term that probably should be avoided in the interests of general understanding. I personally have no difficulty in accepting the formulation of the Second Vatican Council (in the fifth and final redaction of its formulation) that "the books of Scripture must be acknowledged as teaching firmly, faithfully, and without error that truth which God wanted put into the sacred writings for the sake of our salvation." I can hardly conceive of any adherent to the mainline tradition of biblical religion having any difficulty with the formulation. It treats the Bible for what it is, a record of religious experience, a fairly narrow experience, it must be admitted, in view of the far wider dimensions of human existence throughout the millennia, but nevertheless an experience that is entirely respectable and deserving of acknowledgment. This is biblical religion, and it is a responsible religion among the other religions of man.

"Biblical inerrancy" or "infallibility" as it is interpreted in some fundamentalist minds, however, means something quite different. The Bible is no longer a source-book for religion, it is primarily a source of knowledge, sacred and profane. It is no longer a testimonial to religious experience that can be checked against other experience and weighted accordingly, it is instead the one and only source of every human affirmation in every conceivable field of such affirmation, in whatever area of affirmation—social, religious, the totally secular areas of profane history, chronology, current scientific hypotheses of processes—in short, a divine encyclopedia of all relevant knowledge dropped down from the heavens as the only righteous guide to life.

This is not the place, and we do not have the space, to explore the philosophical and historical routes by which this perversion of biblical religion, this bibliolatry, has succeeded in fobbing itself off as the only defense of biblical integrity. It has succeeded, of course. Only that could convince the Madilyn Murray O'Hairs of our time, the Robert Ingersolls of time now past, that by exposing its absurdities they have disposed of any claims biblical faith might possess to intelligent consideration. By disposing of the "Billy Joe Bobs" of the Bible-thumped Sunday morning airwaves, they feel dispensed from assembling the somewhat more formidable armament needed for jousting with types like Aquinas, Scotus, Cajetan, Luther, Calvin, Pascal, Buber, Bonhoeffer, to think of a few.

"Biblical inerrancy" or "infallibility" in the fundamentalist sense, as has often been observed, is the product of the scientific age and the age of rationalism, a simplistic response to both. It is definitely not one of the authentic heritages of mainline Christianity. Attempts to find it in the tradition of the church fathers—fundamentalists do not ordinarily know or care much about the church fathers—have largely been abandoned. Augustine in his *De Genesi ad litteram* could, it is true, rejoice in the apparent harmony between the creation story of Genesis and the rudimentary science of his day; but in the same work he ridicules those who expose religion to scorn by forcing the Bible to say what intelligent readers know it cannot be saying. The fathers did of course believe that the Bible was an inerrant and, if you will, an infallible repository of revealed religion; but from right to left, from John Chrysostom, let us say, to Theodore of Mopsuestia, by theological recourses like *synkatabasis*, "condescension," to be discerned in the inspired word, they recognized its limitations and time-conditionedness in respect to a continually developing human awareness and factual knowledge which is also the gift of God.

When the trivial is deemed equally important with the essential, all becomes trivial. When the floating axe-head of the Elisha tale is to be affirmed with no less certitude than the moral judgments of the great prophets, when the historicity of Darius the Mede is quite as significant as the Deuteronomic theology of covenant, then the Bible has indeed been trivialized. This is what I meant by saying earlier that the Bible itself constitutes a literary form to which the biblical literalist has made himself impervious. Its magic, its poetry, its performative and evocative genius, all these vanish into a chrestomathy of tedious commonplaces. Conrad Hyers has recently said of our situation, quite correctly, I think:

> The symbolic richness and power—the religious meaning of creation—are largely lost in the cloud of geological and paleontological dust stirred up in the confusion. . . . The literalist, instead of opening up the treasure-house of symbolic imagination, digresses into ingenious and fantastic attempts at defending literalism itself.

Creation versus Evolution

The assertion of my second proposition will not take much time. The creationists proceed on the bland assumption that belief in a Creator God is incompatible with acceptance of the scientific hypothesis of biological evolution. As one of them, Henry Morris, has put it: "It is impossible to devise a legitimate means of harmonizing the Bible with evolution." Setting aside the obvious escape-hatch implied by the use of the adjective "legitimate," it suffices to say that such a statement is false and that its underlying premise is unsound. The evidence for this conclusion is to be found virtually everywhere in the wide, wide world of reality that surrounds the tight little enclave of true believers who will not come to terms with this world. As Judge Overton ruled:

> The emphasis on origins as an aspect of the theory of evolution is peculiar to creationist literature. Although the subject of origins of life is within the province of biology, the scientific community does not consider origins of life a part of evolutionary theory. The theory of evolution assumes the existence of life and is directed to an explanation of *how* life evolved. Evolution does not presuppose the absence of a creator or God. . . . The idea that belief in a creator and acceptance of the scientific theory of evolution are mutually exclusive is a false premise and offensive to the religious views of many.

All this does not mean, of course, that there is in practice a full-fledged synthesis on creation and evolution to which both scientists and religious believers can easily assent. The most valiant effort in recent times to achieve such a synthesis has undoubtedly been that of the late priest-scientist Pierre Teilhard de Chardin, in his renowned work *The Phenomenon of Man*. Though warmly welcomed, however, by religionist and scientist alike—as has been poignantly remarked, the English edition of Teilhard's remarkable book, published posthumously, bore the imprimatur of no Catholic bishop but rather of Sir Julian Huxley—no one would claim that either science or religion, on reflection, has accepted the effort as leading to a completely satisfactory result. Indeed, as is well known, the Congregation of the Holy Office, the watchdog of orthodoxy of Teilhard's own church, was moved in 1962 to issue a *monitum*, a caution against hasty and wholehearted acceptance of his theses. It should be added that in 1981, the centenary of Teilhard's birth, in a letter to Archbishop Paul Poupard, rector of the Institut Catholique of Paris where celebrations were being held, the Papal Secretary of State, Cardinal Agostino Casaroli, put this *monitum* into a far more positive context by stressing the great values of Teilhard's contribution to human vision and the daring profundities of his thought.

The fact is, evolutionary theory, while seemingly an inescapable theorem dictated by the observed phenomena, does not have its house sufficiently in order to present the believer in creation with a coherent image of that "how" of which Judge Overton spoke, which he is asked to consolidate with his faith. Some popular presentations of evolution, both in print and in the visual media, seem to be more mystical than scientific. The process is spoken of in teleological terms, venturing into areas where science has no right to intrude. There is marvel over the design in nature, which is really to make a theological affirmation abstracted from the entity that gives theology its name. Design leads to the extraordinary assumption—really contradictory to classical evolutionism—that the evolutionary change somehow took place by some creature's willing or wishing it so, as though reptiles substituted feathers for scales when they decided to fly. It even appears to be taken for granted at times that acquired characteristics were transformed into genetic ones, a notion that is otherwise rejected by the biological consensus. In truth, the evolutionary theory long enshrined in such terms as "natural selection," "survival of the fittest," and the like, now is subject to concepts like "punctuated equilibrium," "genetic drift," and even "evolution from space." These contrarieties partly represent confusion in the ranks of science, partly its legitimate attempt to substitute working hypotheses for those no longer workable. They have been exploited by creationism as an embarrassment to evolutionism, but taken all together in no way do they validate "creation science" as a viable alternative to evolution science. Philosophically, it remains true that evolution, however ultimately it may be plotted, stands in no opposition to a belief in creation as accounting for the "how" of that religious affirmation.

Creation versus Science

The invocation of philosophy—no science in the modern sense of the word, though in earlier times both philosophy and theology were at the apex of "the sciences" in the sense that they were organized and systematized bodies of knowledge—leads me to my final proposition. The notion of creation science is, in fact, absurd. Science, in the modern acceptation of the word, the acceptation intended by the creationists, is by definition inner-cosmic, guided by and responsible to the observed laws of nature, empirically testable and falsifiable. It is not metaphysical: it is self-precluded from venturing into areas whose spectrum lies beyond those governed by, controlled by, and explained by the workings of the universe about us. These are conventional and agreed definitions of what science means, and obviously creationism is no such thing.

There are said to be, and I do not doubt it, respectable scientists in their own right who are also creationists. I do find it hard to believe, however, that there is much correlation between their scientific attainments and their belief in creation. To the extent that I have read the literature, I have observed these scientists who are also creationists adept at their own proper métier, in this instance to poke holes in the vulnerabilities of evolutionary theory, to display the same vulnerabilities which the evolutionists acknowledge. I have not observed on their part any positive scientific argument that furthers the cause of creationism, nor do I believe that by the nature of the case there can be any.

Indeed, as it was noted by Judge Overton in his opinion:

> The scientific community consists of individuals and groups, nationally and internationally, who work independently in such varied fields as biology, paleontology, geology and astronomy. Their work is pub-

lished and subject to review and testing by their peers. The journals for publications are both numerous and varied. There is, however, not one recognized scientific journal which has published an article espousing the creation science theory described in Section 4(a) [of Act 590 of the Acts of Arkansas of 1981]. Some of the State's witnesses suggested that the scientific community was "close-minded" on the subject of creationism and that explained the lack of acceptance of the creation science arguments. Yet no witness produced a scientific article for which publication had been refused.

"Creation science" is the ruse of well-intentioned but very naive religious believers to gain acceptance of their convictions under the coloration of a purely secular discipline which would be given equal time with the scientific consensus concerning the origins and development of biological life. Well-intentioned, yes, but also tragic—theologically, philosophically, religiously. Demonstrably, it has done nothing so well so far as to bring biblical religion into disrepute and make it sound ridiculous and obscurantist. The proverbial bull in the china shop may not be the exact metaphor I am seeking here, but it will serve.

Logically, we have already seen that creationism is an absurdity. What the creationists are really groping towards, with all the deficiencies of their intellectual and historical resources, is the God of the philosophers, a concept which goes back at least to Aristotle in the fourth century B.C. Philosophy, let me remind you again, is not science in the modern sense of the word, the sense that creationists think they know. Philosophy extrapolates from scientific knowledge and is not limited by it. Aristotle thought, as the creationists think, that it is perfectly legitimate to argue from that which is to that which caused it to be, that behind all that is there must be a first being, a first cause, a prime mover. So far so good, one might think, but the evidence would be deceptive.

Blaise Pascal was not the first to recognize that the God of philosophers is not the God of biblical theology. Only with the concept of creation in time—*creatio ex nihilo sui et subiecti*, a term which creationists would like to find in Genesis 1-3 but which is not there—could Thomas Aquinas in the thirteenth century bring Aristotle into conformity with data he regarded could only come through divine revelation. His religious insight was decisive. Etienne Gilson has eloquently outlined the history of Aristotelianism-without-Aquinas:

The world of Aristotle owes its divine maker everything, except its existence. And this is why it has no history, not even in history. . . . Because theology was, before anything else, a history full of unpredictable events, it [i.e., the world of Aristotle] has branded theology as a myth, and science itself has felt the weight of its hostility. Itself scientifically sterile, there is not a single scientific discovery against which, so long as it lasted, it did not raise an indignant protest. And no wonder, for, since the world of Aristotle has no history, it never changes and it is no one's business to change it.

The God of Aquinas, a God who is Father of all and to whom one can pray, is not the Prime Mover of Aristotle. He is the God of the creationists, but he is their God by virtue of no philosophical reasoning but through the same biblical media through which Aquinas met God.

In the final issue I would like to address the question of out-and-out heresy, potentially the destruction of the whole Christian enterprise through the ham-handed activities of well-intentioned but historically and theologically illiterate Christians. In the "Findings of Fact" filed by the Defendants in the Arkansas Case prior to adjudication, a truly deplorable statement was asserted in paragraph 35:

> Creation-science does presuppose the existence of a creator, to the same degree that evolution-science presupposes the existence of no creator. As used in the context of creation-science, as defined by 54(a) [*sic*] of Act 590, the terms or concepts of "creation" and "creator" are not inherently religious terms or concepts. In this sense, the term "creator" means only some entity with power, intelligence, and a sense of design. Creation-science does not require a creator who has a personality, who has the attributes of love, compassion, justice, etc., which are ordinarily attributed to a deity. Indeed, the creation-science model does not require that the creator still be in existence.

It would be hard to set emotional priorities, from bitter sorrow to deep anger, which this wretched formulation and its obvious and cynical compromise with mammon should evoke in any sensitive theological soul. Let us say nothing about the hypocrisy of good people who have obviously convinced themselves that a good cause can be supported by any mendacious and specious means whatsoever. The passage is perverse, however, not only because it says things that are untrue, namely that creationism presupposes a creator whereas evolutionism necessarily does not, and not only because "creation" and "creator" are proffered speciously secular, nonreligious definitions.

The worst thing about these unthinking and unhistorical formulations is what Langdon Gilkey pointed out at the Arkansas trial in December of 1981. The concept of a creator God distinct from the God of love and mercy is a reopening of the way to the Marcionist and Gnostic heresies, among the deadliest ever to afflict Christianity. That those who make such formulations do not seriously intend them save as a debating ploy does not mitigate their essential malevolence.

Conclusion

Is there, finally, any good issue that has been served by this creationism versus evolutionism performance? There is, I think, at least the shadow of one.

The controversy has reminded us, if we needed reminding, how deeply rooted in our society is biblical religion. Misconceived and wrongly defended though it may be by the creationists, it remains a living force that must be reckoned with by our secular society and can by no means be airily dismissed by anyone as the eccentricity of a sectarian few.

I can be more generous than this. If the creation scientists—and as we have seen, there are some genuine scientists who are creationists—have not succeeded in making creation out to be a science, they have succeeded in raising questions about the propriety of an uncritical acceptance of evolutionism on its own terms. In their branding of evolutionism as a rival religion, the creationists are often not far from the mark. That this is so is not, generally, the fault of true scientists but rather of the scientific popularizers, the proponents of a scientism which is often the superstition of the modern age. We have been taught, I think, not to take refuge in the glib assertion that we take our science from the scientists and acknowledge no difficulty in reconciling it with biblical faith. The creationists have contributed to the self-examination of science itself, namely by reminding the more naive of us that there is no monolithic science and that there is no single and undisputed entity called evolutionism. We are forced, in other words, to a fresh evaluation of the perennial theological task, which is to explain the ways of God to man in terms that contemporary man can understand and relate to.

This is not a small contribution, however much it may be the by-product of a controversy which, on the merits of the case itself, should never have taken place.

Chapter 5

Christianity and the Age of the Earth

DAVIS A. YOUNG

Davis A. Young's arguments against creation-science are essentially double edged, arising as they do from a conservative evangelical understanding of the Bible and from his professional credentials as a geologist. Professor of Geology at Calvin College, with extensive field experience in geology, he has published numerous articles in scientific journals. On the theological side, he has in a sense continued the work of his father, the late Edward J. Young, longtime Professor of Old Testament Studies at Westminster Theological Seminary in Philadelphia, with whom he had intended to collaborate in relating science and theology. Augmenting his father's instruction with a continuing study of the Bible and the Christian tradition, Davis Young has authored two books devoted to separating evangelical theology from young-earth and creation-science theories: Creation and the Flood, An Alternative to Flood Geology and Theistic Evolution *appeared in 1977 (Baker), and was followed in 1982 by* Christianity and the Age of the Earth *(Zondervan), from which the present essay is extracted in a slightly revised form.*

Christians have always believed, as they still do, that God created and sustains the entire universe. But many and perhaps most Christians regret, as I do, that the words "creationist" and "creationism" are being used today by a relatively small group for very special purposes. My opposition to these creationists does not imply in any way a denial of creation or the Christian faith. Quite the contrary, my disagreements with them involve my different understanding (as a Christian) of Scripture and doctrine, and my different approach (as a geologist) to scientific evidence.

Scientific arguments that are said by creationists to indicate that the Earth is only a few thousand years old, at most, are based on incomplete information, wishful thinking, ignorance of real geological situations, selective use of data to support the favored hypothesis, and faulty reasoning. Scientific evidence, considered as a whole, and as we have it now, compellingly argues for the great antiquity of the Earth.

Where then does this conclusion lead Christians? Specifically, what does the scientific evidence mean with reference to the truth of the Christian religion? With reference to the truth of the Bible? Is the Genesis account really reliable after all? Does the Bible contain only fables of creation rather than accurate information about it? Or are there perhaps other ways of understanding Genesis when it speaks of creation? Does the Bible contain mistakes about the nature of the world in which we live?

Is Faith Damaged by an Ancient Earth?

Many Christian people cannot understand why God should have taken so long to make the world. Indeed some may feel that if the antiquity of the Earth is accepted then somehow or other God's power and sovereignty are limited. Some feel that we scientists badly misinterpreted the evidence and hope that something will turn up to convince us that the Earth is young. And there is even the impression that scientists are somehow engaged in a conspiracy to doctor the evidence. I have been asked, "Why do you want the Earth to be that old?" as if I had some preference in selecting an age I thought the Earth ought to be. It is shattering for many Christians to face the idea that the Earth really is old because they have been persuaded that the Bible emphatically, unequivocally teaches that the Earth is very young. To establish conclusively the antiquity of the Earth, as I have been attempting to do, would in their minds suggest that the Bible might really be wrong about creation and therefore not reliable. This is a consequence that large numbers of Christian people simply cannot face. Their faith would be damaged, and so because of an unnecessary connection between the antiquity of the Earth and the possibility of error in the Bible, they steadfastly resist the conclusion that the Earth is old.

With such Christian people I have the utmost sympathy. I can appreciate the struggles and anguish such a person must go through, for I have gone through some of those struggles myself. I do, however, want to persuade them that they should not fear the idea of the antiquity of the Earth. They should not be afraid that the overwhelming available evidence that the Earth is billions of years old is somehow damaging to Christianity. The available evidence from science in no way undermines the Bible or our Christian faith.

On the other hand, what is much more likely to undermine Christian faith is the dogmatic and persistent effort of creationists to present their theory before the public, Christian and non-Christian, as in accord with Scripture and nature, especially when the evidence to the contrary has been presented again and again by competent Christian scientists.[1] It is sad that so much Christian energy has to be wasted in proposing and refuting the false theory of catastrophic Flood geology. But Christians need to know the truth and to be warned of error. Creationist articles constantly make sweeping statements to the effect that Christianity is now on surer ground because of the discoveries and theories that creationists have concocted.[2] . . . "Proving" the Bible or Christianity with a spurious scientific hypothesis can only be injurious to the cause of Christ. We do not defend truth by arguing error in its behalf. . . .

The faith of many Christian people could be hindered when they ultimately realize that the teachings of the creationists are simply not in accord with the facts. But imagine the trauma for some believers of accepting the possibility of an old Earth. Believing that the Bible is God's Word and is free of error, many have been thoroughly indoctrinated to believe also that creation occurred in six twenty-four-hour days, that the entire globe was completely submerged for an entire year by the Flood, that uniformitarian geology is based on a godless philosophy, that Flood geology offers a superior explanation of the facts of nature, and that "genuine science" supports the creationist-catastrophist view of the Bible. Imagine the trauma and shock of finally realizing that Flood geology, which has been endorsed so enthusiastically by some well-meaning Christian leaders, is nothing more than a fantasy. A Christian could easily become disillusioned in circles where Flood geology has been regarded as an article of faith or as *the* biblical view of nature.

Furthermore, creationism and Flood geology have put a serious roadblock in the way of unbelieving scientists. Although Christ has the power to save unbelievers in spite of our foolishness and poor presentations of the gospel, Christians should do all they can to avoid creating unnecessary stumbling blocks to the reception of the gospel. Some people who might otherwise be open to the gospel could be completely turned off by Flood geology. If acceptance of Christianity means accepting Flood geology, some will not want to become Christians. No non-Christian geologist is ever going to accept Flood geology or the young-Earth theory today: the flaws and weaknesses are obvious to any practicing geologist.

The Scriptures do not require us to believe in six twenty-four-hour days of creation. There is legitimate internal biblical evidence to indicate that the days of creation may have been indefinite periods of time.[3] Moreover, the genealogies of Genesis 5 and 11 need not be taken in a rigidly literal fashion.[4] Christians also need to realize that accepting the universality of the Flood hardly requires one to adopt Flood geology as the only possible explanation. Moreover, it is not entirely clear that the Bible is talking about a geographically universal flood.[5] Why then are some Christians so rigidly dogmatic about matters on which the Bible itself is not dogmatic? There is considerable room for legitimate variation of interpretation of the Creation and the Flood. Christians should not paint themselves into a corner by being more rigid than the Bible.

Just suppose for the sake of argument that the Bible and the scientific evidence do not seem to agree at every point. Does it really advance the Christian cause to force the facts of nature to fit into a preconceived theory of the Earth as is done by the creationist movement? No, it harms our cause. Christ has called us to truth and honesty. We are to tell the truth in love, but we are not telling the truth if we insist that the facts of nature indicate that the Earth is very young and that the Earth was totally covered and renovated in one year by the Flood as described by Flood geologists.

I am *not* accusing creationists of lying or deliberate distortion. No doubt they have honorable intentions, but if they continue to espouse their theories when other Christians have repeatedly called attention to the falsity of their theories, they must be challenged to stop. It is a far better procedure to follow the evidence of nature wherever it may lead, even if it seems, at first, to run counter to our interpretations of Scripture. Let me indicate why this procedure is better, and in so doing point out why the antiquity of the Earth does not at all undermine Christian faith.

We are dealing with God's world and with God-created facts. . . . We must handle the data reverently and worshipfully, yet we should not be afraid of where the facts may lead. God made those facts, and they fit into His comprehensive plan for the world. God has brought the world into its current state of existence, and thus the facts of geology and all other facts owe their existence to His sovereign counsel. When a geologist finds a rock composed of 30% quartz, 40% alkali feldspar, 20% plagioclase, and 10% biotite, the rock is that way because God willed it to be so, not because the geologist made it up or because of fate or ultimate chance. The fact about that rock's composition is every bit as much a fact as any fact that can be found in the Bible. It is as true as any fact in the Bible. It is just as much a fact as the fact that Christ died for our sins. To be sure, it is a much less important fact. One's life will not be significantly different for either being aware of it or not being aware of it, but it is nonetheless still just as much a fact. It is a very different kind of fact from the facts we find in the Bible. The facts of the Bible are expressed verbally; those in nature are not. The facts of the Bible primarily tell us what we are to believe concerning God and what duty He requires of us. The facts of the Bible are ethically normative for our lives; the facts of nature are not. The Bible generally tells us what we ought to do; nature generally does not. Thus in the Bible and in nature we are dealing with different kinds of revelation of God, with different kinds of facts, but we are dealing in both cases with facts of divine origination.

We see much the same thing on the human level, for mankind has been made in God's image. People can express themselves both verbally and creatively. For example, the monumental Ninth Symphony of Gustav Mahler is very expressive of the personality of its creator. In listening to the music again and again we gain insight into the nature of Mahler himself. We sense something of the kind of person he was. . . . When, for example, we listen to the poignant introspection, the exquisite, almost unbearable nostalgia of the Finale of the Ninth Symphony, we sense something of the tragic inner life of Mahler, of his inner turmoil, of the struggle of his entire life to find meaning in existence, particularly as he faces imminent death. This symphony is a genuine revelation of the character, of the being, of

Gustav Mahler, every bit as much as the letters he wrote and the words he spoke. While the music is revelatory of its composer, it does not express his will in a directly recognizable way. If Mahler's wife, Alma, wanted to know his purposes and character, what he thought of her, and what she should really think of him, she would not learn this so much from his music as from his verbal expressions. His verbalizing would be normative for her, but not his music, even though both the verbalizing and the music were equally genuine expressions of the character of the composer. In a similar way if we want to know what God wants us to do we listen to His words in the Bible, but in the study of nature the redeemed Christian also learns to appreciate the character of God as Psalm 19 and Romans 1 make plain. Creation reveals God's character and expresses His nature, although not in the same direct way that the Bible does.

The facts of the Bible and the facts of nature, therefore, do not disagree but form one comprehensive, unified expression of the character and will of our Creator and Redeemer. Nature and Scripture form a unity, for God is one. Although man, because of his sinful nature, reveals himself in inconsistent and contradictory ways, God *cannot* do so. But the fact that God's words and works are a perfect unity does not by any means indicate that we can always see how they agree or fit together.

We must of necessity engage in the interpretation of both nature and Scripture in order that we might see how the facts fit together, in order that we might see the interrelationships of those facts. In the matter of interpretation God has no problem, because for Him the universe, His word and works, is wholly transparent. Inasmuch as He is creator of the world and author of Scripture, He comprehensively sees and knows all the facts of His universe at a glance. His "interpretation" of the facts coincides with the facts. God sees the interrelationships of the facts as He sees the facts themselves, for He has created in accordance with His plan. All is light to Him; no facts are new. No facts are discovered by Him. No facts are unknown to Him. No facts are unintelligible to Him. The case, however, is much different for us, for we are creatures. Our interpretations of the facts do not coincide with our knowledge of the facts, but must be constructed by reasoning processes from the facts. For us the facts precede the understanding of interrelationships. We collect the facts and then think about their meaning. As creatures, too, we do not have immediate access to all the facts, and our fullest knowledge is incomplete. Then, too, we are sinners and sin mars our interpretations of God's truth. Our intellects, warped by sin, resist to some degree dealing in a responsible way with God's works and words. Our interpretations do not always wholeheartedly accept the facts God has given us. At times we distort their meaning. Sometimes we do this unconsciously. The fact that we must interpret the unified world in which God has placed us means that we do not always understand how everything fits together. Because of our creatureliness and our sinfulness, we do not always see that unity. Hence it may on occasion appear to us that the Bible and nature do not agree, but the disagreement is not between the Bible and nature: it is between our understanding of the Bible and our understanding of nature. It is our interpretation of the God-given data that leads us into discrepancy, conflict, and disagreement. And so, as Christians, we should not be dismayed if such conflicts seem to appear between nature and the Bible. They are not real conflicts between nature and the Bible, but only conflicts between natural science and theological exegesis.

For other reasons we should not be upset over such discrepancies. We recognize that the Bible is a unity, too. We believe that the Bible has one redemptive story to tell from Genesis to Revelation. The Bible story begins in the garden of God and it ends there. We affirm that all parts of the Bible agree and are in perfect harmony with one another, but we do not always see this harmony fully. There is much in the Bible that from our limited perspective does not seem to fit together too well. There are, for example, parallel accounts of the same event in the different gospels. We cannot fully reconcile the differences in detail between the accounts. In God's mind there are no loose ends, no tensions, but in our theology there are. Theology cannot be an air-tight, closed system. We must learn to live with loose ends in our theology.

At the same time, we should not thereby become careless in our theologizing and satisfied with an increasing number of dangling facts. Although as creatures engaged in creaturely interpretation of God's world we will forever be faced with some tensions and loose ends in our theological interpretive endeavors, we should do our best to eliminate them, not artificially, but by becoming more faithful to the truths God has given us.

The same kind of tensions exist in our understanding of nature. Very frequently there are loose ends in natural science because of our limited understanding of the facts of nature. One prominent illustration of such a tension comes from nineteenth-century science.

Geologists were generally of the opinion that the facts gleaned from the rocks suggested that the world was several hundred million years old. On the other hand the evidence of physics in the eyes of Lord Kelvin[6] suggested that the world was less than a hundred million years old. Here were two bodies of facts drawn from different parts of nature which when interpreted by competent scientists indicated two mutually exclusive ideas regarding the age of the Earth. There was tremendous controversy, especially between geologists and physicists. Each group was convinced the other was badly misinterpreting the evidence at hand. Yet at the same time there remained a deep persuasion that nature was a unity and that nature was only giving one answer regarding the age of the Earth. Attempts were made to work out a plausible "harmonization" of the discrepancies between the facts of physics and the facts of geology. Geologists have always been a little bit intimidated by the mathematical sophistication of physics, and so perhaps they were not so sure of themselves as the physicists were. Hence geologists made a real effort to reexamine the data of the Earth to see if it was possible to come up with a legitimate age that would fit the facts and be satisfying to the physicists. Toward the end of his life Kelvin was suggesting that the Earth was probably not much more than 20 million years old; hence, physicists were greatly pleased when the outstanding geologist, Clarence King, proposed on geological grounds an age of 24 million years for the Earth. Presumably a harmonization was achieved.

We must note what did not happen. Geologists did not abandon facts of nature, nor did physicists. No one accused nature of contradicting itself or being in error. They admitted the tension and tried to resolve it, fully persuaded of the unity of nature. Now it turns out that the geologists were right and the physicists wrong, not because either of them had badly misinterpreted evidence or distorted facts. When the phenomenon of radioactivity was discovered a whole new set of facts had to be taken into account. Radioactivity provided a source of heat that was wholly unknown to Kelvin and which therefore he could not have considered in his calculations on the age of the Earth. The old "harmonization" was abandoned, and the scientific tension was eventually resolved in this case because of the discovery of new facts with attendant new and improved interpretations of those facts.

As a geologist, I have developed a detailed regional map of an area in which I had a good understanding of the basic relationships of the rocks. Knowing how they behaved, I was usually able to predict what kind of rock I would find at the top of the next hill. But once in a while I would find an outcrop that did not fit into my larger, generally valid picture of the geology. The outcrop just did not make sense to me. I could neither deny the existence or factuality of the outcrop, nor completely overthrow all the other work I did. I cannot reject the large regional picture simply because I have been unable to figure how one fact fit into it. I accept all the facts, but with a certain unresolved tension, with a loose end. I simply confess that there is an outcrop I do not know what to do with and hope that in time I or another geologist will be able to figure out what it's doing there and how it fits in with all the other outcrops.

There are always loose ends, discrepancies, contradictions in natural science, owing to the fact that scientists are human, our understanding of nature is limited, and we don't always have access to all the facts that are pertinent to the situation. Nevertheless even though I may not have all the facts or may not have apprehended all the facts I still proceed to develop my natural science or my theology on the basis of the facts that I do have. I should be very much surprised if we ever had a natural science without loose ends.

In the same way, I should be very much surprised if we had a unified knowledge of both the Bible and the world that had no loose ends. Why should theology and natural science ever be expected to agree fully when each by itself has plenty of loose ends? The problems and apparent contradictions do not exist between nature and the Bible, but between our understandings of these two very different revelations of God. We should be content to let both bodies of revelation speak for themselves and listen as carefully as we can. Nor should this situation cause us to reject nature or attempt to falsify the evidence to make it come into conformity with what we think is in Genesis.

The same principle must apply to the Bible. It must finally be interpreted in its own terms even though information from other sources may help us to ask proper questions of the biblical text in our interpretive task. The data of nature can only make us take another hard look at the data of the Bible to see if we have interpreted them correctly. Nature, however, cannot force upon us an interpretation of the Bible. The question of the length of the days of Genesis 1 must be decided by the text of Scripture and the analogy of Scripture. It cannot be decided by information from nature. Sometimes a deeper study of Scripture, prompted by the investigation of nature, may lead us to change our interpretation of Scripture, as was certainly the case in the days of the Copernican controversy.

What has been popularly believed by Christians is not necessarily what the Bible teaches. Even though most people in past centuries incorrectly believed the Earth to be only a few thousand years old, it is also true that the great antiquity of the Earth suggested by nature is not at variance with the Bible. There are sound exegetical grounds for maintaining that the six days of creation were long, indeterminate periods of time. This interpretation, long ago suggested by Augustine and other church fathers, has been repeatedly evoked by Christians through the centuries,[7] and it eliminates any conflict with scientific investigation of the age of the Earth. Although this exegesis still leaves areas of tension and unsolved problems, it certainly leaves far fewer contradictions than does the twenty-four-hour-day view of the six days, which is not the only possible interpretation of the text. We have every right to state that the long, figurative day interpretation is legitimate, and has been supported by many of the greatest theologians in church history. We should in all fairness employ those legitimate exegeses of Scripture that allow for plausible harmonizations with scientific thinking.

We must not distort Scripture or the findings of nature in order to obtain a forced agreement between the two. Far too many Christians are willing to distort science in order to gain an accommodation with what they are persuaded is the only possible legitimate interpretation of Scripture. This is the case with the modern creationist movement. Creationists have generally persuaded themselves that the days of Genesis 1 must be twenty-four hours long, and that the genealogies of Genesis allow for only a few thousand years at the most. They have persuaded themselves that the story of the Flood in Genesis can be interpreted only as a flood that completely covered the entire globe and that the mountaintops all around the world were under water. They typically have not recognized other valid interpretations of Creation and the Flood. Having locked themselves into these rigid interpretations they are in disagreement with modern scientific ideas. Not willing to allow tensions to exist, they have sought for harmonization with the facts of nature or with science not by reevaluating their biblical exegeses but by wholesale distortion of science and the facts of nature. They have tried to make nature say things it is not saying. Elsewhere I have documented that creationists have ignored data when convenient and have been very selective in the use of other data. They have attempted to develop a wholly new science. Their wholly new science agrees with their biblical interpretation, but it has almost nothing to do with the facts of the Earth, rocks, chemical element distribution, fossils, and so on, except in the most superficial way. Their theory of a young Earth and a global-Flood catastrophe has been superimposed not only on the Bible, but on nature as well. Such an approach to the harmonization of the Bible with nature is no harmonization at all, for it harmonizes by ignoring the real world in which God has placed us, which God himself made and controls, a real world whose factuality has been determined and given by the sovereign God of the universe.

People must recognize that this modern, young-Earth, Flood-geology creationism is simply not truthful. It is simply not in accord with the facts that God has given. Creationism must be abandoned before even greater harm is done. The persistent attempts of the members of the creationist movement to get their points of view established in educational institutions can only damage both the Christian cause and education. This forcing of creationism on the public will simply lend credence to the idea already entertained by many intellectual leaders that Christianity, at least in its modern form, is sheer anti-intellectual obscurantism.

Nature is also from God, and nature would lead us to believe that the Earth is extremely old. Scientific investigation of the world God gave us is an exciting enterprise that God would have us engage in. We do not need the flight-from-reality science of creationism. We need a more vigorous approach to both nature and Scripture. May I plead with my brethren in Christ who are involved in the young-Earth movement to abandon misleading the public. I urge them to study geology more thoroughly. Geology cannot be learned from a few elementary textbooks. There is far more to it than that. I also urge creationists to be less dogmatic about Scriptural texts over which there has been substantial diversity of interpretation within the historic Christian church. If they would be of service to Christ's kingdom, they should do some honest-to-goodness scientific thinking that takes facts seriously, facts that were created by the God they wish to defend and serve. We Evangelical Christians need to stop expending our energies in defending a false creationism and in refuting a false creationism. Let us spend our energies on interpreting the Bible and the world that God in His mercy and grace has given us.

Notes

1. E.g., Davis A. Young, *Creation and the Flood* (Grand Rapids, Mich.: Baker, 1977); D. E. Wonderly, *God's Time-Records in Ancient Sediments* (Flint: Crystal, 1977), and numerous articles published over the years in *Journal of the American Scientific Affiliation*.
2. For an extreme example, see R. L. Whitelaw, "Radiocarbon Confirms Biblical Creation (And So Does Potassium-Argon)," in W. E. Lammerts, ed., *Why Not Creation?* (Philadelphia: Presbyterian and Reformed, 1970), pp. 90–100.
3. Young, *Creation and the Flood*, pp. 81–89.
4. W. H. Green, "Primeval Chronology," in *Bibliotheca Sacra* (1890), 47: 284–303.
5. See the appendix in an article by A. C. Custance, "Flood Traditions of the World," in *Symposium on Creation IV* (Grand Rapids, Mich.: Baker, 1972), pp. 9–44.
6. See J. D. Burchfield, *Lord Kelvin and the Age of the Earth* (New York: Science History Publications, 1975).
7. See Davis A. Young, *Christianity and the Age of the Earth* (Grand Rapids, Mich: Zondervan, 1982), pp. 13–15, 55–67.

Chapter 6

Biblical Literalism: Constricting the Cosmic Dance

CONRAD HYERS

*Professor of Comparative Mythology and the History of Religions at Gusta-
vus Adolphus College, Conrad Hyers is one of the impressively broad-ranging
scholars working in theology today. He has consistently objected, in his own
words, to "a tendency in modern Western thought, either to identify truth
with 'the facts,' understood in a very literal, prosaic, historicist manner, or
with high level abstractions, emptied of all flesh-and-blood reality, and almost inaccessible to experience," which he describes as a "curious kind of
intellectual schizophrenia." He has written numerous articles on comparative mythology and on non-Western religions, as well as on Christian themes,
and his most notable recent book is* The Comic Vision and the Christian
Faith: A Celebration of Life and Laughter *(Pilgrim Press, 1981).*

> Woe to him who strives with his Maker,
>   an earthen vessel with the potter!
> Does the clay say to him who fashions it,
>   'What are you making?'
>   or 'Your work has no handles'? [Isa. 45:9].

With all the decades of scientific research and biblical scholarship that have intervened since the Scopes "monkey trial" in 1925, one might have thought that the issues were by now passé. Yet the recent wave of school-board hearings, legislative bills and court cases suggests that literalism is a persistent phenomenon. Indeed, we may be seeing only the top of the turnip.

The literalist mentality does not manifest itself only in conservative churches, private-school enclaves, television programs of the evangelical right, and a considerable amount of Christian bookstore material; one often finds a literalist understanding of Bible and faith being assumed by those who have no religious inclinations, or who are avowedly antireligious in sentiment. Even in educated circles the possibility of more sophisticated theologies of creation is easily obscured by burning straw effigies of biblical literalism.

But the problem is even more deep-rooted. A literalist imagination—or lack of imagination—pervades contemporary culture. One of the more dubious successes of modern science—and of its attendant spirits technology, historiography and mathematics—is the suffusion of intellectual life with a prosaic and pedantic mind-set. One may observe this feature in almost any college classroom, not only in religious studies, but within the humanities in general. Students have difficulty in thinking, feeling and expressing themselves *symbolically*.

The problem is, no doubt, further amplified by the obviousness and banality of most of the television programming on which the present generation has been weaned and reared. Not only is imagination a strain; even to imagine what a symbolic world is like is difficult. Poetry is turned into prose, truth into statistics, understanding into facts, education into note-taking, art into criticism, symbols into signs, faith into beliefs. That which cannot be listed, outlined, dated, keypunched, reduced to a formula, fed into a computer, or sold through commercials cannot be thought or experienced.

Our situation calls to mind a backstage interview with Anna Pavlova, the dancer. Following an illustrious and moving performance, she was asked the meaning of the dance. She replied, "If I could say it, do you think I should have danced it?" To give dance a literal meaning would be to reduce dancing to something else. It would lose its capacity to involve the whole person. And one would miss all the subtle nuances and delicate shadings and rich polyvalences of the dance itself.

The remark has its parallel in religion. The early ethnologist R. R. Marett is noted for his dictum that "religion is not so much thought out as danced out." But even when thought out, religion is focused in the verbal equivalent of the dance: myth, symbol and metaphor. To insist on assigning to it a literal, one-dimensional meaning is to shrink and stifle and distort the significance. In the words of E. H. W. Meyerstein, "Myth is my tongue, which means not that I cheat, but stagger in a light too great to bear." Religious expression trembles with a sense of inexpressible mystery, a mystery which nevertheless addresses us in the totality of our being.

The literal imagination is univocal. Words mean one thing, and one thing only. They don't bristle with meanings and possibilities; they are bald, clean-shaven. Literal clarity and simplicity, to be sure, offer a kind of security in a world (or Bible) where otherwise issues seem incorrigibly complex, ambiguous and muddy. But it is a false security, a temporary bastion, maintained by dogmatism and misguided loyalty. Literalism pays a high price for the hope of having firm and unbreakable handles attached to reality. The result is to move in the opposite direction from religious symbolism, emptying symbols of their amplitude of meaning and power, reducing the cosmic dance to a calibrated discussion.

One of the ironies of biblical literalism is that it shares so largely in the reductionist and literalist spirit of the age. It is not nearly as conservative as it supposes. It is *modernistic,* and it sells its symbolic birthright for a mess of tangible pottage. Biblical materials and affirmations—in this case the symbolism of Creator and creation—are treated as though of the same order and the same literary genre as scientific and historical writing. "I believe in God the Father Almighty" becomes a chronological issue, and "Maker of heaven and earth" a technological problem.

To suggest that the first chapters of Genesis ought to be read in the classroom as an alternative to evolutionary theories presupposes that these chapters are yielding something *comparable* to scientific theories and historical reconstructions of empirical data. Interpreting the Genesis accounts faithfully, and believing in their reliability and significance as divine revelation, is understood to mean taking them literally as history, as chronology, as scientific truth. In the words of Henry Morris, a leading "scientific creationist": "The Biblical record, accepted in its natural and literal sense, gives the only scientific and satisfying account of the origins of things. . . . The creation account is clear, definite, sequential and matter-of-fact, giving every appearance of straightforward historical narrative" (*The Remarkable Birth of Planet Earth* [Bethany, 1978], pp. iv, 84).

Two further ironies result from such literalism. The biblical understanding of creation is not being pitted against evolutionary theories, as is supposed; rather, evolutionary theories are being juxtaposed with literalist theories of biblical interpretation. Doing this is not even like comparing oranges and apples; it is more like trying to compare oranges and orangutans. Even if evolution is only a scientific theory of interpretation posing as scientific fact, as the creationists argue, creationism is only a religious theory of biblical interpretation posing as biblical fact. And to compound the confusions, these biblical "facts" are then treated as belonging to the same level of discourse and family of concerns as scientific facts, and therefore supportable by scientific data, properly interpreted. Yet if one is unable to follow all these intertwinings, let alone bow the knee, a veritable Pandora's box of dire fates awaits:

> Belief in evolution is a necessary component of atheism, pantheism, and all other systems that reject the sovereign authority of an omnipotent personal God. [It] has historically been used by their leaders to justify a long succession of evil systems—including fascism, communism, anarchism, nazism, occultism, and many others. [It] leads normally to selfishness, aggressiveness, and fighting between groups, as well as animalistic attitudes and behavior by individuals [*ibid.*, vii].

But the greatest irony is that the symbolic richness and power—the *religious* meaning—of creation are largely lost in the cloud of geological and paleontological dust stirred up in the confusion. If one were to speak of a hermeneutical fall, it would have to be the fall into literalism. Literalism diverts attention from, as well as flattening out, the symbolic depth and multidimensionality of the biblical texts. The literalist, instead of opening up the treasurehouse of symbolic imagination, digresses into more and more ingenious and fantastic attempts at defending literalism itself. Again and again the real issue turns out to be not belief in divine creativity but belief in a particular theory of Scripture, not faith but security. The divine word and work ought to have better handles!

Even among interpreters who do not identify with the literalism of the creationists, one often finds a sense of relief expressed in noting that the sequence of days in Genesis 1, if viewed as eons, offers a rough approximation to modern reconstructions of the evolution of matter and life. It is a *very* rough approximation, considering such difficulties as that the sun, moon and stars were not created until the fourth "eon," following the earth and vegetation in the third. And even if all rough correlations could be made smooth by convoluted arguments about cloud covers and the like, the two Genesis accounts themselves, taken as chronologies, do not agree. In Genesis 2, for example, Adam is created *before* plants and animals, and Eve after. Still, no matter how close the approximations, the entire line of argument is a lapse into literalism and its assumption that this account is in some way comparable to a scientific, historical one.

A case in point is the supposition that the numbering of days in Genesis is to be understood in an arithmetical sense. The use of numbers in ancient religious texts was usually numerological rather than numerical; that is, their symbolic value was more important than their secular value as counters. To deal with numbers in a religious context as an actual numbering of days, or eons, is an instance of the way in which a literal reading loses the symbolic richness of the text.

While the conversion of numerology to arithmetic was essential for the rise of modern science, historiography and mathematics, in which numbers had to be neutralized and emptied of any symbolic suggestion in order to be utilized, the result is that numerological symbols are reduced to signs. The principal surviving exception is the number thirteen, which still holds a strange power over Fridays, and over the listing of floors in hotels and high rises.

Biblical literalism, in its treatment of the days of creation, substitutes a modern arithmetical reading for the original symbolic one. Not only does the completion of creation in six days correlate with and support the religious calendar and Sabbath observance (if the Hebrews had had a five-day work week, the account would have read differently), but also the seventh day of rest employs to the full the symbolic meaning of the number seven as wholeness, plenitude, completion.

The religious meaning of the number seven is derived in part from the numerological combination of the three zones of the cosmos (heaven, earth, underworld) seen vertically, and the four directions, or zones, of the cosmos seen horizontally. Thus seven (adding three and four) and twelve (multiplying them) are recurrent biblical symbols of totality and perfection. The liturgically repeated phrase "And God saw that it was good," and the final capping phrase "And behold it was very good," are paralleled and underlined by being placed in a structure climaxed by a seventh day.

A parallelism of two sets of three days is also being employed, with the second set of days populating the first: light and darkness

(day one) are populated by the greater and lesser lights (four); firmament and waters (two) by birds and fish (five); earth and vegetation (three) by land animals and humans (six). Two sets of three
days, each with two types of created phenomena, equaling twelve,
thus permitted the additional association with the corresponding numerological symbol of wholeness and fulfillment. The totality of nature is created by God, and is to be affirmed in a hymn of celebration and praise for its "very goodness."

While it is true that the biblical view of creation sanctifies time
and nature as created by God—and therefore good—it does not follow that the creation accounts as such are to be understood chron-
ologically or as natural history. And while it is true that history is
seen as the context and vehicle of divine activity, it does not follow
that the creation accounts are to be interpreted as history, or even
prehistory. One of the symbolic functions of the creation accounts
themselves is to give positive value to time and to provide the staging
for history. They are no more historical than the set and scenery of
a play are part of the narrative of the drama, or than the order in
which an artist fills in the pigment and detail of a painting is part
of the significance of the painting.

The symbolic function of creation in valuing time and history becomes clearer when the Genesis accounts are compared with myths
whose purpose is to legitimate cyclical time (as in the Babylonian
myth of the primeval conquest of Tiamat by Marduk, alluded to in
Genesis 1:2), or to those in which time itself is a negative aspect of
a fallen order (as in Plato's myth of the fall of the soul, or similar
myths favored by Hindu and Buddhist mysticism).

When one looks at the myths of surrounding cultures, in fact, one
senses that the current debate over creationism would have seemed
very strange, if not unintelligible, to the writers and readers of Genesis. Scientific and historical issues in their modern form were not
issues at all. Science and natural history as we know them simply
did not exist, even though they owe a debt to the positive value given
to space, time, matter and history by the biblical affirmation of
creation.

What did exist—what very much existed—and what pressed on
Jewish faith from all sides, and even from within, were the *religious*
problems of idolatry and syncretism. The critical question in the creation account of Genesis 1 was polytheism versus monotheism. *That*
was the burning issue of the day, not some issue which certain
Americans 2,500 years later in the midst of a scientific age might
imagine that it was. And one of the reasons for its being such a

burning issue was that Jewish monotheism was such a unique and
hard-won faith. The temptations of idolatry and syncretism were
everywhere. Every nation surrounding Israel, both great and small,
was polytheistic; and many Jews themselves held—as they always
had—similar inclinations. Hence the frequent prophetic diatribes
against altars in high places, the Canaanite cult of Baal, and "whor-
ing after other gods."

Read through the eyes of the people who wrote it, Genesis 1 would
seem very different from the way most people today would tend to
read it—including both evolutionists who may dismiss it as a pre-
scientific account of origins, and creationists who may try to defend
it as the true science and literal history of origins. For most peoples
in the ancient world the various regions of nature were divine. Sun,
moon and stars were *gods*. There were sky gods and earth gods and
water gods. There were gods of light and darkness, rivers and vegetation, animals and fertility. Though for us nature has been "de-
mythologized" and "naturalized"—in large part because of this very
passage of Scripture—for ancient Jewish faith a divinized nature
posed a fundamental religious problem.

In addition, pharaohs, kings and heroes were often seen as sons of
gods, or at least as special mediators between the divine and human
spheres. The greatness and vaunted power and glory of the successive waves of empires that impinged on or conquered Israel (Egypt,
Assyria, Babylon, Persia) posed an analogous problem of idolatry in
the human sphere.

In the light of this historical context it becomes clearer what Genesis 1 is undertaking and accomplishing: a radical and sweeping affirmation of monotheism vis-à-vis polytheism, syncretism and idolatry. Each day of creation takes on two principal categories of divinity
in the pantheons of the day, and declares that these are not gods at
all, but creatures—creations of the one true God who is the only one,
without a second or third. Each day dismisses an additional cluster
of deities, arranged in a cosmological and symmetrical order.

On the first day the gods of light and darkness are dismissed. On
the second day, the gods of sky and sea. On the third day, earth gods
and gods of vegetation. On the fourth day, sun, moon and star gods.
The fifth and sixth days take away any associations with divinity
from the animal kingdom. And finally human existence, too, is emptied of any intrinsic divinity—while at the same time *all* human
beings, from the greatest to the least, and not just pharaohs, kings
and heroes, are granted a divine likeness and mediation.

On each day of creation another set of idols is smashed. These, O

Israel, are no gods at all—even the great gods and rulers of conquering superpowers. They are the creations of that transcendent One who is not to be confused with any piece of the furniture of the universe of creaturely habitation. The creation is good, it is very good, but it is not divine.

We are then given a further clue concerning the polemical design of the passage when the final verse (2:4a) concludes: "These are the generations of the heavens and the earth when they were created." Why the word "generations," especially if what is being offered is a chronology of days of creation? Now to polytheist and monotheist alike the word "generations" at this point would immediately call one thing to mind. If we should ask how these various divinities were related to one another in the pantheons of the day, the most common answer would be that they were related as members of a family tree. We would be given a genealogy, as in Hesiod's *Theogony*, where the great tangle of Greek gods and goddesses were sorted out by generations. Ouranos begat Kronos; Kronos begat Zeus; Zeus begat Prometheus.

The Egyptians, Assyrians and Babylonians all had their "generations of the gods." Thus the priestly account, which had begun with the majestic words, "In the beginning God created the heavens and the earth," now concludes—over against all the impressive and colorful pantheons with their divine pedigrees—*"These* are the generations of the heavens and the earth when they were *created."* It was a final pun on the concept of the divine family tree.

The fundamental question at stake, then, could not have been the scientific question of how things achieved their present form and by what processes, nor even the historical question about time periods and chronological order. The issue was idolatry, not science; syncretism, not natural history; theology, not chronology; affirmation of faith in one transcendent God, not creationist or evolutionist theories of origin. Attempting to be loyal to the Bible by turning the creation accounts into a kind of science or history is like trying to be loyal to the teachings of Jesus by arguing that the parables are actual historical events, and only reliable and trustworthy when taken literally as such.

If one really wishes to appreciate more fully the *religious* meaning of creation in Genesis 1, one should read not creationist or anticreationist diatribes but Isaiah 40. For the theology of Genesis 1 is essentially the same as the theology of Deutero-Isaiah. They are also both from the same time period, and therefore part of the same interpretive context. It was a time that had been marked, first, by the conquest of most of Palestine—save Jerusalem—by the Assyrians under Sennacherib (ca. 701 B.C.). And a century later the Babylonians under Nebuchadnezzar had in turn conquered the Middle East, Palestine and even Jerusalem.

The last vestige of Jewish autonomy and Promised Land had been overrun. The Holy City had been invaded, the temple of Solomon destroyed, the city burned, and many of the people carried off into exile, leaving "the poorest of the land to be vine-dressers and plowmen" (II Kings 25:12). Those taken into Babylonian captivity, as well as those left behind, now had even greater temptations placed before them to abandon faith in their God, and to turn after other gods who were clearly more powerful and victorious.

Given the awesome might and splendor and triumphs of Assyria and then Babylon, was it not obvious that the shepherd-god of Israel was but a local spirit, a petty tribal god who was hardly a match for the likes of Marduk, god of Babylon? Where *was* this god, or the people of his hand, or the land of his promise? Faith was hard and idolatry easy. And now a new and greater power, Persia, loomed on the horizon. Yet despite the littleness and powerlessness of a conquered people before the might and majesty of the great empires of the day, a prophet dared to stand forth and declare what Genesis 1 in its own way also declares:

> Who has measured the waters in the hollow of his hand,
> and marked off the heavens with a span,
> enclosed the dust of the earth in a measure
> and weighed the mountains in scales in a balance?
> Who has directed the Spirit of the Lord,
> or as his counselor has instructed him? [Isa. 40:12, 13]

Here too is a poetic affirmation which no literalism can reduce to its own scales and balances, and no symbolism or imagery exhaust.

> To whom then will you liken God,
> or what likeness compare with him? . . .
> Have you not known? Have you not heard?
> Has it not been told you from the beginning?
> Have you not understood from the foundations of the earth?
> It is he who sits above the circle of the earth,
> and its inhabitants are like grasshoppers;
> who stretches out the heavens like a curtain,

and spreads them like a tent to dwell in;
who brings princes to nought,
and makes the rulers of the earth as nothing. [Isa. 40:21-23]

Had there been a controversy in the Babylonian public schools of the day—and had there been Babylonian public schools—these would have been the issues in debate.

part three

Affirmations, Scientific and Christian

Chapter 7

Natural Science and Religion

ASA GRAY

Asa Gray (1810–1888) is one of the acknowledged folk heroes of science, one whom it would be very difficult to debunk. The only essayist in this anthology who is not still living, his words and insights are as valuable today as they were one hundred years ago. Fisher Professor of Natural History at Harvard, he was one of the great botanists of his time. Probably the most powerful and persuasive advocate of evolution in this country, his view of the evolution of life over millions of years was inherently Christian, demonstrating that an eminent scientist could coordinate his acceptance of biological evolution with a vital Christian faith. His lectures at the Yale Divinity School were published as Natural Science and Religion *in 1880 by Charles Scribner's Sons, only a little more than a century before the same firm publishes this anthology on the same general subject. The following essay is extracted from that original volume.*

I am invited to address you upon the relations of science to religion,—in reference, as I suppose, to those claims of natural science which have been thought to be antagonistic to supernatural religion, and to those assumptions connected with the Christian faith which scientific men in our day are disposed to question or to reject.

While listening weekly—I hope with edification—to the sermons

which it is my privilege and duty to hear, it has now and then occurred to me that it might be well if an occasional discourse could
be addressed from the pews to the pulpit. But, until your invitation
reached me, I had no idea that I should ever be called upon to put
this passing thought into practice. I am sufficiently convinced already that the members of a profession know their own calling better than any one else can know it; and in respect to the debatable
land which lies along the borders of theology and natural science,
and which has been harried by many a raid from both sides, I am
not confident that I can be helpful in composing strifes or in the fix-
ing of boundaries; nor that you will agree with me that some of the
encounters were inevitable, and some of the alarm groundless. Indeed upon much that I may have to say, I expect rather the charitable judgment than the full assent of those whose approbation I
could most wish to win.

But I take it for granted that you do not wish to hear an echo from
the pulpit nor from the theological class-room. You ask a layman to
speak from this desk because you would have a layman's thoughts,
expressed from a layman's point of view; because you would know
what a naturalist comes to think upon matters of common interest.
And you would have him liberate his mind frankly, unconvention-
ally, and with as little as may be of the technicalities of our several
professions. Frankness is always commendable; but outspokenness
upon delicate and unsettled problems, in the ground of which cher-
ished convictions are rooted, ought to be tempered with consideration. Now I, as a layman, may claim a certain license in this regard;
and any over-free handling of sensitive themes should compromise
no one but myself.

As a student who has devoted an ordinary lifetime to one branch
of natural history, in which he is supposed to have accumulated a
fair amount of particular experience and to have gained a general
acquaintance with scientific methods and aims,—as one, moreover,
who has taken kindly to the new turn of biological study in these
latter years, but is free from partisanship,—I am asked to confer
with other and younger students, of another kind of science, in respect to the tendencies of certain recently developed doctrines,
which in schools of theology are almost everywhere spoken against,
but which are everywhere permeating the lay mind—whether for
good or for evil—and are raising questions more or less perplexing
to all of us.

But our younger and middle-aged men must not think that such perplexities and antagonisms have only recently begun. Some of them are very old; some are old questions transferred to new ground, in which they spring to rankness of growth, or sink their roots till they touch deeper issues than before,—issues of philosophy rather than of science, upon which the momentous question of theism or non-theism eventually turns. Some on the other hand are mere *survivals*, now troublesome only to those who are holding fast to theological positions which the advance of actual knowledge has rendered untenable, but which they do not well know how to abandon; yet which, in principle, have mostly been abandoned already. . . .

As connected with this class of questions, many of us remember the time when schemes for reconciling Genesis with Geology had an importance in the churches, and among thoughtful people, which few if any would now assign to them; when it was thought necessary—for only necessity could justify it—to bring the details of the two into agreement by extraneous suppositions and forced constructions of language, such as would now offend our critical and sometimes our moral sense. The change of view which we have witnessed amounts to this. Our predecessors implicitly held that Holy Scripture must somehow truly teach such natural science as it had occasion to refer to, or at least could never contradict it; while the most that is now intelligently claimed is, that the teachings of the two, properly understood, are not incompatible. We may take it to be the accepted idea that the Mosaic books were not handed down to us for our instruction in scientific knowledge, and that it is our duty to ground our scientific beliefs upon observation and inference, unmixed with considerations of a different order. Then, when fundamental principles of the cosmogony in Genesis are found to coincide with established facts and probable inferences, the coincidence has its value; and wherever the particulars are incongruous, the discrepancy does not distress us, I may add, does not concern us. I trust that the veneration rightly due to the Old Testament is not impaired by the ascertaining that the Mosaic is not an original but a compiled cosmogony. Its glory is, that while its materials were the earlier property of the race, they were in this record purged of polytheism and Nature-worship, and impregnated with ideas which we suppose the world will never outgrow. For its fundamental note is, the declaration of one God, maker of heaven and earth, and of all things, visible and invisible,—a declaration which, if physical science is unable to establish, it is equally unable to overthrow. . . .

Half a century ago, when I began to read scientific books and journals, the commonly received doctrine was, that the earth had been completely depopulated and repopulated over and over, each time with a distinct population; and that the species which now, along with man, occupy the present surface of the earth, belong to an ultimate and independent creation, having an ideal but no genealogical connection with those that preceded. This view, as a rounded whole and in all its essential elements, has very recently disappeared from science. It died a royal death with Agassiz, who maintained it with all his great ability, as long as it was tenable. I am not aware that it now has any scientific upholder. It is certain that there has been no absolute severance of the present from the nearer past; for while some species have taken the place of other species, not a few have survived unchanged, or almost unchanged. And it is most probable that this holds throughout; for certain species appear to have bridged the intervals between successive epochs all along the line, surviving from one to another, and justifying the inference that species—however originated—have come in and gone out one by one, and that probably no universal catastrophe has ever blotted out life from the earth. Life seems to have gone on, through many and great vicissitudes, now with losses, now with renewals, and everywhere at length with change; but from first to last it has inhered in one system of nature, one vegetable and one animal kingdom, which themselves show indications of a common starting-point. . . .

All animals vary more or less: agriculturists improve domesticated animals by selection. What is thus done by art is done with equal efficacy, though more slowly, by Nature, in the formation of varieties of mankind, fitted for the country which they inhabit. . . .

Now, this simple principle,—extended from races to species; from the present to geological ages; from man and domesticated animals to all animals and plants; from struggle with disease to struggle for food, for room, and against the diverse hardships which at times beset all living things, and which are intensified by the Malthusian law of the pressure of population on subsistence,—population tending to multiply in geometrical progression, while food can increase only in a much lower ratio, and room may not be increasable at all, so that out of multitudinous progeny only the few fittest to the special circumstances in each generation can possibly survive and propagate,— this is *Darwinism;* that is, Darwinism pure and simple, free from all speculative accretions.

Here, it may be remarked that natural selection by itself is not an hypothesis, nor even a theory. It is a truth,—a *catena* of facts and direct inferences from facts. As has been happily said, it is a truth of the same kind as that which we enunciate in saying that round stones will roll down a hill further than flat ones. There is no doubt that natural selection operates; the open question is, what do its operations amount to. The *hypothesis* based on this principle is, that the struggle for life and survival of only the fittest among individuals, all disposed to vary and no two exactly alike, will account for the diversification of the species and forms of vegetable and animal life,—will even account for the rise, in the course of countless ages, from simpler and lower to higher and more specialized living beings. . . .

Natural selection we understand to be a sort of personification or generalized expression for the processes and the results of the whole interplay of living things on the earth with their inorganic surroundings and with each other. The hypothesis asserts that these may account, not for the introduction of life, but for its diversification into the forms and kinds which we now behold. . . .

But, indeed, you are not so much concerned to know whether evolutionary theories are actually well-founded or ill-founded, as you are to know whether if true, or if received as true, they would impair the foundations of religion. And, surely, if views of Nature which are incompatible with theism and with Christianity can be established, or can be made as tenable as the contrary, it is quite time that we knew it. If, on the other hand, all real facts and necessary inferences from them can be adjusted to our grounded religious convictions, as well as other ascertained facts have been adjusted, it may relieve many to be assured of it.

The best contribution that I can offer towards the settlement of these mooted questions may be the statement and explanation of my own attitude in this regard, and of the reasons which determine it.

I accept substantially, as facts, or as apparently well-grounded inferences, or as fairly probable opinions,—according to their nature and degree,—the principal series of changed views which I [have] brought before you. . . . I have no particular predilection for any of them; and I have no particular dread of any of the consequences which legitimately flow from them, beyond the general awe and sense of total insufficiency with which a mortal man contemplates the mysteries which shut him in on every side. I claim, moreover, not merely allowance, but the right to hold these opinions along with the doctrines of natural religion and the verities of the Christian faith. There are perplexities enough to bewilder our souls whenever and wherever we look for the causes and reasons of things; but I am unable to perceive that the idea of the evolution of one species from another, and of all from an initial form of life, adds any new perplexity to theism. . . .

I am not going to re-argue an old thesis of my own that Darwinism does not weaken the substantial ground of the argument, as between theism and non-theism, for design in Nature.[1] I think it brought in no new difficulty, though it brought old ones into prominence. It must be reasonably clear to all who have taken pains to understand the matter that the true issue as regards design is not between Darwinism and direct Creationism, but between design and fortuity, between any intention or intellectual cause and no intention nor predicable first cause. It is really narrowed down to this, and on this line all maintainers of the affirmative may present an unbroken front. The holding of this line secures all; the weakening of it in the attempted defence of unessential and now untenable outposts endangers all.

I have only to add a few observations and exhortations addressed to Christian theists. . . . The anatomical and physiological difference between man and the higher brutes is not great from a natural-history point of view, compared with the difference between these and lower grades of animals; but we may justly say that what corporeal difference there is is extremely important. The series of considerations which suggest evolution up to man, suggest man's evolution also. We may, indeed, fall back upon Mr. Darwin's declaration, in a case germane to this, that "analogy may be a deceitful guide." Yet here it is the only guide we have. If the alternative be the immediate origination out of nothing, or out of the soil, of the human form with all its actual marks, there can be no doubt which side a scientific man will take. Mediate creation, derivative origination will at once be accepted; and the mooted question comes to be narrowed down to this: Can the corporeal differences between man and the rest of the animal kingdom be accounted for by known natural causes, or must they be attributed to unknown causes? And shall we assume these unknown causes to be natural or supernatural? As to the first question, you are aware, from my whole line of thought and argument, that I know no natural process for the transformation of a brute mammal into a man. But I am equally at a loss as respects the processes through which any one species, any one variety, gives birth to another. Yet I do not presume to limit Nature by my small knowledge of its laws and powers. I know that a part of these still

occult processes are in the every-day course of Nature; I am persuaded that it is so through the animal kingdom generally; I cannot
deny it as respects the highest members of that kingdom. I allow,
however, that the superlative importance of comparatively small corporeal differences in this consummate case may justify any one in
regarding it as exceptional. In most respects, man is an exceptional
creature. If, however, I decline to regard man's origin as exceptional
in the sense of directly supernatural, you will understand that it is
because, under my thoroughly theistic conception of Nature, and my
belief in mediate creation, I am at a loss to know what I should
mean by the exception. I do not allow myself to believe that immediate creation would make man's origin more divine. And I do not
approve either the divinity or the science of those who are prompt
to invoke the supernatural to cover our ignorance of natural causes,
and equally so to discard its aid whenever natural causes are found
sufficient.[2]

It is probable that the idea of mediate creation would be more
readily received, except for a prevalent misconception upon a point
of genealogy. When the naturalist is asked, what and whence the origin of man, he can only answer in the words of Quatrefages and
Virchow, "We do not know at all." We have traces of his existence
up to and even anterior to the latest marked climatic change in our
temperate zone: but he was then perfected man; and no vestige of
an earlier form is known. The believer in direct or special creation
is entitled to the advantage which this negative evidence gives. A totally unknown ancestry has the characteristics of nobility. The evolutionist can give one satisfactory assurance. As the wolf in the fable
was captious in his complaint that the lamb below had muddied the
brook he was drinking from, so those are mistaken who suppose
that the simian race can have defiled the stream along which evolution traces human descent. Sober evolutionists do not suppose that
man has descended from monkeys. The stream must have branched
too early for that. The resemblances, which are the same in fact under any theory, are supposed to denote collateral relationship.

The psychological differences between man and the higher brute
animals you do not expect me now to discuss. Here, too, we may say
that, although gradations abridge the wide interval, the transcendent character of the superadded must count for more than a host of
lower similarities and identities; for, surely, what difference there is
between the man and the animal in this respect is supremely important.

If we cannot reasonably solve the problems even of inorganic nature without assuming initial causation, and if we assume for that supreme intelligence, shall we not more freely assume it, and with all the directness the case may require, in the field where intelligence at length develops intelligences? But while, on the one hand, we rise in thought into the supernatural, on the other we need not forget that one of the three old orthodox opinions,—the one held to be tenable if not directly favored by Augustine, and most accordant to his theology, as it is to observation,—is that souls as well as lives are propagated in the order of Nature. Here we may note, in passing, that since the "theologians are as much puzzled to form a satisfactory conception of the origin of each individual soul as naturalists are to conceive of the origin of species," and since the Darwinian and the theologian (at least the Traducian) take similar courses to find a way out of their difficulties, they might have a little more sympathy for each other. The high Calvinist and the Darwinian have a goodly number of points in common.[3]

View these high matters as you will, the outcome, as concerns us, of the vast and partly comprehensible system, which under one aspect we call Nature, and under another Providence, and in part under another, Creation, is seen in the emergence of a free and self-determining personality, which, being capable of conceiving it, may hope for immortality.

"May hope for immortality." You ask for the reasons of this hope upon these lines of thought. I suppose that they are the same as your own, so far as natural reasons go. A being who has the faculty—however bestowed—of reflective, abstract thought superadded to all lower psychical faculties, is thereby *per saltum* immeasurably exalted. This, and only this, brings with it language and all that comes from that wonderful instrument; it carries the germs of all invention and all improvement, all that man does and may do in his rule over Nature and his power of ideally soaring above it. So we may well deem this a special gift, the gift beyond recall, in which all hope is enshrined. None of us have any scientific or philosophical explanation to offer as to *how* it came to be added to what we share with the brutes that perish; but it puts man into another world than theirs, both here, and—with the aid of some evolutionary ideas, we may add—hereafter.

Let us consider. It must be that the Eternal can alone impart the gift of eternal life. But He alone originates life. Now what of that life which reaches so near to ours, yet misses it so completely? The perplexity this question raises was as great as it is now before evolution was ever heard of; it has been turned into something much more trying than perplexity by the assurance with which monistic evolutionists press their answer to the question; but a better line of evolutionary doctrine may do something toward disposing of it. It will not do to say that thought carries the implication of immortality. For our humble companions have the elements of that, or of simple ratiocination, and the power of reproducing conceptions in memory, and—what is even more to the present purpose—in dreams. Once admit this to imply immortality and you will be obliged to make soul coextensive with life, as some have done, thereby well-nigh crushing the whole doctrine of immortality with the load laid upon it. At least this is poising the ponderous pyramid on its apex, and the apex on a logical fallacy. For the entire conception that the highest brute animals may be endowed with an immortal principle is a reflection from the conception of such a principle in ourselves; and so the farther down you carry it, the wider and more egregious the circle you are reasoning in.

Still, with all life goes duality. There is the matter, and there is the life, and we cannot get one out of the other, unless you define matter as something which works to ends. As all agree that reflective thought cannot be translated into terms of extension (matter and motion), nor the converse, so as truly it cannot be translated into terms of sensation and perception, of desire and affection, of even the feeblest vital response to external impressions, of simplest life. The duality runs through the whole. You cannot reasonably give over any part of the field to the monist, and retain the rest.

Now see how evolution may help you;—in its conception that, while all the lower serves its purpose for the time being, and is a stage toward better and higher, the lower sooner or later perish, the higher, the consummate, survive. The soul in its bodily tenement is the final outcome of Nature. May it not well be that the perfected soul alone survives the final struggle of life, and indeed "then chiefly lives,"—because in it all worths and ends inhere; because it only is worth immortality, because it alone carries in itself the promise and potentiality of eternal life! Certainly in it only is the potentiality of religion, or that which aspires to immortality.

Here I should close; but, in justice to myself and to you, a word must still be added. You rightly will say that, although theism is at the foundation of religion, the foundation is of small practical value without the superstructure. Your supreme interest is Christianity;

and you ask me if I maintain that the doctrine of evolution is compatible with this. I am bound to do so. Yet I have left myself no time in which to vindicate my claim; which I should wish to do most earnestly, yet very deferentially, considering where and to whom I speak. Here we reverse positions: you are the professional experts; I am the unskilled inquirer.

I accept Christianity on its own evidence, which I am not here to specify or to justify; and I am yet to learn how physical or any other science conflicts with it any more than it conflicts with simple theism. I take it that religion is based on the idea of a Divine Mind revealing himself to intelligent creatures for moral ends. We shall perhaps agree that the revelation on which our religion is based is an example of evolution; that it has been developed by degrees and in stages, much of it in connection with second causes and human actions; and that the current of revelation has been mingled with the course of events. I suppose that the Old Testament carried the earlier revelation and the germs of Christianity, as the apostles carried the treasures of the gospel, in earthen vessels. I trust it is reverent, I am confident it is safe and wise, to consider that revelation in its essence concerns things moral and spiritual; and that the knowledge of God's character and will which has descended from the fountainhead in the earlier ages has come down to us, through annalists and prophets and psalmists, in a mingled stream, more or less tinged or rendered turbid by the earthly channels through which it has worn its way. The stream brings down precious gold, and so may be called a golden stream; but the water—the vehicle of transportation—is not gold. Moreover the analogy of our inquiry into design in Nature may teach us that we may be unable always accurately to sift out the gold from the earthy sediment.

But, however we may differ in regard to the earlier stages of religious development, we shall agree in this, that revelation culminated, and for us most essentially consists, in the advent of a Divine Person, who, being made man, manifested the Divine Nature in union with the human; and that this manifestation constitutes Christianity.

Having accepted the doctrine of the incarnation, itself the crowning miracle, attendant miracles are not obstacles to belief. Their primary use must have been for those who witnessed them; and we may allow that the record of a miracle cannot have the convincing force of the miracle itself. But the very reasons on which scientific men reject miracles for the carrying on of Nature may operate in favor of miracles to attest an incoming of the supernatural for moral ends. At least they have nothing to declare against them.

If now you ask me, What are the essential contents of that Christianity which is in my view as compatible with my evolutionary conceptions as with former scientific beliefs, it may suffice to answer that they are briefly summed up in the early creeds of the Christian Church, reasonably interpreted. The creeds to be taken into account are only two,—one commonly called the Apostles', the other the Nicene. The latter and larger is remarkable for its complete avoidance of conflict with physical science. The language in which its users "look for the resurrection of the dead" bears—and doubtless at its adoption had in the minds of at least some of the council—a worthier interpretation than that naturally suggested by the short western creed, namely, the crude notion of the revivification of the human body, against which St. Paul earnestly protested.

Moreover, as brethren uniting in a common worship, we may honorably, edifyingly, and wisely use that which we should not have formulated, but may on due occasion qualify,—statements, for instance, dogmatically pronouncing upon the essential nature of the Supreme Being (of which nothing can be known and nothing is revealed), instead of the Divine manifestation. We may add more to our confession: we all of us draw more from the exhaustless revelation of Christ in the gospels; but this should suffice for the profession of Christianity. If you ask, must we require that, I reply that I am merely stating what I accept. Whoever else will accept Him who is himself the substance of Christianity, let him do it in his own way.

In conclusion, we students of natural science and of theology have very similar tasks. Nature is a complex, of which the human race through investigation is learning more and more the meaning and the uses. The Scriptures are a complex, an accumulation of a long series of records, which are to be well understood only by investigation. It cannot be that in all these years we have learned nothing new of their meaning and uses to us, and have nothing still to learn. Nor can it be that we are not free to use what we learn in one line of study to limit, correct, or remodel the ideas which we obtain from another.

Gentlemen of the Theological School, about to become ministers of the gospel, receive this discourse with full allowance for the different point of view from which we survey the field. If I, in my solicitude to attract scientific men to religion, be thought to have minimized the divergence of certain scientific from religious beliefs, I pray that you on the other hand will never needlessly exaggerate them; for that may be more harmful. I am persuaded that you, in your day, will enjoy the comfort of a much better understanding between the scientific and the religious mind than has prevailed. Yet without doubt a full share of intellectual and traditional difficulties will fall to your lot. Discreetly to deal with them, as well for yourselves as for those who may look to you for guidance, rightly to present sensible and sound doctrine both to the learned and the ignorant, the lowly and the lofty-minded, the simple believer and the astute speculatist, you will need all the knowledge and judgment you can acquire from science and philosophy, and all the superior wisdom your supplications may draw from the Infinite Source of knowledge, wisdom, and grace.

Notes

1. *Darwiniana: Essays and Reviews Pertaining to Darwinism* (New York: D. Appleton & Co., 1876).
2. See Baden Powell, *On the Order of Nature*, p. 163.
3. See an article on "Some Analogies between Calvinism and Darwinism," by Rev. G. F. Wright, in the *Bibliotheca Sacra* (January, 1880).

Chapter 8

Let There Be Light: Modern Cosmogony and Biblical Creation

OWEN GINGERICH

The preceding piece by Asa Gray and this paper by Owen Gingerich will not necessarily "convert" all advocates of creation-science, but they do demonstrate that modern scientific theories of the origins of the physical universe do not require honest men to reject Christianity, nor does the acceptance of the latter require the rejection of the former. Gingerich exemplifies this point for our time just as Gray did a century ago. Professor of Astronomy and of the History of Science, Gingerich follows Gray in the tradition of distinguished Harvard scientists. A member of such highly selective academies as the American Academy of Arts and Sciences and the American Philosophical Society (whose John Frederick Lewis Prize was awarded to him in 1976), he has made many contributions to the advancement of science and to the understanding of its nature and history. His essay, eloquently combining scientific understanding with Christian perception, was first delivered as the Dwight Lecture in Christian Thought at the University of Pennsylvania in 1982, and in 1983 as the McNair Lecture at the University of North Carolina.

In the early part of this century, when the Harvard philosophy department was graced with such luminaries as William James, Alfred North Whitehead, George Herbert Palmer, and George Santayana, the department members consulted with Harvard's President Charles Eliot about an appropriate motto to be carved on the facade of the proposed new philosophy building. Professor Palmer recommended a quotation from Protagoras, "Man is the measure of all things," but President Eliot didn't commit himself. When Emerson Hall was finally completed in 1905 and the motto unveiled, it read"What is man that thou art mindful of him?" I don't know how those illustrious philosophers reacted to this line from Psalm 8, but I do think it poses a fundamental question for us all. Does man have an essential place in the universe, or is he a cosmical nonentity?

I shall return eventually to that question, but let me begin with the first quotation, "Man is the measure of all things." In a curious dimensional way, which Protagoras could scarcely have intended, we are a kind of yardstick for the universe, standing between the microscopic and macroscopic worlds. Up and beyond, the universe extends twenty-five orders of magnitude larger than the human body, while down and within, the atomic nucleus lies nearly sixteen orders of magnitude smaller.

In the microscopic world of the atom there are marvels to stagger the imagination. Physicists have become modern alchemists, transforming gold to mercury and uranium to strontium. Submicroscopic particles can annihilate antiparticles, transforming matter into a burst of energy, or, in reverse, pure energy can give birth to matter with exotic, newly described properties of charm, color, and strangeness as well as mass and electrical charge. At the other end of the scale, astronomers plumb the world of the large, delineating our Milky Way as a giant pinwheel galaxy containing over 200 billion stars, about fifty for every man, woman, and child on earth. And beyond our own stellar system, countless other galaxies are scattered out to the fringes of the universe, some 10 billion light years away.

These are all discoveries of our own century, most of them scarcely half a century old. Yet none of them is quite as astonishing as the scientific scenario that has now been outlined for the first moments of creation. During this past decade knowledge of the world of the smallest possible sizes, the domain of particle physics, has been combined with astronomy to describe the universe in its opening stages. The physics ultimately fails as the nucleo-cosmologists push their calculations back to Time Zero, but they get pretty close to the beginning, to $10(-43)$ second. At that point, at a second split so fine that no clock could measure it, the entire observable universe is compressed within the wavelike blur described by the uncertainty principle, so tiny and compact that it could pass through the eye of a needle. Not just this room, or the earth, or the solar system, but *the entire universe* squeezed into a dense dot of pure energy. And then comes the explosion. "There is no way to express that explosion," writes the poet Robinson Jeffers.

> . . . All that exists
> Roars into flame, the tortured fragments rush away from
> each other into all the sky, new universes
> Jewel the black breast of night; and far off the outer nebulae
> like charging spearmen again
> Invade emptiness.[1]

It is an amazing picture, of pure and incredibly energetic light being transformed into matter, and leaving its vestiges behind—countless atoms and even more numerous photons of light generated in that mighty blast. It's even more astonishing when we realize that the final fate of the universe, whether it will expand forever or fall back on itself to a future Big Crunch, was determined in that opening moment. Furthermore, that moment has left behind a tell-tale imprint in the ratios of hydrogen, deuterium, and helium abundances, imprints which, if our astrophysical sleuthing is clever enough, will enable the nucleo-cosmologists to describe the end as well as the beginning of our physical universe.

But, you may well ask, what evidence do we have that this wondrous tale is true? Or is it some kind of strange fiction? "Where wast thou when I laid the foundations of the earth?" the Lord asked Job from the whirlwind (Job 38:4) and, to be sure, none of us was there. So, I must admit, what the scientists in my detective story have devised is an intricate reconstruction, assembled just as the detective in a whodunit thriller systematically reconstructs the crime. That metaphor is not bad, for a great deal of modern science rests on conjecture, albeit rational conjecture. Yet it is not quite adequate to convey the grandeur and extent of modern science. Personally, I believe there is a better metaphor in likening science to a beautiful, panoramic tapestry. It is beautiful in the way the contrasting patterns and themes are organized into a unified, coherent whole. It is panoramic in its scope, the majestic sweep that covers all of nature from the minutest subatomic particle to the vast outer reaches of space and time. Like a tapestry, it is a human artifact, ingeniously and seamlessly woven together. It is not easy to unravel one small part without affecting the whole.

I cannot, in my short compass here, lay in place all the threads of this vast tapestry whose pattern includes the first moments of creation. Nevertheless, let me try to weave several skeins into place. One part of the design concerns our knowledge of distances, another the time-scale of the universe, and both are inextricably woven together.

The ancient Greeks already knew the size of the earth, and by triangulation they got the distance to the moon fairly well. They did not have to travel to lay out the baseline of the triangle; the rotation of the earth carried them to new positions with respect to our satellite, although the ancients would of course not have thought of it in that way since they believed in a fixed earth. Before the end of the seventeenth century, more precise triangulation, made possible with the telescope and refined measuring scales, allowed astronomers to determine distances within the solar system. Then, allowing a moving earth to sweep out a larger baseline, they triangulated to the nearest stars, this delicate feat being accomplished by the middle of the last century. These trigonometric procedures have a practical limitation, however. Proxima Centauri, the first star beyond the sun, is 400 trillion kilometers away; its light takes four years to reach us. Triangulation can barely penetrate a hundred times farther, not even one percent of the distance across the Milky Way system. A thousand light years lie beyond the reach of the geometrical methods.

Nevertheless, we can fathom the vaster depth of space with techniques that use the geometrical diminution of light with distance, well expressed by the aphorism "Faintness means farness." To proceed, we must single out classes of objects that always have the same intrinsic brightness, and then by observing the apparent brightness of one of these objects, we can calculate its farness from its observed faintness. This is of course easier said than done. But in the second decade of this century, Harlow Shapley, a young astronomer at Mount Wilson Observatory, succeeded in calibrating the luminosities of a type of brilliant pulsating star. Because these stars rhythmically varied in light, it was comparatively easy to detect and identify them, and once they were found and measured, their distances could be calculated. In particular, Shapley was studying the immense aggregations of stars called globular clusters, and he found to his intense exhilaration that these stellar congeries were at distances greater than anyone had contemplated before that time, distances of several tens of thousands of light years. Using the spatial arrangement of globular clusters, Shapley inferred that our Milky Way galaxy was a huge disk of stars and star clouds over a hundred thousand light years across.

It remained for his colleague at Mount Wilson, Edwin Hubble, to apply the same variable star technique to the spiral nebulae and to show that these were also disclike pinwheels of stars, comparable to our own Milky Way, but distributed throughout space beginning around a million light years beyond our own system. But at a distance of 10 million light years, even the most brilliant pulsating stars are diminished below the limit of visibility for the largest of the Earth-based telescopes.

To explore even greater depths of space requires some other class of still brighter objects, and here the globular clusters themselves, taken as units, offer a candle in the darkness. This step is slightly risky, because not all globular clusters are equally bright, and it takes some averaging and checking with alternative methods to work with any confidence. Still, it does allow distances of perhaps 50 million light years to be fathomed.

Beyond that, in the inky blackness of space, it requires shrewd scheming and judicious guesswork to probe further. If we assume some uniformity in space and time, then distant galaxies must on the average be like those nearby, and so the galaxies themselves, well chosen, must become the measures for reaching out a few billion light years. And with distances so great, we realize also that unimaginable vistas of time are now also involved.

The problem of ages is closely akin to that of the distances. Around 1917, V. M. Slipher, working at the Lowell Observatory, found that key features in the spectra of the spiral nebulae were shifted toward the red end of the spectral rainbow compared to similar laboratory measurements. When interpreted as a Doppler shift (similar to the change in pitch of a siren as it passes and recedes from us), these red shifts indicated surprisingly high recessional velocities, some exceeding a thousand kilometers per second. Such speeds are high by any terrestrial standard, but slow compared to the speed of light. After Edwin Hubble had determined the distances to some of these spirals, it became apparent that the farther the galaxy, the faster it was rushing away from us.

These data arrived on the scene just as the cosmologists had begun to speculate on the large-scale properties of the universe, and out of this confluence of theory and observation arose the concept of the expansion of the universe. It was a concept of quite awesome beauty: from a super-dense state, "All that exists/Roars into flame, the tortured fragments rush away from/each other into all the sky." What is more, given the rate of expansion and the distances of the galaxies, we can calculate backwards to the time when they were back together, "crushed in one harbor," in Robinson Jeffers' phrase. And the time comes out about 10 to 20 billion years ago, a time that can be interpreted as the age of the universe itself.

There are two other, quite independent ways to get the ages of some very old things in the universe. I have before me a fragment of the Allende meteorite, a ton of which fell in northern Mexico in 1969. It is probably the oldest object I'll ever touch, dated at 4.6 billion years. How is that age determined? The meteorite contains trace amounts of several radioactive isotopes such as palladium–107, which very gradually changes to silver. In the early stages of the solar system, certain minerals crystallized out as the meteorite formed and cooled, and these crystals contained specific but different amounts of the isotopes, depending on the mineral. Once the atoms were locked up in the crystal structure, they couldn't move, but the radioactive palladium would slowly disintegrate at a known rate, increasing the silver–107. But the original amount of the other silver isotopes remain unchanged, so careful analyses of the isotope ratios in several of the minerals can give the time of crystallization. According to this analysis, the minerals in the small white nodules within the Allende meteorite crystallized 4.6 billion years ago.

Not only has it been possible to determine the age of a specific object such as the Allende meteorite, but even the elements themselves can be dated. If the atoms were infinitely old, then radioactive uranium and thorium would have turned to lead. Their very existence tells us that they were formed at a finite time past. Long ago a supernova may have gone off in our neighborhood of the Milky Way, spewing forth within its nuclear ashes a wide variety of elements. We are all recycled star stuff. The iron in our blood is a typical sample of reused cosmic wastes. Included among that stellar ejecta were a variety of radioactive atoms, and the nuclear physicists can calculate the original ratios of these isotopes. Then, from the currently observed ratios, they can calculate back to the time of the supernova explosion. Careful modeling of the pattern of multiple supernova explosions and the examination of isotopes such as iodine–129 and plutonium–244 yields an age of about 10 billion years. These radioactive dating methods do not give a highly precise answer, but what seems to me very impressive is that the results fall in the same ball park as the expansion age, that is, roughly 10 billion years. It would really be embarrassing if the ages of the atoms came out, say, 50 billion years, that is, several times older than the universe, but fortunately that hasn't happened.

The third way to arrive at a truly ancient age is to calculate the evolution of stars in a globular star cluster, one of those immense and fundamental units Shapley used for inferring the vastness of our Milky Way system. The globular clusters are gravitationally very stable, and therefore they can hang together for a long time. The brightest stars in these clusters are yellow and orange. That means they're a lot cooler than, for example, the profligate blue stars that make up most of the constellation Orion. We can calculate how fast those blue Orion stars use up their nuclear fuel; the most luminous will spend their energy in a few million years. If the dinosaurs were smart enough to have looked up to the stars, they wouldn't have seen the constellation Orion—if it had been there then, it wouldn't be here now, for its stars would have long since burned out. (I don't think the dinosaurs were smart enough to notice the stars, but on the other hand some birds, who might be considered descendants of the dinosaurs, do use the stars to navigate in their long migrational flights!)

In the globular clusters the brightest blue stars have long since burned out, and our calculations show that the cluster stars somewhat fainter have now evolved into the yellow giants that bejewel these celestial brooches. The calculations of a star's evolving structure are complex, and could scarcely be made without high-speed electronic computers, but they do show that the globulars are very ancient objects: at least 10 billion, but probably not over 15 billion years.

I've described three independent ways for dating very old things: globular cluster stars, radioactive isotopes, and the universe itself as established from its expansion. The first two of these indicate that our part of the universe is pretty old, but they don't preclude other parts from being much, much older. Hence we ought to ask if there is any confirming evidence that we live in an evolving universe with a specific beginning.

The quasars, discovered in the 1960s, furnish evidence that the universe is changing, and was far different 10 billion years ago. To see how this works, let's first consider stars, rather than galaxies. If we count the first magnitude stars—Sirius, Vega, Spica, and so on—

we find twenty of them. If we extend our count to the fainter and hence more distant stars of second magnitude, we would be probing a much larger volume and would expect to find a substantially larger number of stars. When we count the stars of second magnitude and brighter, there are just over eighty, or about four times as many. In fact, we can show mathematically that if we have a galaxy in which the stars are uniformly distributed and if space is perfectly transparent, then we must find four times as many stars each time we go one magnitude fainter. However, if we count the stars of the fifteenth magnitude and brighter, we would get about 40 million, but if we go a magnitude fainter, there are not four times, but only about twice as many stars. One of the assumptions must not hold: either space is not transparent, or the stellar distribution is not uniform. The reason is easy to find: the space within our Milky Way galaxy is slightly foggy, and this cuts down the number of fainter, more distant stars that we can actually see.

But now consider the sixteenth-magnitude quasars—it turns out that there are about eight times as many as the brighter fifteenth-magnitude ones. This time it must be the other assumption that fails. We can explain the extra abundance of the quasars by assuming that they really are more frequent in the farther depths of space. Of course, as we look out into space, we are looking backwards into time, and thus we conclude that the quasars were actually more abundant in times long past, some billions of years ago. In other words, the universe was different then; the quasars, the most brilliant of the cosmic fireworks, were far more plentiful in the early stages of the universe. Now they are spent, and their dying embers have perhaps vanished into vast black holes. Their distribution thus provides evidence that the universe is evolving on a grand scale, but it does not force us to conclude that the universe had a definite beginning, even though that seems to be an inviting corollary.

The evidence that the universe had a definite, superdense beginning is somewhat different in nature, and we must approach it more circuitously. Suppose we run time backward in our calculations, to see what the universe is like as its density increases. The total mass and energy will remain the same, but the temperature will rise as the matter-energy is compressed. Finally the temperature becomes so high, and the mean energy of the components so great, that the presently-known laws of physics no longer apply. This happens when we are a split second from squashing the universe into nothingness.

Now let us run the clock forward again, and let me briefly describe the action. In the first few minutes things happen much faster than we can possibly describe them. In the first microseconds the high-energy photons vastly outnumber particles of matter, but there is a continual interchange between the photons and heavy particles of matter and antimatter. Einstein's famous $E = mc^2$ equation helps describe this situation in which the energy of the photons is converted into mass and vice versa. By the end of the first millisecond, the creation of protons and antiprotons is essentially finished, and the vast majority of them have already been annihilated back into photons. As the universe loses its incredible compression, the average energy per photon drops, and during this first second electrons and antielectrons (called positrons) are repeatedly formed and annihilated, finally leaving about 100 million photons of light for every atom, a ratio that still remains.

The thermonuclear detonation of the universe is now on its way, and in the next minute fusion reactions take place that build up deuterium and helium nuclei. After the first few minutes the explosive nuclear fireworks are over, but the headlong expansion continues, and the cosmic egg gradually cools. Still, the temperature remains so high for the next 300,000 years that whenever an electron and proton combine into a neutral hydrogen atom, it is almost immediately split apart by one of the abundant, omnipresent photons. Gradually, however, the average energy of the photons drops, and they lose their potency for ionizing the hydrogen. This detail I would have omitted from my sketch, except for its interesting observational consequence. At that moment when the photons lose their potency, the universe becomes transparent. This happens because the photons no longer interact so intensively with the atoms; the photons fly across space unimpeded, although their color is redshifted by the expansion of the universe. They are ours to observe, and they have been observed by looking out every direction into space, the fossil evidence of the primeval fireball of the Big Bang. This observed background radiation is one piece of evidence supporting the contemporary scientific picture of creation, and the other is the observed abundance of helium and of deuterium, which match well the predicted amounts that would be formed in that cosmic explosion.

This is indeed a thrilling scenario of all that exists roaring into flame and charging forth into emptiness. And its essential framework, of everything springing forth from that blinding flash, bears a striking resonance with those succinct words of Genesis 1:3: "And

God said, Let there be light." Who could have guessed even a hundred years ago, not to mention two or three thousand years ago, that a scientific picture would emerge with electromagnetic radiation as the starting point of creation! According to the NASA astrophysicist Robert Jastrow, the agnostic scientists should sit up and take notice, and even be a little worried. But let us look a little more carefully at the extent of the convergence. Both the contemporary scientific account and the age-old biblical account assume a beginning. The scientific account concerns only the transformation of everything that now is. It does not go beyond that, to the singularity when there was nothing and then suddenly the inconceivably energetic seed for the universe abruptly came into being. Here science seems up against a blank wall. In one memorable passage in his book, *God and the Astronomers,* Jastrow says:

> At this moment it seems as though science will never be able to raise the curtain on the mystery of creation. For the scientist who has lived by his faith in the power of reason, the story ends like a bad dream. He has scaled the mountains of ignorance; he is about to conquer the highest peak; as he pulls himself over the final rock, he is greeted by a band of theologians who have been sitting there for centuries.[2]

The band of theologians has an answer: God did it!

But for either a self-professed agnostic like Jastrow or for a believer, such an answer is unrevealing and even superficial, for it cloaks our ignorance beneath a name and tells us nothing further about God beyond the concept of an omnipotent Creator. Perhaps for that reason even the book of Genesis tacitly ignores that mind-boggling step when something came from nothing. What the Bible has to say concerns what happened next and, in fact, both the scientific and the biblical accounts portray the latent creativity as the universe begins to unfold, beginning with the grand and simple, and leading to the immediate and complex. The scientific picture sketches the creation of atoms, of galaxies, of stars, of life, even of man. Likewise, Genesis speaks of the sun and moon, of plants and animals, and of man.

But there is a truly fundamental difference in their viewpoints. The great tapestry of science is woven together in a grand and awesome design with the question "How?" How can the universe end up with a preponderance of positively charged nuclei? How can fluctuations arise to give birth to galaxies? How can the presence of iron atoms be explained? How can hemoglobin come about? The scientific account starts with our present, everyday universe. Detailed observations of the natural world provide the warp of our tapestry, and the theoretical explanations provide the "how," the weft that holds the picture together.

The biblical picture also concerns the universe around us, but it addresses an entirely different question, not the interconnections of "how" but the motivations and designs of the "who." The Bible brilliantly affirms that our universe has come to be, not by chance, but by a grand design, and that the designer was Almighty God.

In our country today there is a vocal minority which is confused by the separate roles of the scientific way of building up a worldview and the biblical story of creation. Somehow these people feel threatened by the ascendancy of a system of looking at the world that does not explicitly include the designing hand of God in the construction. Science is, by its very nature, godless. It is a mechanistic system, contrived to show how things work, and unable to say anything about the who, the designer. I can sympathize if a deeply religious person finds this incomplete and unsatisfying, and I can even sympathize mildly with the frustration of the creationists, who wish that some broader philosophical framework could be placed into biology textbooks. But they are mistaken when they take scientific explanations as such to be anti-God or atheistic, they are wrong when they think that the Genesis account can substitute for the "how" of scientific explanations, and they err when they think that a meaningful tack is to brand evolution as a "mere hypothesis." In a certain sense *all* of the theoretical explanations of science, the weft that holds the tapestry together, are hypotheses, and to unthread one section risks destroying the entire fabric.

The conflicts in California, Arkansas, and Louisiana might well have been avoided if teachers of science spent a little less time on the scientific answers and a little more time on the process of inquiry, because the process is the heart of the matter. But perhaps it is naive to suppose that children could grasp some of the distinctions that have escaped their elders. Perhaps I can make my point clearer with a bit of digression.

When I first began to prepare this lecture, I received in the mail a colorful poster offering a $1000 cash reward for "scientific proof-positive that the earth moves." In an accompanying letter to me, the potential donor, Mr. Elmendorf wrote: "As an engineer, I am astounded that the question of the earth's motion is apparently not 'all settled' after all these years. I mean, if we don't know *that*, what do we know?"

The question, of course, goes back to Copernicus and Galileo and to the birth of modern science. Most of the scholars in the generations immediately following Copernicus assumed that his heliocentric system was merely a hypothetical arrangement for explaining the apparent motions in the heavens, and not that the earth *really* moved. Galileo was intrigued by the Copernican system, but he was only a timid Copernican until he turned the newly devised telescope to the heavens and found there a miniature Copernican system in the satellite system of Jupiter. Galileo found a succession of other instances where the heliocentric system could nicely explain his observations, and so he began to argue for the reality of the sun-centered arrangement. But he was completely unable to prove it in any strict sense. All he could do was make the heliocentric system appear increasingly probable. The Catholic Church objected to Galileo's line of reasoning, pointing out correctly that just because certain observations were explained by the Copernican system did not mean that some other hypothesis might not equally well explain them, and the Inquisition ordered certain changes in Copernicus' book.

Meanwhile, north of the Alps, Johannes Kepler also accepted the physical reality of the Copernican arrangement, and went to work to show that each planet had an elliptical orbit with the sun at one focus. He could not prove the truth of the earth's motion, but without the assumption of a fixed central sun, his orbital system didn't make much sense.

Then along came Isaac Newton who, with some simple but powerful assumptions concerning the nature of matter and motion and with some powerful new mathematics, was able to build up a marvelous system of both explanation and prediction. Still, Newton had no proof of the earth's motion. What he had was an elaborate picture of how the physical world worked. It was so thorough and so probable that most people had no difficulty in accepting it as truth. Everyone knew that if the earth was really moving around the sun, the positions of nearby stars should show an annual displacement, but the failure to find it did not discredit the heliocentric theory. Thus, when the discovery of annual stellar parallax finally took place around 1840, people could hardly get excited about this purported proof of the motion of the earth.

"At the end of the last century," and here I quote from a most perceptive book by Jacob Bronowski, *The Origins of Knowledge and Imagination*, "there were physicists who were perfectly willing to say that there was no need to produce another Newton because there was nothing as fundamental as gravitation for another Newton to discover. . . . Since then," he continues, "the world has fallen about our ears."[3] Why? Because Einstein's general relativity showed us another way of looking at gravitation, and brought the scientific community to the realization that there was no way to know when any scientific theory was final and therefore true in some ultimate sense. Science simply does not offer "scientific proofs positive," and that is why it is unlikely that anyone will ever collect Mr. Elmendorf's thousand dollars for a "scientific proof-positive" that the earth moves.

Einstein's work has forcefully awakened us to the provisional nature of our scientific picture. As he himself said of science, "the sense-experiences are the given subject-matter. But the theory that shall interpret them is man-made. It is the result of an extremely laborious process of adaptation: hypothetical, never completely final, always subject to question and doubt."

This is why I have continually referred to the scientific worldview as a grand tapestry. It is an interlocked and coherent picture, a most workable explanation, but it is not ultimate truth. Robinson Jeffers puts it well in another poem when he says,

> The mathematicians and physics men
> Have their mythology; they work alongside the truth,
> Never touching it; their equations are false
> But the things *work*.[4]

I know, just as the Catholic Church in Galileo's day knew, that there can be alternate explanations for certain observations. For example, I accept as a working hypothesis the Big Bang model of the universe, but I know that the evidence I have cited concerning the background radiation and the abundances of the elements might have any number of other explanations. But what I am not willing to accept—and this is very important—is some special explanation that does not fit the rest of the picture. All of science is in a sense hypothetical. But the tapestry is of a piece, and it cannot be shredded easily. That is why I am uninterested in the ad hoc and particular claims made here or there by the advocates of "creation science." Perhaps the ultimate truth is that the world was created only 6,000 years ago, but since the Creator has filled it with wonderful clues pointing back 10 or 20 billion years, I am content to do my science by building a coherent picture of a multibillion-year-old creation, even though that may be only a grand hypothesis. Because it is the coherency of the picture and the systematic procedures for getting there—not the final truth—that science is all about.

I have been describing science as a tapestry with a grand design; let me now turn to the idea of a designer. I am personally persuaded that through the eyes of faith one can see numerous vestiges of the designer's hand in the universe. I have many good friends who cannot see it that way, so I am rather doubtful that one can argue a skeptic into faith with the evidences of science. Nevertheless, I find some of these circumstances of nature impossible to comprehend in the absence of supernatural design.

Let's consider for a moment the complex interaction between the Earth's atmosphere and life. From what astronomers have deduced about solar evolution, we believe that the sun was perhaps 25 percent less luminous several billion years ago. Today, if the solar luminosity dropped by 25 percent, the oceans would freeze solid to the bottom, and it would take a substantial increase beyond the sun's present luminosity to thaw them out again. Life could not have originated on such a frozen globe, so it seems that the earth's surface never suffered such frigid conditions. As it turns out, there is a very good reason for this. The original atmosphere would surely have consisted of hydrogen, by far the most abundant element in the universe, but this light element would have rapidly escaped, and a secondary atmosphere of carbon dioxide and water vapor would have formed from the outgassing of volcanoes. This secondary atmosphere would have produced a strong greenhouse effect, an effect that might be more readily explained with a locked car parked in the sun on a hot summer day than with a greenhouse. When you open the car, it's like an oven inside. The glass lets in the photons of visible light from the sun. Hot as the interior of the car may seem, it's quite cool compared to the sun's surface, so the reradiation from inside the car is in the infrared. The glass is quite opaque for those longer wavelengths, and because the radiation can't get out, the car heats up inside. Similarly, the carbon dioxide and water vapor partially blocked the reradiation from the early earth, raising its surface temperature above the mean freezing point of water.

Over the ages, as the sun's luminosity rose, so did the surface temperature of the earth, and had the atmosphere stayed constant, our planet would now have a runaway greenhouse effect, something like that found on the planet Venus; the earth's oceans would have boiled away, leaving a hot, lifeless globe.

How did our atmosphere change over to oxygen just in the nick of time? Apparently the earliest widely successful life form on earth was a single-celled prokaryote, the so-called blue-greens, which survive to this day as stromatolites. Evidence for them appears in the preCambrian fossil record of a billion years ago. In the absence of predators, these algaelike organisms covered the oceans, extracting hydrogen from the water and releasing oxygen to the air. Nothing much seems to have happened for over a billion years, which is an interesting counterargument to those who claim intelligent life is the inevitable result whenever life forms. However, about 600 million years ago the oxygen content of the atmosphere rose rapidly, and then a series of events, quite possibly interrelated, took place: 1) eukariotic cells, that is, cells with their genetic information contained within a nucleus, originated, which allowed the invention of sex and the more efficient sharing of genetic material, and hence a more rapid adaptation of life forms to new environments; 2) more complicated organisms breathing oxygen, with its much higher energy yield, developed; and 3) the excess carbon dioxide was converted into limestone in the structure of these creatures, thus making the atmosphere more transparent in the infrared and thereby preventing the oceans from boiling away in a runaway greenhouse effect as the sun brightened. The perfect timing of this complex configuration of circumstances is enough to amaze and bewilder many of my friends who look at all this in purely mechanistic terms—the survival of life on earth seems such a close shave as to border on the miraculous. Can we not see here the designer's hand at work? Should we not perhaps rephrase the description of this concatenation of events, substituting "created" for "originated" and "developed"? Eukariotic cells were created, which allowed the creation of sex and the more efficient sharing of genetic material and more rapid adaptation of life forms; more complicated organisms breathing oxygen were created; and so on. The first form of these phrases gave the scientific elaboration of the book of Genesis, which adds the "who" to the scientific picture and to the phrase "were created."

It would take more than one lecture to elaborate the exceedingly precarious route to intelligent life on earth. The current version would include the impact of an asteroid at the end of the Cretacious period 70 million years ago, giving the *coup de grâce* to numerous life forms, including the dinosaurs who had ruled the earth since a similar extinction 130 million years earlier; the elimination of these forms opened the environment to the proliferation of mammals and the animal forms we know today, but to describe all this would lead me too far beyond my own expertise. There is, nevertheless, another example of design I wish to touch on.

Early in this century, after the work of Darwin, which emphasized the fitness of organisms for their various environments, the chemist L. J. Henderson wrote a fascinating book entitled *The Fitness of the Environment*, which pointed out that the organisms themselves would not exist except for certain properties of matter. He argued for the uniqueness of carbon as the chemical basis of life, and everything we have learned since then, from the nature of the hydrogen bond to the structure of DNA, reinforces his argument. But today it is possible to go still further and to probe the origin of carbon itself, through its synthesis in the nuclear reactions deep inside evolving stars.

Carbon is the fourth most common atom in our galaxy, after hydrogen, helium, and oxygen, but it isn't very abundant; there are 250 helium atoms for every carbon atom. A carbon nucleus can be made by merging three helium nuclei, but a triple collision is tolerably rare. It would be easier if two helium nuclei would stick together to form beryllium, but beryllium is not very stable. Nevertheless, sometimes before the two helium nuclei can come unstuck, a third helium nucleus strikes home, and a carbon nucleus results. And here the details of the internal energy levels of the carbon nucleus become interesting: it turns out that there is precisely the right resonance within the carbon that helps this process along. Without it, there would be relatively few carbon atoms. Similarly, the internal details of the oxygen nucleus play a critical role. Oxygen can be formed by combining helium and carbon nuclei, but the corresponding resonance level in the oxygen nucleus is *half a percent too low* for the combination to stay together easily. Had the resonance level in the carbon been 4 percent higher, there would be essentially no carbon. Had that level in the oxygen been only half a percent higher, virtually all of the carbon would have been converted to oxygen. Without that carbon abundance, neither you nor I would be here tonight.

I am told that Fred Hoyle, who together with William Fowler discovered this remarkable nuclear arrangement, has said that nothing has shaken his atheism as much as this discovery. Occasionally Fred Hoyle and I have sat down to discuss one or another astronomical or historical point, but I have never had enough nerve to ask him if his atheism had really been shaken by finding the nuclear resonance structure of carbon and oxygen. However, the answer has come rather clearly in the November 1981 issue of *Engineering and Science,* the Cal Tech magazine, where he writes:

> Would you not say to yourself, "Some supercalculating intellect must have designed the properties of the carbon atom, otherwise the chance of my finding such an atom through the blind forces of nature would be utterly minuscule"? Of course you would. . . . A common sense interpretation of the facts suggests that a superintellect has monkeyed with physics, as well as with chemistry and biology, and that there are no blind forces worth speaking about in nature. The numbers one calculates from the facts seem to me so overwhelming as to put this conclusion almost beyond question."[5]

Indeed, some of these circumstances seem so impressive that those scientists who wish to deny the role of design have had to take into account its ubiquitous signs. They have even given it a name: the anthropic principle. Briefly stated, they have turned the argument around. Rather than accepting that we are here because of a deliberate supernatural design, they claim that the universe simply must be this way *because* we are here; had the universe been otherwise, we would not be here to observe ourselves, and that is that. As I said, I am doubtful that one can convert a skeptic by the argument of design, and the discussions of the anthropic principle seem to prove the point.

In any event, Sir Fred and I differ about lots of things—he is not sure, for example, that the universe had a beginning—but on this we agree: the picture of the universe is far more satisfying if we accept the designing hand of a superintelligence.

There is, however, something more in Genesis 1 that does not, and probably cannot, emerge in a scientific picture of creation. Natural theology can argue for the existence of God the Creator and Designer, but it falls short in revealing the essential significance of the biblical creation story. Without doubt the most crucial sentence of the chapter is verse 27, so quintessential that the idea is immediately repeated lest we miss it: "God created man in his own image, in his own image created he him, male and female created he them." Succinctly put, the stance of the biblical account is that God is not only Creator and Designer, but there is within us, male and female, a divine creative spark, a touch of the infinite, consciousness, and conscience. It is not so easy to fathom within ourselves those same divine evidences that appear in the external world. As the astronomer Johannes Kepler wrote: "There is nothing I want to find out and long to know with greater urgency than this. Can I find God, whom I can almost grasp with my own hands in looking at the universe, also in myself?"[6]

What Kepler longed to know with such urgency in 1620 is even more urgent for our agenda today. As scientific human beings, we have grasped the harmony of creation, we have learned the secrets of the stars, and we have in a terrifying way brought those secrets to earth. As Arthur Eddington wrote so presciently in 1920, "If, indeed, the sub-atomic energy in the stars is being freely used to maintain their great furnaces, it seems to bring a little nearer to fulfillment our dream of controlling this latent power for the well-being of the human race—or for its suicide."[7]

I have spoken tonight of the integrity of the great tapestry of science, how rational man can fill in the details of the working out of God's incredible design. For me, the coherency of my own view demands a step further, toward accepting something even more incredible and mind-boggling than cosmology or the evolution of intelligent life on earth, namely, that God has given us something more, a demonstration of his sacrificial love in the life and death of Jesus. Created in the image of God, we are called not to power or personal justice, but to sacrificial love. I confess that this is not the logical conclusion of my line of argument; indeed, it is the beginning, the point of departure for a way of perceiving science and the universe. But unless we can see the universe in those terms, I believe that we are headed with the rest of the fallen human race to nuclear suicide.

I cannot bring myself to believe that is God's plan for humankind. When the Psalmist asks, "What is man that thou art mindful of him," I think the question not only reminds us of our place in the immensity of the cosmos, but it affirms our place in the universe as intelligent beings created in the image of God. I certainly hope that as sentient, moral creatures we have enough intelligence, enough conscience, and even enough sacrificial love to avoid nuclear confrontation and catastrophe.

Concerning these arguments, and in keeping with the image of intelligent, creative, and moral beings, I can do no better than to close with a quotation from the seventeenth-century English virtuoso, Thomas Browne: "The wisdom of God receives small honor from those vulgar heads that rudely stare about, and with a gross rusticity admire his workes; those highly magnifie him whose judicious enquiry into his acts, and deliberate research into his creatures, returne the duty of a devout and learned admiration."[8]

Notes

1. From "The Great Explosion," in Robinson Jeffers, *The Beginning and the End and Other Poems* (New York: Random House, 1963).
2. Robert Jastrow, *God and the Astronomers* (New York: Warner Books, 1978).
3. Jacob Bronowski, *The Origins of Knowledge and Imagination* (New Haven: Yale University Press, 1978).
4. From "The Great Wound," in Robinson Jeffers, *The Beginning and the End and Other Poems.*
5. Fred Hoyle, "The Universe: Past and Present Reflections," *Engineering & Science* (November 1981), pp. 8–12.
6. Johannes Kepler, *Gesammelte Werke,* vol. 17, p. 80; Carola Baumgardt, *Johannes Kepler: Life and Letters* (New York: Philosophical Library, 1951), pp. 114–15.
7. Arthur Eddington, "The Internal Constitution of the Stars," *Nature* (1920), 106:14–20.
8. Thomas Browne, *Religio Medici* (London, 1642), p. 28.

part four

Affirmations, Biblical and Theological

Chapter 9

Science and Christianity

POPE JOHN PAUL II

Most religious leaders disapprove of creation-science primarily because of what they perceive to be, at best, its religious inadequacies and oversimplifications. Judged by the standards of accepted Jewish and Christian understandings of the Bible and of belief, the creationist conception seems to be warped in various degrees, like images reflected in a broken mirror or even in a mirror made to show puzzling images, distorting the reality it supposedly reflects. Such mirrors represent some truth, but the total effect is a deformed and misleading vision. In order to place the rejection of creationism in the full context of religious thought and belief, we need to understand the attitudes toward creation and the created order held by the mainstreams of Judaism and Christianity. It is therefore appropriate that the final group of essays in this anthology should be chosen to present affirmations, both theological and biblical. The essays which follow indicate the major under-

Part I of this chapter is extracted from the pope's address on November 10, 1979, to the Pontifical Academy of Sciences, an academy in which "believing and nonbelieving scientists collaborate, agreeing in the search for scientific truth and in respect for the beliefs of the other," as the pope put it (p. 392). Part II is taken from the pontiff's address to German scholars and university students in Cologne Cathedral on November 15, 1980. These copyright pages (142–153) are reproduced with permission of *Origins*. Part III (prepared and published by the "Osservatore Romano," Vatican City) contains his remarks on "Scripture and Science" on October 3, 1981, to a study session of the Pontifical Academy in that year. Full texts of these three addresses may be found in *Origins*, the weekly magazine of the National Catholic News Service, as follows: "Faith, Science and the Search for Truth" (1979–80), 9:389–92; "Science and the Church: A Dialogue" (1980), 10:395–98; and "Science and Scripture: the Path of Scientific Discovery" (1981), 11:277–80.

standings of Roman Catholic, Jewish, and Protestant beliefs. On no other principal doctrine is the ecumenical consensus so impressive.

We shall begin with the pope, who heads the largest communion of Christian believers in the world, as well as in America. Himself a distinguished philosopher, John Paul II has consistently expressed concern for mutually constructive relations between Christianity and science. The following pages represent his thoughtful analysis of the theological and ethical bases of those relations, as human creatures systematically study the creation in its many aspects. The broad theological and biblical conceptions which the pope outlines generally represent not only the contemporary Roman Catholic understanding, but also that of many and probably most other Christians.

Faith, Science and the Search for Truth

Pure and Applied Science

The search for truth is the fundamental task of science. The researcher who moves on this first slope of science feels the whole fascination of the words of St. Augustine: *"Intellectum valde ama"*—"Love understanding greatly"—(Epist. 120, 3, 13: PL 33, 459), and the function proper to it, of knowing the truth. Pure science is a good, worthy of being very well loved, for it is knowledge and therefore perfection of man in his intelligence. Even before its technical applications, it ought to be honored for itself as an integral part of culture. Fundamental science is a universal good, which all people must cultivate in full liberty in relation to every form of international servitude or of intellectual colonialism.

Fundamental research must be free in relation to economic and political powers, which must cooperate in its development without hobbling its creativity nor enslaving it for their own ends. Like every other truth, scientific truth has in fact no accounting to make except to itself and to the supreme truth which is God, creator of man and of everything.

On its second slope, science is turned toward practical applications, which find their full development in various technologies. In the phase of its concrete realizations, science is necessary for humanity to satisfy the just requirements of life and to overcome the various evils which threaten it. There is no doubt that applied science has rendered and will render immense services to man, if only it be inspired by love, ruled by wisdom, accompanied by courage which defends it against undue interference by all tyrannical powers. Applied science must be allied with conscience so that, in the trinomial science-technology-conscience, it may be the cause of the true good of man that is served.

Unfortunately, as I had the occasion to say in my encyclical *Redemptor Hominis*, "the man of today seems always threatened by what he produces. . . . This seems to make up the main chapter of the drama of present-day human existence" (n. 15). Man must emerge victorious from this drama which threatens to degenerate into tragedy, and he must regain his authentic kingship over the world and his full dominion over the things he produces. At the present time, as I wrote in the same encyclical, "the essential meaning of this 'kingship' and 'dominion' of man over the visible world, which the Creator himself gave man for his task, consists in the priority of ethics over technology, in the primacy of the person over things, and in the superiority of spirit over matter" (n. 16).

This triple transcendence is maintained to the degree that the meaning of the transcendence of man over the world and of God over man is preserved. In exercising its mission as guardian and advocate of both transcendences, the church considers that it is helping science to preserve its ideal purity on the side of fundamental research and to fulfill its service to man on the side of its practical applications.

The church gladly recognizes, moreover, that it has benefited from science. It is to science, among other things, that what the [Second Vatican] council said in regard to certain aspects of modern culture must be attributed: "Finally the new conditions affect religious life itself . . . the critical spirit purifies it of a magical conception of the world and of surviving superstitions and exacts a more and more personal and active adherence to the faith. As a result many persons are achieving a more vivid sense of God" (*Gaudium et Spes*, n. 7).

Collaboration between religion and modern science is to the advantage of both, without at all violating their respective autonomy. Just as religion requires religious freedom, so science legitimately claims freedom of research. The ecumenical council Vatican II, after having reaffirmed, with the First Vatican Council, the just freedom of human arts and disciplines in the sphere of their own principles and their own method, solemnly recognizes "the legitimate autonomy of culture and particularly that of the sciences" (*Gaudium et Spes*, n. 59). On the occasion of [this solemn commemoration of the centenary of the birth of Albert Einstein,] I would like to confirm anew the declarations of the council on the autonomy of science in its function of research on the truth inscribed in creation by the finger of God. Filled with admiration for the genius of the great scholar in whom the imprint of the creating spirit is revealed, the church, without intervening in any way by a judgment that is not up to it to make on the teaching concerning the great systems of the universe, nevertheless proposes this teaching for the reflection of theologians in order to discover the harmony existing between scientific truth and revealed truth.

The Tragic Case of Galileo

[The President of this Academy] said very rightly that Galileo and Einstein characterized an epoch. The greatness of Galileo is known by all, as is that of Einstein; but unlike him whom we honor today before the College of Cardinals in the Apostolic Palace, the first had much to suffer—we could not hide it—from the men and agencies of the church. The Vatican Council recognized and deplored certain undue interventions: "We cannot but deplore"—it is written in Number 36 of the conciliar constitution *Gaudium et Spes*—"certain attitudes which have existed among Christians themselves, insufficiently attentive to the legitimate autonomy of science. Sources of tensions and conflicts, they have led many minds to conclude that faith and science are mutually opposed." The reference to Galileo is clearly expressed in the note attached to this text, which cites the volume *Life and Works of Galileo Galilei* by Msgr. Pio Paschini, edited by the Pontifical Academy of Sciences.

In order to go beyond this position taken by the council, I wish that theologians, scholars and historians, animated by a spirit of sincere collaboration, might examine more deeply the Galileo case and, in an honest recognition of wrongs on whatever side they occur, might make disappear the obstacles that this affair still sets up, in many minds, to a fruitful concord between science and faith, between church and world. I give my entire support to this task which will be able to honor the truth of faith and of science and open the door to future collaborations.

Permit me, gentlemen, to submit to your attention and to your reflection some points that appear to me important in order to place again in its true light the Galileo affair, in which the agreements between religion and science are more numerous and above all more important than the lacks of understanding from which resulted the bitter and painful conflict that has been prolonged throughout the following centuries.

He who is rightly called the founder of modern physics explicitly declared that the two truths, of faith and of science, can never contradict one another, "holy scripture and nature alike proceeding from the divine word, the first as dictated by the Holy Spirit, the second as most faithful executor of God's orders," as he wrote in his letter to Father Benedetto Castelli, Dec. 21, 1613 (*The Works of Galileo*, national ed., vol. V, pp. 282–285). The Second Vatican Council expresses itself no differently; it even makes use of similar expressions when it teaches: "If methodical investigation within every branch of learning is carried out in a genuinely scientific manner and in accord with moral norms, it never truly conflicts with faith. For earthly matters and the concerns of faith derive from the same God" (*Gaudium et Spes*, n. 36).

Galileo feels in his scientific research the presence of the Creator who stimulates him, who anticipates and helps his intuitions, by acting in the depths of his mind. With regard to the invention of the telescope, he writes at the beginning of *Sidereus Nuncius*, recalling some of his astronomical discoveries: *"Quae omnia ope Perspicilli a me excogitati divina prius illuminante gratia, paucis abhinc diebus reperta, atque observata fuerunt"*—"All that has been discovered and observed in recent days is thanks to the telescope that I invented, after having been enlightened by divine grace" (*Sidereus Nuncius*, Venice, in the works of Thomas Baglio, MDCX, fol. 4).

The Galilean confession of divine illumination in the mind of the scholar finds an echo in the text already quoted of the conciliar constitution *Gaudium et Spes:* "The one who strives, with perseverance and humility, to penetrate the secret of things, that same one, even if he is not aware of it, is like one led by the hand of God" *(loc. cit.).* The humility on which the conciliar text insists is a virtue of mind necessary both for scientific research and for adherence to the faith. Humility creates a climate favorable to dialogue between the believer and the scientist; it calls for the enlightenment of God, already known or still unknown but loved in one case as in the other by the one who humbly seeks the truth.

Galileo formulated important norms of an epistemological character which prove to be indispensable for putting holy scripture and science in agreement. In his letter to the grandduchess of Tuscany, Christine of Lorraine, he reaffirms the truth of scripture: "Holy scripture can never lie, on condition however that it be penetrated in its true meaning, which—I don't believe that it can be denied—is often hidden and very different from the one which the simple signification of the words seems to indicate" (*The Works of Galileo*, national ed., vol. V, p. 315). Galileo introduces the principle of an interpretation of the sacred books which goes beyond the literal meaning, but is in conformity with the intention and with the type of exposition proper to each of them. It is necessary, as he affirms, that "the wise men who explain it show the true meaning of it."

The ecclesiastical magisterium admits the plurality of rules of interpretation of holy scripture. It teaches expressly, in fact, with the encyclical *Divino Afflante Spiritu* of Pius XII, the presence of different literary genres in the sacred books and therefore the necessity of interpretations in conformity with the character of each of them.

The various agreements that I have recalled do not resolve of themselves all the problems of the Galileo affair, but they contribute to creating a point of departure favorable to their honorable solution, a state of mind favorable to the honest and fair solution of old oppositions.

The existence of this Pontifical Academy of Sciences, with which Galileo was in some way associated through the ancient institution which preceded the one to which eminent scientists belong today, is a visible sign which shows to the peoples, without any form of racial or religious discrimination, the profound harmony which can exist between the truths of science and the truths of faith.

Science and the Church

The Hopeful Example of Albertus Magnus

Our encounter today* ought to be understood as a sign of readiness for dialogue between science and the church. The day itself and the place itself give a special meaning to this meeting. On this day 700 years ago, in the Dominican convent not far from this cathedral, at whose founding he was present, died Albert the German, as his contemporaries called him. Those who came after his time gave him the title of "the Great" because of his peerless learning. Albert did many kinds of work in his life as a religious and as a preacher, as superior in his religious order and as bishop, and as a peace intermediary in his city of Cologne. But he also won worldly greatness as a thinker and teacher, as one who embraced and mastered the

---

*John Paul II is speaking at Cologne Cathedral to "representatives of many researchers, teachers, assistants and students in the universities, academies, and other research institutions"—ED.

knowledge of his time and gave it new form in his life's work. Contemporaries already described him as *auctor*, as author or founder of an increase of scientific knowledge. The following age marked him out as *doctor universalis*. The church, who reckons him among her saints, turns to him as one of her teachers, her doctors, and celebrates him liturgically under this title.

But our commemoration of Albert the Great should be only an act of due piety. It is more important to make present the real nature of his life work. We must give it its basic and permanent significance. Let us look briefly at the mental and spiritual situation in Albert's time.

You know how there was increasing knowledge of the writings of Aristotle and Arab science. The Christian West had so far relived the tradition of late Christian antiquity and developed its thought. Now it came into contact with a well-extended non-Christian explanation of the world, one that rested upon profane rationality alone. Many Christian thinkers, and very significant ones, saw this challenge above all as a danger. They believed that they must guard the historical identity of the Christian tradition against it. Then there were also radical individuals and groups who saw an unresolved contradiction between that scientific rationality and the truth of faith; they decided for themselves in favor of this "scientific thought."

Albert took the middle way between those two extremes. The claim of truth made by rationally founded science was acknowledged; indeed it was substantially adopted, completed, corrected and further developed in its autonomous rationality. Thus it became a possession of the Christian world.

The Christian world found its understanding of the world to be uncommonly enriched, but it must not let go any element of its tradition or any ground of faith. For no basic conflict can exist between reason—which tends toward truth through its God-given nature, and is ready to acknowledge the truth—and faith, which devotes itself to the always divine source of all truth. Faith actually assures the autonomy of natural reason. It presupposes that autonomy for its postulate assumes such freedom, which is only proper to the nature of reason.

It is clear at the same time, therefore, that faith and knowledge belong to differing orders of understanding and that these orders cannot be confused with one another. But then it is also clear that reason can do nothing of itself. It is bounded. It must proceed through numerous single points of knowledge; it is involved with a great number of single sciences. The unity of world and truth with their origin can be grasped only by ever differing lines of knowledge. Philosophy and theology themselves are limited activities as means of knowledge. They can establish the unity of truth only in differentiation, as in an open, ordered system.

We repeat: Albert accomplished recognition and adoption of rational knowledge in an orderly system. Each element keeps to its proper place in this and yet remains subordinate to the authority of the object of faith. Thus Albert wrote a charter for Christian intellectuality, and its principles can be seen today to be still applicable. We do not belittle the significance of this innovation when we remark at the same time that Albert's work is intrinsically time-bound, and so belongs in that respect to history. The "synthesis" introduced by him has an exemplary character, and we do well to keep its basic tenets in mind when we turn to the question of science, faith and church in our own day.

Many see the kernel of this question in the relationship between church and modern science. They feel the weight of it through those famous conflicts that arose from the intervention of church authorities in the process of the advance of scientific knowledge. The church remembers that with regret; today we acknowledge the errors and deficiencies involved in that affair. We may say today that they have been overcome, thanks to science's power of conviction, thanks above all to the work of some scientist-theologians, who deepened the understanding of the faith and freed it from its bonds with time.

The church's magisterium has often given reminders of those principles since the days of the First Vatican Council. Its most recent and most explicit reminder came in the Second Vatican Council (*Gaudium et Spes*, 36). Those principles and reminders are already discernible in the work of Albert the Great. He expressly stated the differentiation between the orders of knowledge of faith and reason. He acknowledged the autonomy and liberty of the sciences and spoke in favor of freedom of research. We have no fear, indeed we regard it as excluded, that a science or branch of knowledge, based on reason and proceeding methodically and securely, can arrive at knowledge that comes into conflict with the truth of faith. This can be the case only where the differentiation between the orders of knowledge is overlooked or denied.

If such a view were wholly adopted by thinkers in all branches of knowledge, then it would help to overcome the historical taint with which relations between the church and the natural sciences are charged, and it would enable a dialogue between partners to be undertaken, as is already going on in many ways. It is not a question of going back over disputes of the past, but of facing fresh problems which arise in general culture today from the role played by the sciences.

Modern Scientific Culture: Problems and Opportunities

In this situation the church does not counsel prudence and holding back. She counsels courage and resolve. There are no grounds for not facing the truth or fearing it. Truth and all that is true is a lofty good; we ought to turn to it with love and joy. Science too is a way to what is true, for it entails God-given reason, which is conditioned by its nature not toward error but toward the truth of knowledge.

This must hold good for technically and functionally orientated science as well. To understand knowledge only as a "method giving results" is a diminishment; contrariwise, however, it is legitimate to value results as a sign of the worth of the knowledge whence they flow. We cannot regard the technical world, which is man's work, as a realm quite distant from truth. That world is not at all meaningless. It is true to say that it has decidedly improved human living relationships. And the hardships that result from the advance of technical civilization do not justify forgetting the good things that such advance itself brought.

We have no reason to regard our scientific and technical culture as inimical to the world of God's creation. It is, of course, clear that technical knowledge can be turned to good as well as to evil use. Someone engaged in research into poisons can turn this knowledge to healing as well as to killing. But there can be no doubt that we must see to separating the good from the bad. Technical science, directed toward changing the world, is justified through its service to mankind.

We may not say that progress has gone too far so long as many human beings, indeed many peoples, live in depressed conditions, even conditions unworthy of human beings, which can be improved with the help of scientific and technical knowledge. Weighty tasks lie before us and we cannot avoid them. Fulfillment of them is a fraternal service to our fellow man and we owe this to him in the same way that the work of mercy is owed to those who stand in need by those who can do that work.

We do fraternal service to our fellow man because we recognize those values in him which belong to him as a moral being. We speak of personal dignity. Faith teaches us that it is man's characteristic to be God's image. Christian tradition adds that man exists for his own sake, not for the purposes of some other. Hence human personal dignity is that basis on which all cultural applications of technical and scientific knowledge have to be judged.

The development of modern sciences has added wings to the spirit of modern awareness. The modern mind has set itself the goal of scientific examination of man and his social and cultural ambience or life environment. A range of full information such as cannot be overlooked is produced today and has its effect on public and private life. The social systems of contemporary states, health and education, economic processes and cultural forces, all are stamped in many ways by the influence of these sciences. But the point is that the sciences not put man under tutelage. In technical culture as well man must remain free in accordance with his dignity. Indeed the meaning of this culture must be to give him ever more freedom.

This insight into the personal dignity of man and his overriding significance is not something possible only through the faith. It is not excluded from the powers of natural reason, which distinguishes between true and false, good and bad, and recognizes freedom as the basic condition of man's being. It is an encouraging sign and one that is spreading through the world. The idea of the rights of man attests nothing else, and even those who oppose those rights by their deeds cannot do without them. This gives hope, and we wish to encourage that hope.

The voices are becoming more numerous of those who will not be content with the immanent restriction imposed on the sciences and who make a quest for the one whole truth in which man's life is fulfilled. It is as if knowledge and scientific search expanded endlessly, yet ever returned unceasingly to their origin. The old question of the connection between knowledge and belief has not been overcome by the development of modern sciences, but shows all its vital and powerful significance in a more and more scientific world.

The Mutual Freedom of Science and Religion

We have so far deliberately spoken of science that is in service to culture and thereby to man. But to restrict it to this aspect would be too little. We must remind ourselves, exactly in regard to the crisis, that science is not only a service for other purposes. Knowledge of the truth bears its sense within itself. It is a power with a human and personal character, a human good of high rank.

Pure "theory" is itself a manner of human "praxis." The believer expects a supreme "praxis" that will unite him with God forever. It is a vision; it is thus "theory." We speak of the "legitimation of science"; yes, science has its sense and its rights, if it is recognized as capable of truth and if the truth is recognized as a human good. Then striving for the freedom of science is also legitimated, for how else can a human good assert itself than through freedom? Science must be free as well in the sense that no intermediate goal, social requirements or economic interests shall condition its capacities. This does not mean that it must be separated from the principal "praxis." But, in order to have influence upon the praxis, it must be conditioned thereto through truth, and be free for truth.

Science committed to the truth does not let itself be tied to the model of functionalism or some other model which restricts understanding to scientific rationality. Science must be open, it must be manifold. We need to have no fear of the detriment of having a one-sided orientation. This forms part of the threesome of personal reason, freedom and truth. Manifold and concrete development is thus founded and protected.

I have no worry about seeing the science of the faith also on the horizon of a rationality so understood. The church desires autonomous theological research, distinguished from the church's magisterium, yet knowing that it is pledged with it to common service to the truth of faith and to the people of God. It is not to be excluded that tensions and conflicts occur. But these are never to be excluded in the relationship between church and science. They have their basis in the limitedness of our reason. It is restricted in its scope, and so is exposed to error. However, we may always have hope in a reconciling solution, if we build up this reason exactly on our capacity for truth.

In past epochs, the champions of modern science fought against the church with the slogans: reason, freedom and progress. The battlefronts have changed today in view of the crisis in direction which science is facing, the multiple threats to its freedom and doubts about progress. Today it is the church that is the portal:

—For reason and science that trust in the capacity for truth, which legitimizes them as human capacities;

—For the freedom of science, through which it has its dignity as a human, personal good;

—For progress in service to mankind, which needs it for the safety of its life and its dignity.

The church and all Christians stand with this task in the center of the vicissitudes of our age. A solution capable of bearing the pressing question of the meaning of human existence, the dimensions of the matter and the prospects of a far-reaching hope, is possible only in renewed linking of scientific thought with man's power in faith to seek truth. The struggle for a new humanism upon which the development of the third millennium may be founded can be fruitful only if scientific understanding is brought into vital relationship with the truth, which is revealed to man as a gift from God. Man's reason is a grand instrument for knowing and figuring the world. But in order to bring the whole fullness of human capabilities to realization, it needs to be open toward the word of everlasting truth, which became flesh in Christ.

I said at the beginning that our coming here today is a sign of readiness for dialogue between science and church. Has it not become clear from these reflections how urgent such dialogue is? Both sides should profit by it, by listening, to make steady progress. We need each other.

Seven hundred years ago the bones of the Wise Men of the East were given shelter and reverenced in this cathedral. They were those men who, at the beginning of the new age which was launched with the incarnation of God, set themselves to worship the true Lord of the world.

Those men united the knowledge of the time in their persons, and so they became an example for truth-seeking men generally. The knowledge that reason attains finds its fulfillment in worshiping the divine truth. The man that goes toward this truth suffers no diminution of his freedom, but is led to full freedom and to truly human fulfillment of his existence, in trusting commitment to the Spirit who is promised to us through Jesus Christ's work of salvation.

Scientists and students and all others who are together here today, I appeal to you and ask you to keep the final goal of your work and of the whole of your lives constantly before your eyes in your striving after scientific knowledge. To this end I recommend to you especially the virtues of fortitude and humility. Fortitude defends science in a world of doubts that is alienated from the truth and is in need of meaning.

Humility is that virtue whereby we acknowledge the limits of reason in the face of overtowering truth. These virtues are those of Albert the Great.

Science and Scripture: The Origins of the Cosmos

Cosmogony and cosmology have always aroused great interest among peoples and religions. The Bible itself speaks to us of the origin of the universe and its makeup, not in order to provide us with a scientific treatise, but in order to state the correct relationships of man with God and with the universe. Sacred scripture wishes simply to declare that the world was created by God, and in order to teach this truth it expresses itself in the terms of the cosmology in use at the time of the writer. The sacred book likewise wishes to tell men that the world was not created as the seat of the gods, as was taught by other cosmogonies and cosmologies, but was rather created for the service of man and the glory of God. Any other teaching about the origin and makeup of the universe is alien to the intentions of the Bible, which does not wish to teach how heaven was made but how one goes to heaven.

Any scientific hypothesis on the origin of the world, such as the hypothesis of a primitive atom from which derived the whole of the physical universe, leaves open the problem concerning the universe's beginning. Science cannot of itself solve this question: There is needed that human knowledge that rises above physics and astrophysics and which is called metaphysics; there is needed above all the knowledge that comes from God's revelation. Thirty years ago, on November 22, 1951, my predecessor Pope Pius XII, speaking about the problem of the origin of the universe at the study week on the subject of microseisms organized by the Pontifical Academy of Sciences, expressed himself as follows:

> In vain would one expect a reply from the sciences of nature, which on the contrary frankly declare that they find themselves faced by an insoluble enigma. It is equally certain that the human mind versed in philosophical mediation penetrates the problem more deeply. One cannot deny that a mind which is enlightened and enriched by modern scientific knowledge and which calmly considers this problem is led to break the circle of matter which is totally independent and autonomous—as being either uncreated or having created itself—and to

rise to a creating mind. With the same clear and critical gaze with which it examines and judges the acts, it discerns and recognizes there the work of creative omnipotence, whose strength raised up by the powerful fiat uttered milliards of years ago by the creating mind, has spread through the universe, calling into existence, in a gesture of generous love, matter teeming with energy.

Chapter 10

Understanding Creation in Genesis

NAHUM M. SARNA

One of the most eminent Hebraic scholars in America today, Nahum Sarna has taught at the University of London, at the Jewish Theological Seminary in New York, and since 1967 has been Dora Golding Professor of Biblical Studies at Brandeis University. The recipient of many honors, he has published widely, including books devoted to Genesis, the Psalms, and Job, and since 1974 he has been general editor of the Jewish Publication Society's Bible Commentary series. His interpretation of the creation accounts in Genesis provides a masterly introduction to the ancient Near Eastern contexts for Hebrew beliefs, and uses these pre-scientific and mythological materials to highlight the really important substance of the Genesis accounts. He thus conveys to the reader a clear sense of the original and revolutionary contributions of the Hebrew accounts of creation, contributions of perennial value for human life and society.

The Bible does not constitute an ideological monolith. This fact is often overlooked. Ancient Israel encountered the world in many dif-

This chapter is excerpted from pp. 1–23 of Professor Sarna's *Understanding Genesis* (New York: Schocken, 1970). Reprinted by permission of the Melton Research Center, The Jewish Theological Seminary of America.

ferent ways and its varying responses to the stimuli of cosmic phenomena gave rise to several cosmologies or descriptions of the manner in which the world and its contents came into being.[1] Not all are
equally prominent in biblical literature and some are merely fragmentary. Yet it is clear that the Bible reflects different notions current in Israel, some of which awaken memories of ancient Near
Eastern mythologies.

The most famous is to be found in Genesis 1:1–2:4a.[2] It opens
with the phrase, "when God began to create the heaven and the
earth," and it closes with the formula, "such is the story of heaven
and earth as they were created." Within this literary framework are
described the divine activities within a seven-day period. The creative process is successively unfolded in the following stages: 1) light,
2) sky, 3) earth, seas and vegetation, 4) luminaries, 5) living creatures in the sea and the sky, 6) animal life on earth and man "created in the image of God." The account culminates in the Sabbath,
or divine cessation from creation which, to the Torah, is as much a
part of the cosmic order as is the foregoing creativity.

The second biblical account of Creation (2:4b–24) opens with the
formula, "When the Lord God made earth and heaven," and goes on
to tell how the entire surface of the earth was watered by a flow that
would well up from subterranean springs. But the main topic in this
account is the formation of man and his placement in the Garden of
Eden. The narrative ends with the creation of woman because of divine recognition of the human need for companionship.

From many scattered allusions in biblical literature—prophetic,
poetic and wise—it is certain that there were prevalent in Israel
other notions about the events connected with the creation of the
world. Among these is the popular belief that in days of old, prior
to the onset of the cosmogonic process, the forces of watery chaos,
variously designated Yam (Sea), Nahar (River), Leviathan (Coiled
One), Rahab (Arrogant One) and Tannin (Dragon), were subdued
by God.[3] There does not seem to be any unanimity in these accounts
about the ultimate fate of these creatures. According to one version,
they were utterly destroyed.[4] According to another, the chaotic
forces, personalized as monsters, were put under restraint.[5] It must
be remembered, however, that this combat myth, once fully developed, appears in a very attenuated and fragmentary form in the
biblical sources and the several allusions have to be pieced together
into some kind of coherent unity. Nevertheless, there is ample witness to the fact that the myths to which these allusions refer found

literary expression in ancient Israel and were sufficiently well known to be used as reference points in literary compositions.[6]

Not Science

It should be obvious that by the nature of things, none of these stories can possibly be the product of human memory, nor in any modern sense of the word scientific accounts of the origin and nature of the physical world.

Biblical man, despite his undoubted intellectual and spiritual endowments, did not base his views of the universe and its laws on the critical use of empirical data. He had not, as yet, discovered the principles and methods of disciplined inquiry, critical observation or analytical experimentation. Rather, his thinking was imaginative, and his expressions of thought were concrete, pictorial, emotional, and poetic.[7] Hence, it is a naive and futile exercise to attempt to reconcile the biblical accounts of creation with the findings of modern science. Any correspondence which can be discovered or ingeniously established between the two must surely be nothing more than mere coincidence. Even more serious than the inherent fundamental misconception of the psychology of biblical man is the unwholesome effect upon the understanding of the Bible itself. For the net result is self-defeating. The literalistic approach serves to direct attention to those aspects of the narrative that reflect the time and place of its composition, while it tends to obscure the elements that are meaningful and enduring, thus distorting the biblical message and destroying its relevancy.

Whether the Hebrew Genesis account was meant to be science or not, it was certainly meant to convey statements of faith. As will be shown, it is part of the biblical polemic against paganism and an introduction to the religious ideas characteristic of the whole of biblical literature. It tells us something about the nature of the one God who is the Creator and supreme sovereign of the world and whose will is absolute. It asserts that God is outside the realm of nature, which is wholly subservient to Him. He has no myth; that is, there are no stories about any events in His life. Magic plays no part in the worship of Him. The story also tells us something of the nature of man, a God-like creature, uniquely endowed with dignity, honor and infinite worth, into whose hands God has entrusted mastery over His creation. Finally, this narrative tells us something about the biblical

concept of reality. It proclaims the essential goodness of life and assumes a universal moral order governing human society.

To be sure, these affirmations are not stated in modern philosophical terms. But, as we have already pointed out, the audience of the
biblical writers had its own literary idiom. Therefore, to understand
them properly we must not confuse the idiom with the idea, the
metaphor with the reality behind it. The two have to be disentan-
gled from each other and the idea conveyed must be translated into
the idiom of our own day. If this is to be successfully accomplished,
the biblical narrative has to be viewed against the background of the
world out of which it grew and against which it reacted.[8]

A comparison with Near Eastern cosmogonies shows the degree
of indebtedness of the Israelite version to literary precedent, even as
Shakespeare was greatly obligated to his predecessors. Yet, at the
same time, the materials used have been transformed so as to become the vehicle for the transmission of completely new ideas.

Competing Pagan Accounts

One of the most famous myths emanating from the ancient world
is the Babylonian epic known by its opening words, *Enuma Elish*
("when on high"). For the purposes of our study this particular cosmology is the most important of all since it has been preserved more
or less in its entirety, and because it belongs to the same ancient
Near East of which ancient Israel was a part.[9]

The Babylonian creation epic tells how, before the formation of
heaven and earth, nothing existed except water. This primal generative element was identified with Apsu, the male personification of
the primeval sweetwater ocean, and with his female associate Tiamat, the primordial saltwater ocean, represented as a ferocious
monster. From the commingling of the two waters were born the
divine offspring. These, in turn, gave birth to a second generation of
gods and the process was repeated successively. Then came a time
when the young gods, through their unremitting and noisy revelry,
disturbed the peace of Tiamat and Apsu. The latter decided to destroy the gods, but the evil design was thwarted by the quick action
of the all-wise Ea, the earth-water god.

Tiamat now planned revenge and organized her forces for the attack on the gods. The latter, for their part, requested Marduk to lead
them in battle. He acceded provided that he be granted sovereignty

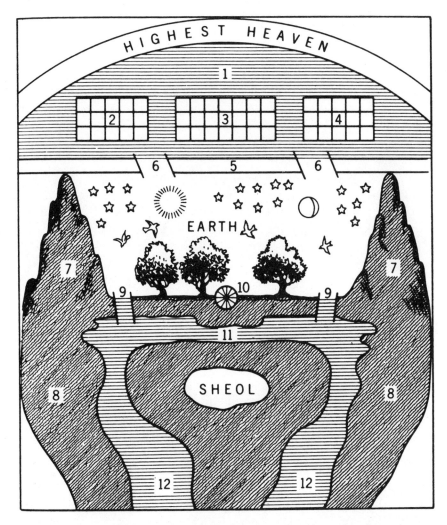

Biblical conception of the world: (1) waters above the firmament; (2) storehouses of snows; (3) storehouses for hail; (4) chambers of winds; (5) firmament; (6) sluice; (7) pillars of the sky; (8) pillars of the earth; (9) fountain of the deep; (10) navel of the earth; (11) waters under the earth; (12) rivers of the nether world.

over the universe. To this condition the assembly of the gods readily agreed and Marduk, invested with the insignia of royalty, thereupon became their champion and took up the cudgels against Tiamat and her helpers. After a fierce battle in which he defeated the enemy forces and slew Tiamat, Marduk sliced the carcass of the monster in

two and created of one half the firmament of heaven and of the
other the foundation of the earth.

The work of creation having thus begun, Marduk then established
the heavenly luminaries, each in its place. This activity is described
in the fifth tablet of the epic which, unfortunately, is fragmentary.
However, from what follows it would appear that the gods com-
plained to Marduk that, each having now been assigned his or her
fixed place and function in the cosmos, there would be no relief
from unending toil. Accordingly, Marduk decided to create man to
free the gods from menial labor and this he proceeded to do, fash-
ioning a human being out of the blood of Kingu, Tiamat's second
husband and captain of her army. The gods showed their gratitude
to Marduk by building for him a great shrine in the city of Babylon,
"the gate of god." The epic ends with a description of a testimonial
banquet tendered by the gods at which they recite an adulatory
hymn of praise to Marduk that confirms his kingship for all eter-
nity. . . .

The Function of the Genesis Narrative

If we have devoted so much space to a discussion of the role of
Enuma Elish in Babylonian civilization, it is only because of the im-
portance of the subject for the proper understanding of the biblical
Genesis account and the perennial significance of its message.

It must be remembered that the Mesopotamian and Hebrew cosmogonies, each in its own way, express through their symbolism the
world-views and values that animated the civilization each represents. The opening chapters of the Bible unveil the main pillars upon
which the Israelite outlook rests. The characteristic trends of the religion of Israel assert themselves in Genesis as powerfully as does the
rationale of Mesopotamian society and religion in *Enuma Elish*.

However, a vital and fundamental distinction must be made at
once between Israel and Mesopotamia. The theme of creation, important as it is in the [Hebrew] Bible, is nevertheless only introductory to what is its central motif, namely, the Exodus from Egypt.
God's acts in history, rather than His role as Creator, are predomi-
nant in biblical thought.

The Bible opens with the account of Creation, not so much because its primary purpose is to describe the process of cosmogony,
nor because its chief concern is with the nature of the physical world

or the origin and constitution of matter. Genesis is but a prologue to the historical drama that unfolds itself in the ensuing pages of the Bible. It proclaims, loudly and unambiguously, the absolute subordination of all creation to the supreme Creator who thus can make use of the forces of nature to fulfill His mighty deeds in history. It asserts unequivocally that the basic truth of all history is that the world is under the undivided and inescapable sovereignty of God. In brief, unlike *Enuma Elish* in Babylon, the Genesis Creation narrative is primarily the record of the event which inaugurated this historical process, and which ensures that there is a divine purpose behind creation that works itself out on the human scene.

This playing of the cosmological theme in a relatively minor key in biblical literature points up other basic distinctions between Genesis and *Enuma Elish*. The former has no political role. It contains no allusion to the people of Israel, Jerusalem or the Temple. It does not seek to validate national ideals or institutions. Moreover, it fulfills no cultic function. The inextricable tie between myth and ritual, the mimetic enactment of the cosmogony in the form of ritual drama, which is an essential characteristic of the pagan religions, finds no counterpart in the Israelite cult. In this respect too, the Genesis story represents a complete break with Near Eastern tradition.

Non-Mythological[10]

The reason for this detachment of cosmogony from the ritual is not hard to find. The supreme characteristic of the Mesopotamian cosmogony is that it is embedded in a mythological matrix. On the other hand, the outstanding peculiarity of the biblical account is the complete absence of mythology in the classical pagan sense of the term. The religion of Israel is essentially non-mythological, there being no suggestion of any theo-biography. . . .

Nowhere is this non-mythological outlook better illustrated than in the Genesis narrative. The Hebrew account is matchless in its solemn and majestic simplicity. It has no notion of the birth of God and no biography of God. It does not even begin with a statement about the existence of God. Such speculation would have been unthinkable [in Israel] at this time.[11] To the Bible, God's existence is as self-evident as is life itself. The Hebrew concept of God is implicit in the narrative, not formulated abstractly and explicitly. The whole of biblical literature is really the attestation of the experiences of individuals and of a nation with the Divine. Genesis, therefore, begins immediately with an account of the creative activity of the pre-exist-ent God.

Far different is the Mesopotamian account. Theogony is inextrica-bly tied up with cosmogony. The gods themselves had to be created. Even Marduk, the head of the pantheon, is not pre-existent. The first supernal beings are demons and monsters, while the god of creation is only born at a fairly late stage in the theogonic process. Moreover, his creative activity is introduced almost casually and incidentally.

Not Magic

This absence or presence of the theogonic motif had profound consequences for the development of the religions of Israel and her Near Eastern neighbors. The birth of the gods implies the existence of some primordial, self-contained, realm from which the gods themselves derive. The cosmos, too, is fashioned from this same ele-ment, personified in *Enuma Elish* as the carcass of Tiamat. That is to say, both the divine and the cosmic are animated by a common source. Moreover, the concept of the immanence of the gods in na-ture was one of the basic convictions of the religions of the pagan world. It meant the existence of divine powers, operative in nature, upon whom the well-being of man and society depended. The peri-odic changes in nature were conceived as episodes in the lives of the gods. Nature and man belonged to the same realm. Hence, the goal of man on earth was to integrate himself harmoniously into the cosmic rhythm.[12]

This all-pervasive dependence upon the material explains the prominence in polytheistic religion of the tales of the personal lives of the gods, their subjection to birth, growth, sex, hunger, disease, impotence, senescence and even death.[13] Now, if there are many gods and these gods are dependent upon physical existence, then they can have neither freedom nor omnipotence. Their immanence in nature limits their scope. Their sovereign powers are circum-scribed by the superior forces inherent in the primordial substance of existence. Since, according to pagan concepts, man's destiny is controlled by two separate forces, the gods and the powers beyond the gods, it was inevitable that magic became an integral part of pagan religion. Man had to be able to devise the means of activating those forces superior even to the gods. Religion, as a consequence, became increasingly concerned with the elaboration of ritual designed to propitiate the numerous unpredictable powers that be.

Anyone who reads the Hebrew Bible, especially the Book of Psalms, is aware that the ancient Israelite was as struck by the majesty of natural phenomena as was any of his pagan neighbors. But unlike them, he did not profess to see God within those phenomena. The clear line of demarcation between God and His creation was never violated. Nowhere is this brought out more forcefully than in the Hebrew Genesis account. Here we find no physical link between the world of humanity and the world of the divine. There is no natural connection between the Creator and his handiwork. Hence, there is no room for magic in the religion of the Bible. The God of Creation is eternally existent, removed from all corporeality, and independent of time and space. Creation comes about through the simple divine fiat: Let there be!

"Let There Be!"

It has been maintained that this notion of the creative power of the word is known to us from elsewhere in the ancient Near East.[14] But the similarity is wholly superficial, for wherever it is found it has a magical content. The pronouncement of the right word, like the performance of the right magical actions, is able to, or rather, inevitably must, actualize the potentialities which are inherent in the inert matter. In other words, it implies a mystic bond uniting matter to its manipulator.

Worlds apart is the Genesis concept of creation by divine fiat. Notice how the Bible passes over in absolute silence the nature of the matter—if any—upon which the divine word acted creatively. Its presence or absence is of no importance, for there is no tie between it and God. "Let there be!" or, as the Psalmist echoed it, "He spoke and it was so,"[15] refers not to the utterance of the magic word, but to the expression of the omnipotent, sovereign, unchallengeable will of the absolute, transcendent God to whom all nature is completely subservient. Such a concept of God and of the process of creation added a new dimension to human thought and marked a new stage in the history of religion. It emancipated the mind from the limitations of mythopoeic thinking, and it liberated religion from the baneful influence of magic.

"Male and Female He Created Them"

This notion of creation by the divine will presents us with yet another radical departure from paganism. In polytheistic mythologies creation is always expressed in terms of procreation. Apparently, paganism was unable to conceive of any primal creative force other than in terms of sex. It will be remembered that in *Enuma Elish*, Apsu and Tiamat represent respectively the male and female powers which, through the "commingling of their waters" gave birth to the first generation of gods. The sex element existed before the cosmos came into being and all the gods were themselves creatures of sex.[16] On the other hand, the Creator in Genesis is uniquely without any female counterpart and the very association of sex with God is utterly alien to the religion of the Bible. When, in fact, Genesis (1:27; 5:2) informs us that "male and female He created them," that God Himself created sexual differentiation, it is more than likely that we are dealing with an intended protest against such pagan notions.

The same may be said in regard to the place of the element of water in the Hebrew cosmogony. The latter shares with *Enuma Elish* the idea of the priority of water in time.[17] Just as Apsu and Tiamat, the two oceans, exist before all things, so in Genesis the existence of water is taken for granted. The darkness is over the surface of the deep; the wind,[18] or the breath of God, sweeps over the waters and the primordial waters are divided into two. Now this concept of the priority of water is fairly widespread among many unrelated mythologies. It most likely arose from the fact that, being amorphous, water seems clearly to represent the state of affairs before chaos was reduced to order and things achieved fixed form. However, since in lower Mesopotamia the earth actually came into being through the sinking of the water level and deposits of silt, it is more than probable that we have in our Genesis account, which gives priority in time to water and envisages the dry land as emerging from it, Babylonian coloration. This is particularly so in view of the contrast between the rich alluvial plains of the Euphrates-Tigris valley and the hilly, rocky soil of Palestine, dependent for its fertility upon seasonal rainfall.[19]

However, the similarity ends here. For in pagan mythologies water is the primal generative force—a notion utterly foreign to the Book of Genesis. Here God wills and the waters obey. At His command they divide.

universal Creator has profound ethical implications. It means that the same universal sovereign will that brought the world into existence continues to exert itself thereafter making absolute, not relative, demands upon man, expressed in categorical imperatives—"thou shalt," "thou shalt not."

It is not to be wondered at that Mesopotamian society suffered from a malaise which scholars have characterized as "overtones of anxiety." The nature of the gods could give no feeling of certainty and security in the cosmos. To make matters worse there were also environmental factors that had to be taken into account. Man always found himself confronted by the tremendous forces of nature, and nature, especially in Mesopotamia, showed itself to be cruel, indiscriminate, unpredictable. Since the gods were immanent in nature, they too shared these same harsh attributes. To aggravate the situation still further, there was always that inscrutable, primordial power beyond the realm of the gods to which man and gods were both subject. Evil, then, was a permanent necessity and there was nothing essentially good in the pagan universe. In such circumstances there could be no correlation between right conduct and individual or national well-being. The universe was purposeless and the deities could offer their votaries no guarantee that life had meaning and direction, no assurance that the end of human strivings was anything but vanity. History and time were but a repeating cycle of events in which man played a passive role, carried along relentlessly by the stream of existence to his ineluctable fate.[33]

Far different is the outlook of Genesis. One of its seemingly naive features is God's pleasure at His own artistry, the repeated declaration, after each completed act of creation, that God saw how good His work was (1:4 etc.). Following the creation of living things, we meet with the climactic observation that God saw all that He had made and found it to be "*very* good" (1:31). But this naiveté of idiom cloaks a profundity of thought that marks off the mood of Hebrew civilization from that of Mesopotamia in a most revolutionary manner. The concept of a single directing Mind behind the cosmic machine, with all its ethico-moral implications, emancipated Israel from thralldom to the vicious cycle of time. In place of a fortuitous concatenation of events, history has become purposeful and society has achieved direction. A strong streak of optimism has displaced the acute awareness of insecurity. The all-pervasive pagan consciousness of human impotence has given way to a profound sense of the significance of man and the powers he can employ. Contemplating

the awesome majesty of cosmic phenomena, the Psalmist can yet ex-
tol the glory and dignity with which God has adorned man and the
authority He has placed in his hands.[34]

This basic belief in the essential goodness of the universe was, of
course, destined to exert a powerful influence upon the direction of
the religion of Israel and to affect the outlook on life of the people.
It found its expression in the concept of the covenant relationship
between God and His people and ultimately achieved its most glorious manifestation in the notion of Messianism—two uniquely Israelite contributions to religion. The God of Israel, being a deity
whose will is absolute and incontestable and whose word is eternal,
was able to give assurances that human strivings were decidedly not
in vain. Israelite society did not suffer from "overtones of anxiety."

The Sabbath

This unshakable conviction in the essentially benign nature of divine activity, is reflected, too, in the description of the cessation from
creativity. We are told God

> ceased on the seventh day from all the work which He had done. And
> God blessed the seventh day and declared it holy, because on it God
> ceased from all the work of creation which He had done.

. . . It will doubtless have been noted at once that the statement
about God here cited contains no mention of the sabbath as a fixed,
weekly institution. It refers only to the seventh day of Creation, to
the divine cessation from creation, and to the blessing and sanctifi-
cation of that day. But the name "sabbath" is not to be found, only
the cognate verbal form *shabat*, meaning, "to desist from labor." Yet
the connection between the weekly sabbath day and Creation is explicitly made both in the first version of the Ten Commandments:

> For in six days the Lord made heaven and earth and sea, and all that
> is in them and He rested on the seventh day; therefore the Lord
> blessed the sabbath day and hallowed it. . . .
>
> (EXOD. 20:11)

as well as in another passage emphasizing the sabbath as an external sign of the covenant between God and Israel.[35] In other words,
while Genesis ignores the weekly sabbath-day, these texts under-

stood this self-same passage as being the source of the institution.[36]

As a matter of fact, there are no biblical sources recounting the founding of the weekly sabbath-day. The antiquity of its existence is presupposed in all the legislation and even in the narratives. Just one month after the departure from Egypt, and before the Sinaitic revelation, the sabbath is assumed to be already established.[37] Moreover, the very formulations of both versions of the Decalogue—"Remember/observe the Sabbath day"—take for granted an existing institution.[38] There cannot be any doubt that the sabbath belongs to the most ancient of Israel's sacred days. . . .[39]

The seventh day is what it is, because God chose to "bless it and declared it holy." Its blessed and sacred character is part of the divinely ordained cosmic order. It cannot, therefore, be abrogated by man, and its sanctity is a reality irrespective of human activity. Being part of the cosmic order, this day must, like all other divinely created things, be essentially good and beneficial to man. Hence, it is a "blessed" day, the very antithesis of the Mesopotamian notion of evil or ill-omened days. Finally, its connection with the drama of Creation makes the day universal in character. It is not to be wondered at that this combination of blessedness and universality soon expressed itself in the religion of Israel in socio-moral terms, so that the privileges of the sabbath rest were extended equally to all members of the family, to the slave and the stranger, to the beast of burden and to the cattle in the field.[40] Whatever its origins, the biblical sabbath was a unique institution, transformed beyond recognition from any Near Eastern antecedents it may have had.[41]

The Cosmic Battle

We have already stressed the fact that the notion of conflict was inherent in the pagan view of the cosmos. Implicit in the notion of a multiplicity of gods is a plurality of wills which, by human analogy, is bound, in turn, to engender strife. The internecine strife of the gods, the personified forces of nature, is an outstandingly characteristic feature of polytheistic cosmogonies. That is why polytheistic accounts of creation always begin with the predominance of the powers of nature, and invariably describe in detail a titanic struggle between two opposing forces. They inevitably regard the achievement of world order as the outgrowth of an overwhelming exhibition of power on the part of one god who, through a monopoly of violence, manages to impose his will upon all others.[42] This theme of the cosmic battle is the underlying motif of *Enuma Elish*. The existence in Israel of residual fragments of a popular version of this combat myth was pointed out earlier. . . .[43] The Book of Genesis itself has no direct reference to the notion of creation in terms of struggle. Indeed, the very idea is utterly alien to the whole atmosphere of the narrative. Yet one has the feeling that the narrator was not unaware of the place of the combat myth in pagan cosmogony, for he emphatically tells us that God created the "great sea monsters" (1:21), that these mythological beings, which elsewhere are counted among those who rebelled against God[44] were not at all preexistent rivals of the one Supreme Creator, but His own creatures. . . .

Despite the familiarity of the Hebrew account with some of the motifs of the cosmogonic myths of the ancient Near East, all notion of a connection between creation and cosmic battles was banished from Genesis with extreme care. The idea of strife and tension between God and nature is unthinkable. To emphasize the point, the words "and it was so" are repeated after each divine fiat.

Furthermore, it is highly significant that the biblical fragments of a cosmogonic combat myth have survived solely as picturesque metaphors exclusively in the language of poetry, something which strongly indicates a minimal impact upon the religious consciousness of Israel. Never once are these creatures accorded divine attributes, nor is there anywhere a suggestion that their struggle against God in any way challenged God's sovereign rule in the universe.

But the real qualitative difference between the pagan cosmogonic combat myth and the Israelite fragments is evidenced by the use to which the latter are put in biblical literature. They practically always appear as a literary device expressing the evil deeds and punishment of the human wicked in terms of the mythical conflict of God with the rebellious forces of primeval chaos. The plunderers and despoilers of Israel are compared to the noisy seas and the turbulent, mighty, chaotic waters which flee at the divine rebuke.[45] The sinful ones of the earth, the objects of divine wrath, are designated by the names of the mythological monsters,[46] while the defeat of the creature *Yam* in ancient times is cited as evidence of God's overwhelming power in dealing with the wicked.[47] Similarly, God's decisive overthrow of His mythical primeval enemies is invoked as an assurance of His mighty power for the redemption of Israel through a like victory over the present historical enemies of the nation.[48]

The gross polytheism of the combat myth, in all its implications for religion and society, was excluded from biblical literature. The motif itself underwent radical transformation. In Israelite hands, a backward-looking myth of the dim past re-enacted mimetically in the cult became a symbolic affirmation of the future triumph of divine righteousness in human affairs. Evil in the world is no longer apprehended metaphysically, but belongs on the moral plane. The events of pre-history have become in the Bible the pattern for history. The Lord of creation who wholly controls nature is by virtue of that fact an unfailing source of confidence that His word is eternal and His incursions into history effective; so that His absolute power over the forces of chaos carries with it the assurance of the historical triumph of righteousness over evil.[49]

Notes

1. See T. H. Gaster, "Cosmogony," in George A. Buttrick, ed., *Interpreter's Dictionary of the Bible,* 4 vols. (New York: Abingdon, 1962), 1:702ff.
2. Followers of the documentary hypothesis have assigned this section to the P source and the second account to the J source.
3. Cf. Isa. 27:1, 51:9-10; Job 26:12–13. See below for a discussion of the "cosmic Battle."
4. Ibid.
5. Cf. Ps. 104:9; Prov. 8:27; Job 26:10, 38:8–11.
6. See H. Gunkel, *Schöpfung und Chaos in Urzeit und Endzeit* (Göttingen, 1921); U. Cassuto, "Epic Poetry in Israel," *Knesseth* (1943–1944), 8:121–142; U. Cassuto, *Me'Adam ad Noah* (Jerusalem, 1953), pp. 20–23, 30f.; U. Cassuto, *Commentary on the Book of Exodus,* 2nd ed. (Jerusalem, 1953), pp. 119–125.
7. For a comprehensive study of this subject, see J. Pedersen, *Israel: Its Life and Culture,* 4 vols. (London, 1959).
8. For a review of the speculative thought in ancient Egypt and Mesopotamia, see H. Frankfort, et al., *Before Philosophy* (Baltimore, 1961).
9. For an English translation of *Enuma Elish* and other Mesopotamian creation stories, see A. Heidel, *The Babylonian Genesis* (Chicago, 1963); E. A. Speiser in J. Pritchard, ed., *Ancient Near Eastern Texts Relating to the Old Testament,* 2nd ed. (Princeton, 1955), pp. 60–72.
10. This is the central theme of Y. Kaufman, *Toldot Ha'Emunah Ha-Yisre'elit* (Tel-Aviv, 1942–1956), abridged as *The Religion of Israel* (Chicago, 1960). For a summary of his views and arguments on this

particular problem, see his article in *Journal of Biblical Literature* (1951), 70:179–197. See also on this subject H. Gunkel, *The Legends of Genesis* (New York, 1964), p. 15f; B. S. Childs, *Myth and Reality in the Old Testament* (Naperville, Ill., 1960).

11. On this subject in general, see A. B. Drachman, *Atheism in Pagan Antiquity* (Copenhagen, 1922).
12. See E. Voegelin, *Order and History* (Louisiana, 1956), p. 41f; S. Moscati, *The Face of the Ancient Orient* (Garden City, N.Y., 1962), p. 78f.
13. Cf. E. O. James, *The Ancient Gods* (London, 1960), pp. 239, 260.
14. S. N. Kramer, *History Begins at Sumer* (New York, 1959), p. 79f.
15. Pss. 33:9 (cf. v.6); 148:5.
16. On the notion of the "sexualization of the world," see M. Eliade, *The Forge and the Crucible* (New York, 1962), pp. 34–42; T. Jacobsen in H. Frankfort, et al., *Before Philosophy*, pp. 158f., 170ff.; N. O. Brown, *Hesiod's Theogony* (Indianapolis, 1953), pp. 8, 19.
17. See T. Jacobsen in H. Frankfort, et al., *Before Philosophy*, p. 159f.
18. Gen. 1:2, 6f. On the "wind from God," see H. M. Orlinksy, "The Plain Meaning of Ruah in Gen. 1.2," *Jewish Quarterly Review* (1957), 48:174–182.
19. See L. Woolley, "Stories of the Creation and the Flood," *Palestine Exploration Quarterly* (1956), 88:15f.
20. For an explanation of the creation of woman out of Adam's rib, see S. N. Kramer, *History Begins at Sumer*, p. 146.
21. Gen. 11:3 (cf. Lev. 14:41f.); Job 10:9, 27:16, 30:19.
22. Job 4:19, 10:9, 33:6; cf. Isa. 29:16, 45:9, 64:7.
23. For primitive, Near Eastern and classical parallels to this motif, see J. Frazer, *Folklore in the Old Testament*, 3 vols. (London, 1919), 1:3–44.
24. *Enuma Elish*, VI:1–34.
25. *Gilgamesh*, I:II:34f.
26. J. Pritchard, ed., *Ancient Near Eastern Texts Relating to the Old Testament*, p. 99f.
27. See S. N. Kramer, *History Begins at Sumer*, p. 108f; S. N. Kramer, *Sumerian Mythology* (New York, 1961), pp. 68–75; T. Jacobsen in H. Frankfort, et al., *Before Philosophy*, p. 176.
28. J. Pritchard, ed., *The Ancient Near East in Pictures Relative to the Old Testament* (Princeton: Princeton University Press, 1954), pp. 190, 318, No. 569.
29. See the remarks of H. H. Rowley, *The Unity of the Bible* (Cleveland, 1961), pp. 74f., 186nn.53, 55.
30. Isa. 29:16, 45:9ff.; Jer. 18:21.
31. On this subject, see the remarks of M. I. Finley, *The World of Odysseus* (New York, 1959), p. 150; H. Frankfort, *Kingship and the Gods* (Chicago, 1948), p. 277f.; J. J. Finkelstein, "Bible and Babel," *Commentary* (1958), 26:438f.; E. A. Speiser, "Three Thousand Years of Biblical Study," *Centennial Review* (1960), 4(2):219.

32. Cf. Gen. 18:25; Isa. 5:16.
33. T. Jacobsen in H. Frankfort, et al., *Before Philosophy*, p. 137; H. Frankfort, *The Birth of Civilization in the Ancient Near East* (New York, 1956), pp. 54, 63.
34. Cf. Ps. 8:4–9.
35. Exod. 31:12–17.
36. See U. Cassuto, *Me'Adam ad Noah*, p. 39ff.
37. Exod. 16:5, 22–30.
38. Ibid., 20:8; Deut. 5:12.
39. See N. M. Sarna, "The Psalm for the Sabbath Day," *Journal of Biblical Literature* (1962), 81:157, and the literature cited there in note 11.
40. Exod. 20:10f., 23:12; Deut. 5:14.
41. See Y. Kaufmann, *Toldot Ha'Emunah HaYisre'elit*, 1:579, 2:491.
42. See T. Jacobsen in H. Frankfort, et al., *Before Philosophy*, pp. 139f., 153–157, 187–199; N. O. Brown, *Hesiod's Theogony*, p. 40ff.
43. See note 6.
44. Isa. 27:1, 51:9.
45. Isa. 17:12–14.
46. Isa. 27:1.
47. Job 38:4–15.
48. Isa. 51:9f; Hab. 3:8-15; Ps. 74:12-18.
49. See N. M. Sarna, "The Psalm for the Sabbath Day," p. 161f.

Chapter 11

The Earth is the Lord's: An Essay on the Biblical Doctrine of Creation

BERNHARD W. ANDERSON

A widely recognized master of Old Testament study, and one of the great teachers of our time, Bernhard Anderson is Professor Emeritus of Old Testament Theology at Princeton Theological Seminary. His academic appointments have included positions at the University of North Carolina, Colgate-Rochester Divinity School, Drew University, and the American School of Oriental Research in Jerusalem. His many books range significantly over the field of biblical studies: on rediscovering the Bible, on understanding the Old Testament, as well as on the Pentateuch, the Psalms, the prophetic heritage of Israel, and relations of the Old Testament to the Christian faith. The essay included here, a classic of its kind, appeared in an earlier form in 1955. Going beyond the opening accounts of Genesis, Anderson's presentation of the whole biblical doctrine of creation is as relevant today as it was when it first appeared. The author's subsequent discussions of the biblical doctrine of creation include his book Creation versus Chaos: The Reinterpretation of

This essay is reprinted by permission from *Interpretation: A Journal of Bible and Theology* (January, 1955), 9:3–20. The author has made some revisions for its inclusion in this anthology.

Mythical Symbolism in the Bible *(Association Press, 1967); "Creation and Ecology"* (American Journal of Theology and Philosophy [1983] *7:14–30); and "Biblical Theology of Creation," in a volume of Old Testament essays dealing with Creation (forthcoming from Fortress Press).*

To understand creation biblically the premise must be abandoned on which the "science versus religion" battle has been waged: the notion, still popularly held, that the biblical view of creation is either bad science or good science, depending on which side one takes in the controversy. To be sure, the creation-faith does have radical implications for the scientific enterprise, as it does for any phase of human activity. Indeed, this doctrine is the clearest warning against assigning any form of human activity (science, politics, economics, education, art) to a special reservation where it has a supposedly autonomous role. To say that "the earth is the Lord's and the fulness thereof" is to affirm that no area of life escapes the unconditional religious concern which informs our creaturely existence. Nevertheless, the biblical view of creation is not an effort at primitive science. It does not purport to deal primarily with the speculative question of the origin and genesis of the earth, the question which lies properly in the domain of the science of nature. Whatever "science" is found in the biblical creation narratives is a legacy from the cosmological speculation of Israel's neighbors and has been outmoded by the *Weltbild* or world-picture which modern science has brought to view.

But this does not mean that the biblical doctrine is irrelevant to our scientific culture. Actually we shall discover that the doctrine speaks to our condition with greater relevance, since it is not dealing with a speculative question but with *human life here and now*. The affirmation that God is Creator arose originally out of the worship experience of Israel, not out of the reflections of a systematic theologian or a philosopher. The fact that the Genesis creation story reaches its climax in the observance of the Sabbath is clear witness to the existential foundation of the creation-faith in the Israelite cultus. The atmosphere pervading the first chapter of Genesis is that of the community of worship. The language, which moves in the majestic cadenzas of priestly prose, is the language of faith—not that of speculative thought or prescientific reasoning. Therefore, our task is to go behind the *doctrine* to the *experience of worship* out of which has come the affirmation that "the earth is the Lord's"

(Ps. 24:1). In the Bible creation refers not to a distant event which belongs in the field of astrophysics but to an event which now—in this moment of worship—is celebrated in cultic participation, especially in connection with annual religious festivals.

Our method of study will involve, of course, special attention to the accounts found in the first two chapters of Genesis. Literary criticism has singled out two creation stories: one (2:4b-25) found in the Old Epic (Yahwistic or J) narrative which was written in the time of the United Monarchy about 950 B.C., and the other (1:1-2:4a) belonging to the so-called Priestly Writing (P) which is dated in the post-exilic period about 500 B.C. However, to assign dates to these chapters in terms of the literary history of the Pentateuch is not necessarily to indicate the age of the traditions that were written down at these particular times. Both chapters embody traditions that are much older than the time of their literary composition. Indeed, belief in divine creation is one of the oldest elements of Israel's faith and is attested in many biblical passages, not only in historical books (for example, Gen. 14:19, I Kings 8:12 Septuagint) but in Israel's hymns such as Psalms 8, 19, 24, and 104. Therefore our study must range beyond Genesis 1 and 2 and cannot conclude until we have given at least a brief treatment of the New Testament.

Today some interpreters advocate demythologizing the biblical language concerning creation, that is, disengaging the essential content of meaning from the language form in which it is expressed—a prescientific language which is obsolete in terms of the modern scientific outlook.[1] To attempt such a translation into the modern idiom is an important aspect of the apologetic task of the community of faith, which must ever seek a point of contact in secular life and thought in order that the gospel may be communicated to the world. However, in the last analysis it is questionable whether the content of the creation-faith can be abstracted from the biblical form in which it is expressed. Instead of dispensing with the biblical language the interpreter should seek to understand it from within, that is, from within the worshipping community of Israel. The problem of demythology is put in a new light when at the outset one recognizes that the biblical language concerning creation does not purport to give us knowledge about nature, such as can be acquired through science and expressed in scientific terms. Rather, it affirms something about human existence itself—about the scientist as a person involved in the drama of history, about the life of any person regardless of the culture in which he or she lives. It affirms something about my life, your life, which no amount of scientific knowledge could ever disclose. It speaks to the person who is immersed in history and for whom the status of a detached observer is out of the question.

I

In the first place, the creation faith affirms that God alone is the creator of the meaning which supports all human history and the natural world which is the theater of the historical drama. Human history or nature do not secrete their own meaning. Rather, God's revelation creates the meaning which undergirds all existence. God's Creative Word is the source of all being. So the psalmist affirms:

> By the word of the Lord the heavens were made,
> and all their host by the breath of his mouth.

Hence it is folly for peoples and nations to act as though their plans determined the meaning of life.

> Let all the earth fear the Lord,
>   let all the inhabitants of the world stand in awe of him!
> For he spoke, and it came to be;
>   he commanded, and it stood forth. (Ps. 33:6-9)

This psalmist affirms the conviction expressed in Genesis 1 where, in the same kind of universal vision, all existence is seen to be grounded in the meaning disclosed by God's Word.

Both stories of creation are characterized by this universal view which includes the heavens and the earth and all humankind. It is noteworthy, however, that in both cases creation-faith presupposes election-faith, that is, the conviction that God has chosen the history of Israel as the special medium of divine revelation. This is clear in the Old Epic (J) narrative where the movement of primeval history (Gen. 2-11) is toward the decisive moment related in Genesis 12: the call of Abraham and the divine promise that in him and his seed all the families of humankind would be blessed. It is also true in the Priestly (P) scheme where everything points toward the singling out of the holy community, Israel, and God's revelation of the Torah at Sinai. In neither the Old Epic nor the Priestly tradition does creation stand by itself. It is integrally related to the special history of Israel within which God chose to make known "his mighty acts" of salvation. Thus the place of the creation stories in the narrative sequence indicates that the primary concern is about the meaning of history, especially Israel's history in relation to the histories of other peoples. To speak of the "first things" in this context is not to reflect on ancient origins, but is rather to say something about the source and foundation of the meaning discerned within Israel's history. As Ludwig Köhler observes:

> The creation story of the Old Testament does not answer the question, "How did the world come to be?" with the reply, "God has created it," but it answers the question: "Whence has the history of the People of God received its meaning?" with the reply, "God has given to the history of the People of God its meaning by the Creation."[2]

When we open the Bible and begin reading from Creation toward the call of Israel, we are really reading the story backward. Israel came to believe that the Word of God created a historical community, a social order (Ex. 15:16, "the people whom thou hast created"; echoed in Isa. 43:1-2), before she affirmed that "by the word of the Lord were the heavens made." The earlier Old Epic (J) creation story and the later Priestly (P) version are both secondary to the ancient Israelite witness which pointed to Yahweh's saving deeds in the Exodus, the wilderness wandering, and the conquest of Canaan. Israel's early *credo*, as preserved in the little liturgy found in Deuteronomy 26:5-10, makes no reference to the creation but rehearses the mighty acts of the Lord, beginning with the deliverance from Egypt. This silence about the creation is very striking.[3] The inference is justified that in Israel's faith redemption was primary, creation secondary, not only in order of theological importance, but also in order of appearance in the Israelite tradition. In the early stage of Israel's faith attention focused upon what Yahweh had done in history, especially in the crucial event of the Exodus. For in this event Israel was, so to speak, created out of nothing, that is, out of a mass of slaves who were regarded as a historical nonentity in the ancient world. But the Word of God, spoken through Moses and actualized in concrete events, created meaning and order out of desolation. God's Word made history; it created a new people. Israel could have said with Paul: "God chose what is low and despised in the world, even things that are not, to bring to nothing things that are" (I Cor. 1:28). Later prophets rightly pointed back to the Exodus as the time of Israel's beginning (Amos 3:1-2; Hosea 11:1, 12:9, 13:4).

Israel's early faith, while concentrating on Yahweh's redemptive acts in history, did not ignore Yahweh's lordship over nature. According to the tradition Yahweh commanded the plagues in the land of Egypt, was victorious in the cataclysm of the Red Sea, and graciously provided the pilgrim people with food and water in the wilderness. The Song of Deborah (Judges 5) describes Yahweh's coming on the storm to rescue the embattled "people of Yahweh" at Megiddo and portrays the heavenly host—"the stars in their courses"— joining battle in the defeat of Sisera's army. Nature was not removed from Yahweh's sovereignty but was the servant of Yahweh's historical purpose. In the Old Epic (J) tradition the impressive claim is made that the whole earth belongs to Yahweh (Exod. 19:5). Plainly Yahweh's sway, according to Israel's early faith, was as high as the heavens and as wide as the whole earth (see also Josh. 10:12, Gen. 49:25, Exod. 15, Deut. 33:13-16). However, these tremendous affirmations were made from the standpoint of a community which remembered and celebrated the saving deeds of Yahweh in history. The first thing that Israel said was not "In the beginning God created the heavens and the earth," but rather, "In the beginning Yahweh created Israel to be his people and gave us a task and a future in his purpose."

During the first generations of Israel's historical career there was little motive to view the meaning of the Exodus, the Call of Israel, within a universal or cosmic design. When Israel was pressed on every hand by foes that threatened to annihilate her, the burning issue was the meaning of what was happening in the history of *this* people, not the question of Israel's relation to the nations or to the cosmos. However, when historical tensions relaxed and Israel achieved some measure of security in the Palestinian corridor, the time was ripe to affirm that the meaning revealed in Israel's history was actually the meaning undergirding the history of all peoples and the whole creation.

The time for this widening historical vision was, above all, the glorious era of nationalism under David and Solomon. Whatever tendencies there may have been in this direction during the earlier period, it was the great political achievements of these kings, especially David, which widened the political and cultural horizons of Israel. With this expanding national view went also an expanding view of Yahweh's lordship over the world, as expressed preeminently in the Old Epic or Yahwist narrative which, in its written form, probably dates from the reign of Solomon. In this comprehensive history, which extends from the creation (Gen. 2-3) to at least the eve of the conquest of Canaan, the whole past was reviewed in the light of the

Exodus faith and the special history whose theme was the saving deeds of Yahweh. Especially significant for the subject of this essay was the prefacing of the traditions dealing with primeval history (Gen. 2-11) to the stories concerning God's dealings with Israel (Gen. 12 through Joshua). According to Gerhard von Rad, the Yahwist's most original contribution was the incorporation of these traditions into a comprehensive history so that the creation is now seen in the light of Israel's Exodus faith.[4]

Thus a line was traced from where Israel stood in history right back to the remotest beginnings of human history, using the traditional stories that were available. The result of this broadening of the narrative scope was a vision of the whole range of history in the light of the meaning that was revealed within Israel's history. The narratives of Genesis 2-11 do not deal particularly with Israel, but with all peoples. '*Adam* is neither a Hebrew nor an Israelite, but human being (humankind) generically, including both "male and female," as explicitly stated in Genesis 1:26-27 (note the alternation of singular and plural forms of speech). This typical or representative role is further exemplified in the Paradise Story in Genesis 2-3, where the human situation is portrayed in the primeval parents, the man and the woman—Adam and Eve. This universal perspective is evident throughout the primeval history (Gen. 1-11). In the story of the Flood we learn that Noah is not an Israelite but the ancestor from whom sprung the major ethnic groups, of which the Semites are one. In Genesis 2-11, then, the claim is made that Yahweh, who spoke to Moses and delivered Israel from Egypt, is none other than the God of primeval times.[5] The One who created the community Israel is the Creator of humankind. In this way the Yahwist expands and universalizes the meaning that was revealed to Israel in her unique historical experiences. In a similar manner, but with less concern for the dynamic movement and conflict of history, the Priestly Writer affirms that Israel's cultic history is given meaning by the God of the whole creation.

To speak of God as Creator, then, is not to make an affirmation about the manufacture of nature. Were this the case, the old oriental myths which describe the birth of the gods out of the previously existing stuff of chaos and which portray one of these gods making the world in a great battle with the powers of chaos, could be replaced rationally by the doctrine of evolution.[6] But the biblical creation-faith deals primarily with *the meaning of human history*. The great affirmation of the Bible is that the meaning, first disclosed in the events of Israel's history, is the meaning upon which the world is founded. The redemptive Word, by which Israel was created as the People of God, is none other than the creative Word by which the heavens were made. The point bears reemphasis that in the Bible creation is not an independent doctrine, but is inseparably related to the basic story of the people in which Yahweh is presented as the actor and redeemer. Salvation and creation belong together (cf. Isa. 43:14-19, 51:9-10). Therefore, to proclaim God as Creator is, as so often in the Psalms (cf. Ps. 29, 33, 104), a call to worship. It is a summons to acknowledge *now* the foundation and source of the meaning of our history.

II

Closely related to what we have been saying about historical meaning is another facet of the doctrine of creation: the total dependence of the world upon God. The earth is the Lord's; it is not self-sustaining. Everything in it, including human life, partakes of creaturely finitude. Were it not for the fact that the Creator sustains the world, it would lapse back into primeval chaos.

To acknowledge the infinite distance between the Creator and the creature is difficult for people in the modern world who are prone to identify God with some aspect of human consciousness, perhaps the Intelligence that our minds perceive in the cosmos, or the natural processes in which human history is involved, or even "the best in human nature." However, the God of the Bible is not identified with any phenomenon in the world. The God who claims Israel and whom Israel worships is, "God and not a man, the Holy One in your midst," as the prophet Hosea proclaimed (Hos. 11:9). To be sure, we must seek analogies from human experience to witness to the presence of the Holy God in the human world; but the great blasphemy is to identify the image with the One to whom the image points. The doctrine of creation, which stresses the dignity and supremacy of humankind in God's creation (Ps. 8:3-8), also draws the sharpest line between the Creator and the creature (Job 38:2-7).

At first glance this does not seem to be true of the Old Epic story in Genesis 2 in which Yahweh is portrayed in vividly human terms as he forms man, then the animals, and finally a woman. But despite the naïveté of the language there is no doubt about Yahweh's sovereignty. Two divine prerogatives, symbolized by two trees, separate creatures from their Maker: the knowledge of good and evil (i.e., the capacity for responsible decision) and deathless life. To grasp for these prerogatives, and thereby overstep the bounds of humanity, is an act of rebellion against the Lord God. Lest the eating of the fruit of the first tree should tempt the human being to "put forth his hand and take also of the tree of life, and eat and live for ever" (Gen. 3:22), the couple is driven out of the garden. Human beings can assert their independence from their Creator, but they cannot escape being who they are: creatures who exist in relation to God and who are exposed to God's grace and judgment. This theme is developed further in the Old Epic (J) stories dealing with Cain and Abel (Gen. 4:1-16), the Flood (Gen. 6-8), and the Tower of Babel (Gen. 11:1-9).

That God alone is sovereign is affirmed emphatically in the Priestly creation story in Genesis 1. According to this chapter, the creation is totally dependent upon the will of the transcendent God. Here there is not the slightest suggestion that the Creator is identified with any power immanent in nature, as was the case in the nature mythologies of antiquity. God is completely independent from the primeval watery chaos, out of which the habitable world is created. The imperative of the Creator's word is the only connection with the works of creation. Perhaps the belief in "creation out of nothing," implying that even the primeval chaos was created by God, is too sophisticated for Israel's faith; for the primary concern of this chapter is to express the total dependence of everything upon God's ordaining will rather than to answer the question of the origin of the stuff of chaos. It is noteworthy, however, that the verb *bara'* ("create"), which appears in the preface to the creation epic (vs. 1) and again emphatically in the case of the creation of animal life (vs. 21) and human life (vs. 27), is used in the Old Testament exclusively of effortless divine creation which brings into being something absolutely new. This language comes as close to creation *ex nihilo* as one can without actually using the expression which is first found in the late Jewish book, II Maccabees (7:28).[7] In any case, the Priestly creation story affirms the unconditional sovereignty of God and the complete dependence of creation upon God's transcendent will, an affirmation that is only further underscored by later discussions in which creation *ex nihilo* was made explicit.

Once again we must remember that this emphasis upon God's sovereignty over creation belonged to the present experience of the worshipping community, Israel. The unforgettable events of Israel's history, chiefly the deliverance from Egyptian bondage and the giving of the covenant, were impressed upon the people's experience as signs of Yahweh's lordship over them. The covenant itself was not a parity relationship, but was a covenant between unequals: the sovereign and the vassal people. Israel was dependent for her very life upon the will of the One who had taken the initiative to deliver this people and bring them into covenant relationship (Exod. 19:4f). The basic motif of Israelite worship is the confession that Yahweh is Lord.

From this standpoint of present faith Israel looked back to the creation and affirmed that the world itself is dependent upon the same sovereign will, the same Lord of the covenant. All polytheism is, of course, excluded from the creation because Israel was dependent upon only one sovereign will. The regularities of nature are not regarded as natural laws, but as expressions of the same faithfulness which characterized Yahweh's relation to the covenant people (cf. Gen. 8:22). Even as Israel would fall prey to the enemies that constantly threatened her, were it not for Yahweh's sustaining power, so also the world is maintained only by its relationship to God. Apart from the power of the Creator the earth would return to the water chaos from which it was created.

One of the curious aspects of the biblical doctrine of creation is the portrayal of the earth as being established upon the primeval Sea. In one sense, of course, this is only an expression of the world-picture which Israel inherited from her cultural neighbors: the view of the earth as a flat surface, resting upon subterranean waters and overarched by the solid firmament which upholds the heavenly ocean. Obviously this is not good science. However, since the creation-faith does not pretend to deal with natural science the more important issue is whether this mythopoeic language communicates an understanding of the depth of human existence which is perhaps lacking in the modern scientific outlook.

The Priestly (P) creation story begins with a description of the earth in an uninhabitable stage: "the earth was without form and void, and darkness was upon the face of the deep." As in the preface, so in the rest of the Priestly story creation is seen in relation to chaos. By the command of God light is separated from the primeval darkness, a firmament is placed in the midst of the waters to separate the waters (above) from the waters (below), and the waters under the heaven are gathered together into one place so that dry land appears. In this view the watery chaos is not destroyed; rather, the primeval Sea surrounds the habitable earth on every hand. Were it not for the Creator's power, by which the firmament was created and the Sea assigned boundaries, the earth would be engulfed by the flowing together of the waters and would return to primeval chaos (cf. Gen. 7:11, 8:2). No language could express more forcefully the utter dependence of the world upon the Creator.

This imagery recurs throughout the Old Testament.[8] The psalmist who exclaims that "the earth is the Lord's" also marvels that Yahweh has established the earth firmly upon the primeval Deep.

> The earth is the Lord's and the fulness thereof,
> the world and those who dwell therein;
> for he has founded it upon the seas,
> and established it upon the rivers. (Ps. 24:2, cf. 136:6)

Elsewhere we read that God has made firm the firmament above and has assigned boundaries to the sea (Prov. 8:27-29; Ps. 104:7-9; Jer. 5:22). God watches over Chaos (Job 7:12) and if the waters lift themselves up, rebukes them and they flee (Ps. 77:16, 18:15, etc.). God has established the foundations of the earth in the depths of the sea and when the earth shakes with the roaring of the waters, holds its pillars firm (Ps. 75:3, 46:1-3). Ancient peoples knew, perhaps in a more immediate sense than those who live in the modern scientific era, that the goodness and order of human life are constantly threatened by the powers of chaos. Jeremiah could envision God's judgment bringing about a return to primeval chaos in a powerful poem in which the same phrase *(tohu wa-bohu)* is used that is found in Genesis 1:2.

> I looked upon the earth, and lo, a chaotic waste [*tohu wa-bohu*],
>   and unto the heavens, and their light was gone.
> I looked on the mountains, and lo, they were quaking,
>   and all the hills were trembling.
> I looked, and lo, there was no human being,
>   and all the birds of the sky had vanished.
> I looked, and lo, the orchard land was a wilderness,
>   before Yahweh, before his burning wrath.
>   (Jer. 4:23-26—my translation)

In another poem a psalmist, near to death, speaks of being cast into the waters of the primeval Deep (Jonah 2). Were it not for the Creator's sustaining power the waters of chaos would break in upon the earth, destroying all meaning and order. God's work of creation, then, is also God's work of salvation. Moment by moment the creation is supported solely by the will of the Creator. In this perspective, to affirm that God is Creator is to acknowledge utter dependence upon the One who is our Refuge and our Strength.

> Therefore we will not fear though the earth change,
>   though the mountains shake in the heart of the sea;
> though its waters roar and foam,
>   though the mountains tremble with its tumult. (Ps. 46:2-3)

Clearly this biblical language cannot be quickly dismissed as the expression of an outmoded cosmology. Israel had something other than H_2O in mind in describing the earth as resting on the Sea, just as the author of Revelation likewise had something different in view in his vision of the New Heaven and the New Earth where the Sea would be no more (Rev. 21:1). Is it not true that human life indeed rests upon and is surrounded by elemental chaos which constantly threatens the goodness and orderliness of the world? The "chaos and desolation" of Genesis 1:2 is not just a statement about primeval times; it is a statement about a present possibility. Commenting on this verse, Gerhard von Rad observes that human beings have always had a haunting awareness "that behind all creation lies the abyss of formlessness; that all creation is always ready to sink into the abyss of the formless; that the chaos, therefore, signifies simply the threat to everything created." "This suspicion," he continues, "has been a constant temptation" to faith.[9] Today, more than ever, people are becoming aware of this Depth, this Abyss. The threat of "non-being," the anxiety over the possible meaninglessness of life, the fear of chaotic forces that threaten to overwhelm our secure world—this experience has found expression in modern language that has striking affinity with the creation imagery of the Bible. The truth of the matter is that existence is not self-sustaining. The world and all creatures in it are radically dependent upon God. For it is by God's command that order is created and sustained in the midst of the surging forces of the Deep that threaten to burst beyond their assigned boundaries and plunge the world into chaos.

III

Finally, the doctrine of creation affirms that every creature is assigned a place in God's plan in order that it may perform its appointed role in serving and glorifying the Creator.

This is magnificently portrayed in the Priestly creation story. God "calls" each thing by its name, that is, God exercises sovereignty by designating the peculiar nature and function of each creature. The heavenly bodies, for instance, are not celestial beings who control human life, as was supposed in the astrological cults of antiquity; rather, they are servants of God whose appointed function is to designate the seasons and to separate the day from the night. Every creature of heaven and earth participates in the "liturgy," the divine service of which the Sabbath is the climax. "Nature is the order decreed by God in which each part is called to worship."[10] Hence the Psalmist says that the heavens are joining in an inaudible anthem to the Creator (Ps. 19:1-4).

It is human beings, however, who occupy a special place in the liturgy of creation. In the Priestly creation story the creation of *'adam*, consisting of "male and female" (Gen. 1:27), is the last of God's works; therefore they constitute the crown of the creation. The fact that human beings are created on the same day as the animals is an important testimony to the intimate relation between the human and non-human creatures. But humankind is accorded a place of dignity far above the animals; they are given a special divine blessing and are commissioned to have dominion over the nonhuman creatures. Their task is to glorify God by filling the earth and subduing it, thereby acting as the appointed representatives of the Creator.[11] In the Old Epic (J) creation story the same view is presented in more picturesque language. There we see *'adam* placed in the natural environment which the Lord God has provided. This earthly being is intimately related to the animals, the narrator says, for like them *'adam* is a "living creature" (*nefesh hayya*: 2:19, cf. 2:7) who is made from the dust (2:7) and returns to it (3:19) at death. But *'adam* is more than a natural animal, as evidenced by the sovereign power to give the animals names (2:20), and by the special kind of partnership between man and woman (2:21-24). Above all, these human beings, unlike the animals, stand in an "I and thou" relation with their Maker and may be obedient, or disobedient, to the task that is given: to dress and keep the garden as faithful stewards of God's estate (cf. 2:15).

Again we must remember that these two creation stories derived their meaning from the faith of the covenant community, Israel. The purpose of Israel's deliverance from Egypt, according to Exodus 3:12, was that Israel should "serve God" at the sacred mountain. To be sure, the nature of Israel's God-given task was more profoundly understood in later times, especially in the poems of Second Isaiah (Isa.

40-55). However, the consistent witness of Israel's tradition is that Yahweh's gracious deeds bound the people to their God in the obligation of service. Israel was beholden to her Creator and Redeemer. Her calling was for a task: to be obedient to what Yahweh requires (Mic. 6:8). Accordingly, Joshua is represented as rehearsing the story of Yahweh's benevolent deeds and summoning the people assembled at Shechem to covenant decision: "Now therefore fear Yahweh and serve him in sincerity and in faithfulness. . . . Choose this day whom you will serve!" (Josh 24:14f.). This emphasis on volitional response with one's whole being to the gracious overture and sovereign claim of God is characteristic of Israel's faith and was an indispensable basis of the experience of worship.

In the creation stories this view of the relationship between God and people is retrojected to the very beginning of history. Thus the claim is made that the *role of humankind*—not just the role of Israel—is to perform the task given by the Creator. The uniqueness of human beings among other earthly creatures is that they are persons whom God addresses, the "Thou" with whom God enters into personal relationship. Human beings are not bound within the order of nature, experiencing no greater demand upon them than to adjust harmoniously to the rhythms of nature. They are decisional creatures, summoned into dialogue with their Creator. Unlike the animals, who are bound only to the earth, human creatures are historical beings who live vis à vis the God who gives them a task. Since God's word, when responded to, frees humans from the cycles of nature and sets their face toward the future, the creation is truly the beginning of history. Though the Yahwist and Priestly traditions differ from each other in important respects, both agree in regarding the creation as the inauguration of a historical drama in which human beings must reckon with the sovereign power and purpose of the God who is Creator and Lord.[12] History is not a natural process of growth and development; it is the realm of interpersonal relationships (political, economic, social) where peoples and nations cannot escape the sovereign Voice: "Let be then: learn that I am God" (Ps. 46:10, New English Bible).

The natural world, however, is the sphere within which this historical drama unfolds. The creation narratives of Genesis give no hint that the natural environment is intrinsically an evil, material realm from which one should seek escape into a sphere that is presumed to be "higher" and "more spiritual." In the Priestly creation account the world of God's creation is called "exceedingly good"

(Gen. 1:31). This verdict of divine approval is not simply an esthetic judgment, like that of an Artist who looks with satisfaction on a finished painting; more than that, the approving judgment signifies that every creature in the created world corresponds to God's intention, fulfills the function for which it was created, and performs its task as part of the larger whole. To be sure, the Priestly creation account lacks any trace of creaturely rebellion against the Creator which mars the goodness of the creation. This creaturely flaw is mentioned briefly in Psalm 104 (see the concluding reference to wicked people in vs. 35), a psalm that otherwise provides a poetic parallel to the Priestly creation story. The Priestly account in Genesis 1:1-2:3 is now supplemented with the story of Paradise Lost (Gen. 2:4-3:24) so that a fuller picture may be given. However, even in the Old Epic traditions about Paradise, Cain and Abel, the Flood, and the Tower of Babel (Gen. 2-11), the flaw in God's creation lies in the human *will* (freedom), not in the natural or cosmic environment.

This positive view toward "nature" (the environment provided by the Creator) is given poetic expression in the magnificent creation hymn, Psalm 104. The poet urges Yahweh to "rejoice in his works" (vs. 31): the gushing springs, the growing grass, the nocturnal habits of the animals, the daytime activities of human beings, the teeming creatures of the sea—even Leviathan, the dread monster of the Deep (vs. 26) which figures in Melville's *Moby Dick*. Everything has a role in relation to Yahweh's purpose and joins in the anthem of praise to the Creator which the poet verbalizes. The human body, too, shares in the goodness of God's creation. The biblical view of creation provides no basis for a negative attitude toward sex, eating and drinking, and physical enjoyment (see Ps. 104:15!). The world of "nature" is the God-given habitat in which human beings are to find *joy* in performing their task in the service of the Creator.

This view of the task of creatures to serve and glorify God helps us to understand more clearly the crucial statement in the Genesis creation story about "the image of God."

> Then God said:
> "Let us make human beings ['*adam*] in our image, after our likeness, and let them have dominion over the fish of the sea, the birds of the sky, the cattle and all wild beasts, and everything that moves upon the earth.
> So God created humanity ['*adam*] in his own image, in the image of God he created it; male and female he created them."
>
> (Gen. 1:26-27—my translation)

Undoubtedly the word translated "image" *(tselem)* should be taken much more concretely than is often done by those who attenuate its meaning to the "spiritual" part of human nature or, in Greek fashion, to the "soul" as distinguished from the "body." Elsewhere the Hebrew word refers to something concrete and visible, for instance, a picture drawn on a wall (Ezek. 23:14) or a statue of a god (II Kings 11:18; Dan. 3:1). Such concreteness characterizes the usage of *tselem* in Genesis 1:26-27, although the explanatory addition of "likeness" *(demuth)* moves in the direction of greater abstraction.[13] Apparently the view in the Priestly account is that *'adam*, viewed as a total bodily whole (a psychosomatic unity, as we would say), is fashioned after the heavenly beings of God's Council who are addressed in the plural pronouns of Genesis 1:26 ("us," "our"). If this is the correct interpretation, *'adam* is made in the image of the heavenly beings ("angels"; see Ps. 8:5 LXX) who surround God and are members of the heavenly council referred to in Micaiah's vision (I Kings 22:19-23) and the prologue to the Book of Job (Job 1:6). However, the main import of the statement about the *imago Dei* is not to define human *nature* in relation to God but to accent the special *function* that God has assigned human beings in the creation. Human beings, male and female, are designed to be God's representatives, for they are created and commissioned to represent or "image" God's rule on earth. To be made in the image of God is to be endowed with a special task. Gerhard von Rad puts it this way:

> Just as powerful earthly kings, to indicate their claim to dominion, erect an image of themselves in the provinces of their empire where they do not personally appear, so man is placed upon earth in God's image as God's sovereign emblem. He is really only God's representative, summoned to maintain and enforce God's claim to dominion over the earth. The decisive thing about man's similarity to God, therefore, is his function in the nonhuman world.[14]

Hence the statement about the *imago Dei* is appropriately followed immediately by the further announcement that God confers a special blessing on human beings and commands them to exercise dominion over the earth.

The dignity of humankind is not based upon something intrinsic to human nature, such as "the infinite value of the human personality." The worth of human beings lies in their relation to God. They are persons whom God addresses, visits, and is concerned about. But above all they are "crowned" as kings and queens to perform a special task in the Creator's earthly estate. This special dignity of human beings in God's creation excites the wonder and praise of a psalmist:

> When I survey your heavens, your finger-works,
>   the moon and the stars that you have established,
> what are human beings that you remember them,
>   human persons that you seek them out?
> Yet you have placed them slightly below heavenly beings,
>   and with honor and majesty have crowned them.
> You have given them dominion over your handiwork,
>   everything you have put in subjection to them . . .
>
> (Ps. 8:3-6—my translation)

This passage is extraordinarily interesting because it is the only place in the Old Testament, aside from Priestly passages in Genesis (1:26-27, 5:3, 9:6), where the divine image is mentioned—a rather striking fact in view of the importance of the *imago Dei* in Christian theology. The eighth psalm provides a commentary on Genesis 1:26-28. The psalmist affirms that God "has caused humankind to lack a little less than God," or perhaps, "than the angels." As in the Genesis creation story, this high status endows human beings with a function given to no other creature: to have dominion over the nonhuman creation. Human dominion on earth, then, is to be exercised within the sovereign rule of God. The "glory and honor" of human beings is the task that God has given them.

IV

In this essay I have pointed to three aspects of the creation faith, all of which were derived from the worship experience of the covenant community, Israel. The affirmation that God is Creator is actually a corollary of the primary knowledge of God as the Lord of history: the God whose acts gave meaning to Israel's history, bound Israel in dependence upon the Lord of the covenant, and gave Israel a task in the divine plan. From this faith-situation Israel looked back to the primordial beginning, interpreting all history and nature in the light of the Word of God which had been spoken to Israel.

Israel's backward view to the beginning has as its counterpart Israel's forward view to the end when God's purpose will be fulfilled. God is the Lord of time, for

Before the mountains were brought forth,
　　or ever thou hadst formed the earth and the world,
　　from everlasting to everlasting thou art God.

(Psalm 90:2)

It is not without significance that the Priestly creation story is artic-
ulated in the time sequence of a week. The week is governed, not
by an abstract principle of Time, but by the will of God which gives
each day its meaningful content. In Israel's faith time does not move
in a circle, but moves toward the culmination of the Creator's intention, just as the week of creation moves toward the Sabbath rest.
Thus the creation-faith is eschatological. The affirmation "in the beginning" is incomplete without the related affirmation "in the
end."[15]

The eschatological aspect of the creation-faith is more evident in
Old Epic (J) tradition and in the prophetic message than in the
Priestly Writing of the Pentateuch which lacks the story of Adam's
rebellion against the Creator. While the priest emphasizes God's upholding the order of the present world, the prophet sees the present
under the stigma of divine judgment. Because 'adam, whose imagination of the heart is only evil continually (Gen. 6:5, 8:21), mars the
goodness of the creation, he thereby provokes the Creator to act in
judgment to cleanse the earth of corruption and violence. The contrast between God's original intention for the creation and the sorry
reality of the present world is so sharp that, according to Israel's
prophets, God wills to act, bringing judgment upon the world order
in order that there may be a new beginning, indeed a new creation.
The theme of the New Creation is most clearly emphasized in the
poems of so-called Second Isaiah (Isa. 40-55), who understood himself to be standing just beyond the shadow of divine judgment that
fell severely upon Israel and on the threshold of the New Age. Yahweh is not only the Creator of the cosmos, who numbers and names
the myriads of stars (40:26), but Yahweh's redemptive work in history is also creative. Yahweh is Israel's Creator and Redeemer (43:1,
44:1-2, 45:11-12). Even now, says this prophet, Yahweh is beginning
a new work of creation in this historical community (Isa. 41:17-20,
42:9, 43:19, etc.), a creative/redemptive beginning which will shed
blessing and light on the whole world of humanity and nature. Later
prophetic voices in the Isaianic tradition spoke in more apocalyptic
terms of a cosmic re-creation: a "new heaven and a new earth" (Isa.
65:17, 66:2).

The New Testament doctrine of creation, which must be treated here all too briefly, presupposes the view of creation set forth in the Old Testament. Contrary to the second century radical, Marcion, who wanted to make a sharp separation between creation and redemption and even to repudiate Israel's creation faith, it is clear in the pages of the New Testament that the God who acts redemptively in Jesus Christ is none other than the creator of heaven and earth. In the New Testament, however, the theme of creation is reinterpreted, especially under the influence of the prophetic/apocalyptic stream of tradition mentioned above. Paul, the great theologian of the early church, understood the resurrection of Jesus to be the beginning of the New Age, the New Creation which would ultimately be consummated in the transformation of the whole world and even the cosmos. God's act of redemption in the life, death, and resurrection of Jesus Christ not only begins to actualize God's saving purpose manifest to Israel, but also to actualize the intention of the creation "in the beginning" (II Cor. 4:6). Jesus Christ is the eschatological New Adam who is "the likeness of God" (II Cor. 4:4), "the image of the invisible God, the first-born of all creation" (Col. 1:15)—language which clearly recalls the creation story of Genesis. Therefore he is the beginning of a new humanity, a new history; for "if any one is in Christ," says Paul, that one "is a new creation; the old has passed away, behold, the new has come" (II Cor. 5:17; cf. Cal. 6:15). The new community, the church, is the sphere where God's new act of creation/redemption has begun; but the whole creation, human and nonhuman, is also involved, waiting longingly for the finishing of God's new creation (Rom. 8:19-23).[16] Through Christ, we read in the epistle to the Colossians, persons may be invested with "the new nature which is being renewed in knowledge after the image of its creator" (Col. 3:10). These passages and others testify that God's work in Christ has in view the restoration of the original intention of the creation and, therefore, is a foretaste of the final consummation when all things will be made new.

Second, in the New Testament, God's original creation is often understood christologically. Just as in the Old Testament the creation is viewed in the perspective of the Exodus-faith of the covenant community, so Christian interpreters view the whole span of the biblical story, from beginning to end, from the standpoint of God's self-disclosure in the life, death, and resurrection of Jesus Christ. In the light of this revealing event, the community of faith looks backward to the original creation, as in the prologue to the Fourth Gospel which echoes the opening words of Genesis: "In the beginning" (John 1:1). Similarly in the epistle to the Colossians the creation is viewed christologically:

> In him all things were created, in heaven and on earth, visible and invisible, whether thrones or dominions or principalities or authorities—all things were created through him and for him. He is before all things, and in him all things hold together. (Col. 1:16 f.)

Here, again, we see that in the Christian view the doctrine of Creation cannot be separated from its larger narrative context: the whole drama that unfolds from creation to consummation and that has its climactic center in Jesus Christ. The whole of human history and all of nature stand under God's signature in Christ. In Christ is laid bare the meaning which undergirds all existence; through him people acknowledge the God upon whom they are completely dependent; from him they hear anew the summons to a task within God's plan. From this standpoint of faith the Christian community traces the purpose of God backward to the beginning, saying that "in Christ all things were created"; and it traces the purpose forward to the consummation of history, saying that "God will sum up all things in Christ."

Notes

1. See the stimulating essay by Rudolf Bultmann in H. W. Bartsch, ed., *Kerygma and Myth*, trans. by R. H. Fuller (London: Society for the Promotion of Christian Knowledge, 1953).
2. Ludwig Köhler, *Theologie des Alten Testaments* (Tübingen, 1936), p. 70.
3. See also the longer summary found in Joshua 24, where, again, there is no reference to the creation.
4. Gerhard von Rad, *Genesis*, Old Testament Library rev. ed. (Philadelphia: Westminster, 1972), pp. 13–28.
5. This is made explicit in the J narrative by the usage of the special divine name, Yahweh, throughout Genesis and by the claim that people began to worship Yahweh in the antediluvian period; cf. Gen. 4:26.
6. The Babylonian myth of creation, *Enuma Elish*, begins with a theogony. See J. B. Pritchard, *Ancient Near Eastern Texts* (Princeton: Princeton University Press, 1950), pp. 60ff. See also Bernhard W. An-

derson, *Creation versus Chaos: The Reinterpretation of Mythical Symbolism in the Bible* (New York: Association Press, 1967), ch. 1.

7. For a defense of creation *ex nihilo* in Genesis 1, see Walther Eichrodt, "In the Beginning: A Contribution to the Interpretation of the First Word of the Bible," in Bernhard W. Anderson and Walter Harrelson, eds., *Israel's Prophetic Heritage* (New York: Harper, 1962), pp. 1–10; *Theology of the Old Testament*, II (Philadelphia: Westminster, 1967), pp. 101–6.

8. In many passages in the Old Testament there are allusions to the ancient myth of the battle with chaos (Tiamat in Babylonian mythology) portrayed as a dragon or serpent. See Isa. 27:1, 51:9, Ps. 89: 9-10; Job 9:13, 26:12. In Genesis 1:2 *Tehom* (deep) is linguistically related to Babylonian Tiamat, but there is no suggestion of a mythological struggle.

9. *Op. cit.*, p. 51.

10. Wihelm Vischer, *The Witness of the Old Testament to Christ* (London: Lutterworth Press, 1949), p. 46.

11. See Bernhard W. Anderson, "Human Dominion over Nature," in Miriam Ward, ed., *Biblical Studies in Contemporary Thought* (Boston: Greeno, Hadden & Co., 1975), pp. 27–45.

12. See Eichrodt, "In the Beginning," pp. 49–50 for comments on "the inner connection of creation and history."

13. Notice, however, that the explanatory *demuth* does not appear in Genesis 1:27 or 9:6.

14. *Op. cit.*, p. 60. In the above discussion I am indebted to von Rad's insights at a number of points.

15. See Köhler, *Theologie des Alten Testaments*, pp. 70f.

16. See the illuminating book by my colleague, J. Christiaan Beker, *Paul the Apostle* (Philadelphia: Fortress Press, 1980). He shows that Paul's message belongs in the prophetic/apocalyptic context. On the "new creation" (II Cor. 5:17) he writes: "To be 'in Christ' is indeed a 'new act of creation', but this creation must still wait for its future completion in the liberation of the whole creation (Rom. 8:21), when 'we shall always be with the Lord' (1 Thess. 4:17)." Quotation from p. 310; see also pp. 101, 152, 191, *passim*.

Epilogue

Epilogue

The Two Books of God

ROLAND MUSHAT FRYE

Christians affirm in the Apostles' Creed today, as they have for centuries, that "I believe in God the Father almighty, maker of heaven and earth," and in the Nicene Creed that "We believe in one God, the Father all-governing, creator of all things visible and invisible."[1] In those words we recognize that the Bible provides faithful insights into God's creative will and continuing providence. In addition, Christians have also recognized that we have available to us not just one book of God, but two: the book of God's Word in Scripture, which concerns the ultimate nature and destiny of humanity, and the book of God's Works in Nature, which contains the created order. In the early church, the great Saint Augustine in one of his sermons thus called upon his listeners to observe "the great book . . . of created things. Look above you; look below you; read it, note it."[2] Following the same conception, John Calvin in the Reformation period referred to the "duplex cognito," or twofold knowledge of God.[3] In our own century, Pope Pius XII drew on the same idea in his Address to the Pontifical Academy of Science on December 3, 1939: "Man learns from two books: the universe for the human study of things created by God; and the Bible, for the study of God's superior will and truth. One belongs to reason, the other to faith. Between them there is no clash."

The book of God's Word leads to salvation, which is the ultimate concern for mankind, whereas the book of God's Works leads to science, which confers lesser but still very great benefits. This distinction can preserve the integrity both of faith and of science, and forestall unnecessary confrontations between them, confrontations which can only confuse our understanding of both books through which God speaks. If we fail to respect the knowledge of God attainable through either of these books, we neglect his gifts. While one book confers the ultimate grace of salvation, and the other confers the proximate benefits of knowledge, we do not need to choose one to the exclusion of the other, for God has laid both open before us.

It was on the basis of this understanding that Robert Boyle, a great scientist and a devout Christian, was able to say: "If we lay aside all the irrational opinions which are unreasonably fathered on the Christian religion, and all erroneous conceits repugnant to Christianity which have been groundlessly fathered upon philosophy [science], the seeming contradictions between Divinity and true Philosophy [or science], will be but few, and the real ones none at all."[4] Conflicts between the two books of God are not inherent in those books themselves: the books, in the Christian understanding, are traceable to the same author, but they are composed in different styles and concern different subject matters so that the methods of reading them must be different, as are the purposes of such reading. Such conflicts as arise from time to time are the results of misreading, when human proponents of one book claim authority over the subjects properly belonging to the other, or when either book is read in a way appropriate only to the other.

The conception of the two books, authored by a single all-powerful and all-wise God, became a major presupposition in the development of modern science. To cite a single but very significant case in point, let us consider the views of Sir Francis Bacon, who has often been called the first philosopher of science as we know it. Bacon's persuasive and learned arguments contributed to the founding of the Royal Society and to the promotion of modern scientific endeavor. His Christian and biblical beliefs are not only apparent at many points in his writings as a whole, but are privately and individually expressed in his *Personal Confession of Faith*, which aligns him with Reformed theology. Among other things, that *Confession* affirms Bacon's conviction that human problems arise from human rebellion against God and the attempt to control the knowledge of good and evil in purely human terms: "presuming to imagine that the commandments and prohibitions of God were not the rules of good and evil, but that good and evil had their own principles and beginnings . . . he [man] lusted after the knowledge of those imagined beginnings; [so] that he willed to depend no more upon God's will revealed, but upon himself and his own light, as a god."[5]

As a professing Christian, Bacon saw the origin of human evil in these terms: men and women assume that they have sufficient knowledge of good and evil so that they do not need guidance from God through God's disclosures of himself. It is therefore a mark of the sin of pride to exalt one's own preferences and prejudices above the clear evidence of either of the two books of God. Theologically, Bacon knew that the two books are not co-equal in value, and that we should be careful not to confuse them, or to confuse what we can learn from one with what we can learn from the other. He declared that it was simply impossible "to deduce the truth of the Christian religion from the principles of the philosophers, and to confirm it by their authority," and he described such misguided efforts to substitute natural science for biblical religion as "disparaging things divine by mingling with things human."[6]

On precisely the same basis that faith could not be founded on natural philosophy, Bacon also repudiated the possibility of founding science directly upon the Scriptures, and he attacked those who would vainly derive scientific propositions from the Bible. His words on that subject are as pertinent today as they were in the early 1600s:

> This vanity some of the moderns have with extreme levity indulged so far as to attempt to found a system of natural philosophy [in our terms, science] on the first chapters of Genesis, on the Book of Job, and other parts of the sacred writings . . . because from this unwholesome mixture of things human and divine there arises not only a fantastic philosophy [again, science] but also an heretical religion.[7]

To illustrate his point, he cited those narrow-minded dogmatists who argued on the basis of the Genesis accounts that the earth was flat, and who refused to accept the evidence of scientists "who on most convincing grounds (such as no one in his senses would now think of contradicting) maintained that the earth was round."[8] Fortunately, the flat-earth dogmatists did not prevail, but they exemplify a continuing frame of mind which confuses both science and religion.

As a Christian layman, Bacon regarded the promotion of science as his vocation under God. Let no man, he wrote in 1605 in his *Advancement of Learning*,

> think or maintain that a man can search too far or be too well studied in the book of God's Word or in the book of God's Works, divinity or philosophy, but rather let men endeavor an endless progression of proficience in both; only let men beware that they apply both to charity and not to swelling; to use, and not to ostentation. . . .[9]

Bacon immediately went on to warn that we "not unwisely mingle or confound these learnings [of religion and philosophy] together," but that we recognize the integrity of the book of God's Word in Scripture and the book of God's Works in science.

In those statements, Bacon evoked an ancient theme of Christian theology, and he may also have been influenced either directly or indirectly by John Calvin, the major theologian of the period, who declared of the Bible that "the Holy Spirit had no intention to teach astronomy; and in proposing instruction meant to be common to the simplest and most uneducated persons, he made use by Moses and the other prophets of popular language that none might shelter himself under the pretext of obscurity."[10] It is only a literalist reading of the Scriptures which requires a direct conflict with the findings of legitimate science, but Calvin argued persuasively that such a literalistic reading of such passages in the Bible is unnecessary and incorrect. What Calvin said in the sixteenth century about the science of astronomy, we can in principle adapt to the twentieth century by saying that "the Holy Spirit had no intention to teach geology and biology," and conclude that it is a violation of the intention of Scripture to assume otherwise.

Calvin used such an interpretation not only to defend the integrity of Scripture but also to defend the integrity of science. Consistently and repeatedly, he repudiated any possible hint of anti-intellectualism or educational anti-elitism. He fully recognized that science is esoteric, abstract, and removed from the common sense perceptions of most people, that it goes beyond what he called "things that lie open to our eyes" (such as the relative size of sun and moon), but he went on to declare that "nevertheless, this study is not to be reprobated, nor is science to be condemned, because some frantic persons are wont boldly to reject whatever is unknown to them." He continued that science "is not only pleasant, but also very useful to be known: it cannot be denied that this art unfolds the admirable wisdom of God."[11]

In a question which could well be asked of twentieth-century literalists, Calvin wrote "shall we say that the philosophers [scientists] were blind in their fine observation and artful description of nature?" No, he emphatically concluded, because we cannot read these scientific writings "without great admiration. We marvel at them because we are compelled to recognize how preeminent they are. But shall we count anything praiseworthy or noble without recognizing at the same time that it comes from God? Let us be ashamed of such ingratitude. . . ."[12] In the great edifice of human arts and sciences, constructed in part by believers and in part by unbelievers, Calvin thought that we could see "some remaining traces of the image of God, which distinguished the entire human race from the other creatures."[13] Such statements are directly opposite to the constricted narrowness of contemporary American advocates of so-called creation-science.

The best flowering of modern culture, and derivatively of modern technology, grew out of this essentially religious conception of the two books of God. Both books are important, as evidences of God's providence, but they operate in quite different ways. One should not go to science or history or secular literature to find the means of grace or the hope of glory, nor to the Scriptures to find engineering drawings of the universe, its development and operation. Many of the greatest contributions and the greatest opportunities of our culture derive from that simple but profound recognition of the two books of God, and from the parallel but separate pursuit of their meanings.

Yet in America today influential voices call upon us in effect to abandon that healthy and ancient recognition that God has revealed himself in two quite different ways, through Scripture and through nature. School teachers and school boards are placed under pressure either to minimize their teaching of the findings of modern scientists who have investigated the book of the Works of God in Nature, or to introduce in our school curricula an account of the origins of the universe based in a literalistic reading of the parabolic accounts of Creation in the first chapter of Genesis, as though this were a scientific theory.

Just as Christianity does not assume that nature and science can tell us all we need to know about God and man, so too it does not assume that the Bible can tell us all we need to know about science and nature. Neither the Bible itself, nor the Christian tradition as a whole, nor the Protestant tradition in particular, requires that we close our minds to thought, shut off our understandings, and restrict ourselves to a literalistic dogma that the earth is flat, that the whole universe revolves around the earth, and that the moon is one of the great lights of heaven. On precisely the same basis, and for precisely the same reasons, we are not required as Christians to maintain that the earth was created in six calendar days, or by a digital adjustment in six thousand years, when everything which has been learned by the most careful and honest scientific analysis of the book of the Works of God points to different conclusions. Science and faith will conflict irreconcilably only if we insist upon confusing and conflating the two books of God. And if we do that, the result will be either bad for science, or bad for religion, or bad for both. There is only one God, to be sure, but we will both understand him better and honor him more fully if we approach him in terms of both of the two books which he has made available to us.

Notes

1. These creeds may be found in virtually all Christian worship books, and are conveniently contained along with many others in John Leith, ed., *Creeds of the Churches: A Reader in Christian Doctrine from the Bible to the Present* (Garden City, N.Y.: Doubleday Anchor, 1963), see pp. 24 and 30.

2. See Augustine, Sermon 126, and Commentary on Psalm 45.2-3, in *Corpus Christianorum*, Series Latina, vol. 38, p. 522. The Psalm is numbered 46 in Protestant versions of the Bible. The two-book conception was also cited by the desert father St. Antony (see Helen Waddell, ed. and trans., *The Desert Fathers* [New York: Sheed and Ward, 1942], p. 176). Ernst Curtius traces its use from the Middle Ages into the eighteenth century, in his *European Literature and the Latin Middle Ages* (Princeton University Press: Bollingen Series XXXVI, 1973), pp. 319–26, while John Dillenberger picks up some later references in his *Protestant Thought and Natural Science* (Garden City, N.Y.: Doubleday, 1960), esp. pp. 89, 98f., 113f., 130, and 158. See also Arnold Thackray and Jack Morrell, *Gentlemen of Science* (Oxford: Oxford University Press, 1981), pp. 225–27; James R. Moore, *The Post-Darwinian Controversies;*

A Study of the Protestant Struggle to Come to Terms with Darwinism in Great Britain and America, 1870–1900 (Cambridge: Cambridge University Press, 1979), pp. 83f.; and James McCosh, *The Religious Aspects of Evolution*, 2d ed. (New York: Charles Scribner's Sons, 1890), pp. 93f.

3. John Calvin, *Institutes of the Christian Religion*, ed. by John T. McNeill, (Philadelphia: Westminster, 1960), 1.2.1.

4. Quoted by John Dillenberger, *Protestant Thought and Natural Science*, p. 114.

5. Albert-Marie Schmidt, *Calvin and the Calvinistic Tradition*, trans. by Ronald Wallace (New York: Harper and Brothers, 1960), p. 157 for the quotation, and p. 153 for the theological alignment.

6. Francis Bacon, *Novum Organum*, lxxxix, in Edwin A. Burtt, ed., *The English Philosophers from Bacon to Mill* (New York: Modern Library, 1939), p. 63.

7. *Ibid.*, 1xiv, p. 45.

8. *Ibid.*, 1xxix, p. 63.

9. Francis Bacon, *Essays, Advancement of Learning, New Atlantis, and Other Pieces*, ed. by Richard Foster Jones (New York: Odyssey Press, 1937), pp. 179, 222.

10. John Calvin, *Commentary on the Psalms*, ed. by James Anderson (Grand Rapids, Mich.: Baker, 1981) 5:184–85.

11. John Calvin, *Commentaries on Genesis*, ed. by John King (Grand Rapids, Mich.: Baker, 1981), p. 86.

12. John Calvin, *Institutes of the Christian Religion*, 2.2.15.

13. *Ibid.*, 2.2.17.

DATE DUE